Research Methods for Business & Management:

A Guide to Writing Your Dissertation

Firstly ... nothing exists;
secondly ... even if anything exists, it is incomprehensible by man;
thirdly .., even if anything is comprehensible, it is guaranteed to be inexpressible
and incommunicable to one's neighbour.

Gorgias 500 BC, quoted in Aristotle, *De Melisso Xenophane Gorgia* 980a:19–20

THE GLOBAL MANAGEMENT SERIES

Research Methods for Business & Management

Second edition

A guide to writing your dissertation

Kevin O'Gorman and Robert MacIntosh

 Goodfellow Publishers Ltd

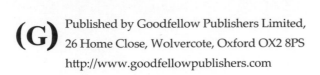

Published by Goodfellow Publishers Limited,
26 Home Close, Wolvercote, Oxford OX2 8PS

http://www.goodfellowpublishers.com

First published 2014

This edition 2015

British Library Cataloguing in Publication Data: a catalogue record for this
title is available from the British Library.
Library of Congress Catalog Card Number: on file.

ISBN: 978-1-910158-51-7

 Design and typesetting by P.K. McBride, www.macbride.org.uk

Cover design by Cylinder

Printed by Marston Book Services, www.marston.co.uk

Contents

Dedications

To my beautiful wife Anne and our children Euan, Eilidh and Eva. There is nothing better in life than to spend time with you. Thank you.

RMacI

To my mother for the constant and continued support, and Diana and Keith for the never ending dinners, and Maggie for some excellent words and rather fine sentences, I could not have done it without you.

KDO

Acknowledgments

The genesis of this book lay in a search for a text that could be used to guide students through the challenges of preparing a dissertation. Having failed to find something which inspired us, we were struck by the vast experience available within our own institution. This book draws upon the talents and accumulated wisdom of our colleagues in the School of Management and Languages at Heriot-Watt University. To our colleagues at Goodfellow Publishers, we remain indebted. Sally, Tim and Mac each showed a willingness to help bring a complex project to market in an unrealistically short time scale. Their calm and stoic acceptance of the production schedule were much appreciated and the professionalism of their work was exceptional. Thomas Farrington played a key role in checking and polishing the manuscript and we are also indebted to him for the speed and accuracy of his work.

KDO & RMacI

Biographies

Norin Arshed is an Associate Professor and the Programmes Director for Leadership and Organisational Performance suite of programmes in the Department of Business Management at Heriot-Watt University. She is an economist by background, with professional experience both in the public and private sectors. Her research concentrates on exploring and understanding the enterprise policy process. Institutional theory is the theoretical lens used in her work to highlight the dynamics of enterprise policy process at the macro and micro-levels. She is involved with numerous stakeholders in undertaking her research which involve government institutions, think tanks and the private sector.

Nigel Caldwell is a Reader at Heriot-Watt School of Management and Languages. He has worked at Bradford, Plymouth and Bath Universities. Prior to his academic career, he worked at a leading UK automotive manufacturer; gaining first-hand experience of Japanese supply techniques such as JIT, Kanban and Total Quality Management implementation. His research today explores the fields of Operations and Supply Management. Nigel publishes in journals such as *International Journal of Operations & Production Management* and *Industrial Marketing Management*. He has generated research income approaching three quarters of a million pounds from the UK Engineering and Physical Research Council.

Ross Curran is a PhD student at Heriot-Watt University, Edinburgh, where he is an active member of the Intercultural Research Centre. His primary research interests focus on improving volunteer management practises in the third sector, while he has published papers exploring PPT in the developed world, and authenticity consumption at tourist sites in Japan. His PhD thesis is concerned with fostering greater utilisation of the heritage inherent in many third sector organisations.

Mike Danson is Professor of Enterprise Policy at Heriot-Watt University and has worked widely on issues about urban and regional economic development, island and rural economies and enterprises, demographic change, volunteering, Gaelic, microbreweries and poverty. He has published 13 edited books and over 200 papers. He has advised parliaments, governments, and such organisations as the OECD, European Commission, Scottish Enterprise. Mike was recently awarded the prize for the best book in regional studies and graduated with the first DLitt from the University of the West of Scotland in 2012. He is Treasurer of the Academy of Social Sciences.

Thomas Farrington is a Post-Doctoral Research Associate in Management and Organisation at Heriot-Watt University. His research examines contemporary issues in business and management, with particular emphasis on marketing and cultural authenticity; management practice and business ethics; consumer identity and tourism; colonial legacies and intercultural studies. Thomas has taught at South East European University in Tetovo and at the University of Edinburgh, from which he received his doctorate, and where he was Co-Director of the Scottish Universities' International Summer School. His work has most recently appeared in the *Journal of American Studies*, *Research in Hospitality Management*, and the *Journal of Marketing Management*.

Keith Gori is a doctoral researcher in the School of Management and Languages at Heriot-Watt University. His doctoral research engages with Consumer Culture Theory, identity and consumer narratives in the context of the British Home Front during World War Two. More widely his research interests lie in consumer and marketing history, the historical development of thinking surrounding the social responsibilities of business, and experiential marketing. He has presented both historical and contemporary research outputs at international marketing conferences and has published work in the *Journal of Marketing Management*. He teaches on global management and marketing courses in the Department of Business Management.

Emma Hill is a PhD student in the department of Languages and Intercultural Studies at Heriot-Watt University. She holds a BA(Hons) in English Studies from the University of Exeter and a MA in English Literary Studies from the University of York. Her current research is focused on the ways in which migrant peoples make themselves heard in both the public and private spheres, particularly with reference to the Somali population in Glasgow. More generally, her interests include topics concerning migration, identity, memory, place and text.

Christian König is a PhD student in the School of Management and Languages at Heriot-Watt University, Edinburgh. He is an active member of the Logistics Research Centre and his primary research interests focus on the outsourcing strategies of focal firms and the continuous development of service providers. In his doctoral thesis, he investigates the role of systems integrators in the logistics industry using an exploratory approach Christian received an MSc. in Logistics and Supply Chain Management with distinction from Heriot-Watt University in Edinburgh in 2012.

Sean Lochrie is a PhD student at Heriot-Watt University, Edinburgh, where he is an active member of the Intercultural Research Centre. His primary research interest focuses on the creation of custodianship behaviours within World Heritage Site management. Sean received an MRes in Business and Management (2012) and a BA Hons in Management and Tourism (2011), both from The University of Strathclyde. Recent publications have explored taverns, inns and economic development in the American West, and stewardship in World Heritage Site management. Sean also teaches on the business research methods course in the Department of Business Management at Heriot-Watt University.

Robert MacIntosh is Professor of Strategy and Head of the School of Management and Languages at Heriot-Watt University. He trained as an engineer and has worked at the Universities of Glasgow and Strathclyde. His research on the ways in which top teams develop strategy and on organizational change has been published in a wide range of outlets. He has a long-standing interest in research methods for business and management studies and has published on the relevance of management research using methods that include ethnography and action research. He has consulted extensively with public and private sector organizations and sits on the board of the charity Turning Point Scotland.

Andrew MacLaren is Programme Director of the MSc in International Fashion Marketing in the Department of Business Management, Heriot-Watt University. His PhD explored business elites in the international hotel industry and his current research remains focussed on service products, informed by literature relevant to leadership, entrepreneurship and consumption. With diverse research links across luxury fashion, aviation and the hotel industry, his outlook is international and he works closely with industry throughout Europe, North America, the Middle East, India and China. He has published widely in the field on multiple topics, contributing in the domains of theory, method and industry practice and he continues to work towards interdisciplinary collaborations that engage with multiple fields of research through his extensive industry network.

Gavin Maclean is a PhD Student in the School of Management and Languages at Heriot-Watt University. His PhD thesis examines the work of professional musicians in terms of labour process theory and Pierre Bourdieu's theory of practice. More widely he is interested in sociological study of work and employment and 'symbolic' forms of work, particularly cultural production, public sector work and multilingualism in the workplace. He teaches on Human Resource and Critical Approaches to Management courses.

Kevin O'Gorman is Professor of Management and Business History and Head of Business Management in the School of Languages and Management in Heriot-Watt University, Edinburgh. He trained in Glasgow, Salamanca and Rome as a philosopher, theologian and historian. His research interests have a dual focus: origins, history and cultural practices of hospitality, and philosophical, ethical and cultural underpinnings of contemporary management practices. Using a wide range of methodological approaches he has published over 80 journal articles, books, chapters, and conference papers in business and management.

Angeliki Papachroni is a Research Associate in the School of Management and Languages at Heriot-Watt University. Her research focuses on issues around strategy implementation, organizational change, paradox management, innovation processes and organizational tensions. She holds a PhD on organizational ambidexterity from Warwick Business School exploring how organizations manage the conflicting demands of encouraging innovation and maintaining focus, a challenging topic with important strategic and organizational implications. Angeliki has co-authored a number of strategic teaching case studies including "Strategic Leadership and Innovation at Apple Inc" which won the ECCH/Case Centre overall prize for 2013.

Rodrigo Perez Vega is an Assistant Professor in Marketing in the School of Management and Languages at Heriot-Watt University Dubai Campus. His research interests are around digital marketing, social media, and consumer behaviour online. He has experience doing qualitative (i.e. interviews, content analysis) and quantitative (i.e. experiments and multivariate testing) research in online environments. Rodrigo received an MRes in Management (2011) by investigating the incidence of positive and negative incidence of electronic word-of-mouth on Twitter; he also has an MSc in Strategic Project Management (2011) and a BA Hons in Marketing (2006). Prior to his PhD, Rodrigo had marketing experience in several digital marketing and brand management roles within FMCG and service industries.

Catherine Porter is an Assistant Professor in the Department of Accountancy, Economics and Finance at Heriot-Watt University. In the past she has been a British Academy Postdoctoral Fellow, and also worked for the public sector in the UK Department for International Development. She is an economist, specialising in the economics of developing countries, with a particular focus on Africa. She has been involved in the design and fieldwork of several large-scale quantitative surveys in Ethiopia, India, Peru and Vietnam. Her research involves the statistical analysis of such quantitative surveys to answer questions around the measurement of poverty, and the effectiveness of policies that aim to reduce poverty.

James Richards is an Associate Professor in Human Resource Management in the School of Languages and Management in Heriot-Watt University, and an Academic Member of the Chartered Institute of Personnel and Development. James has published research in human resource management journals, edited book collections and consultancy based reports. James' research interests are grounded in industrial sociology and employment relations. Early research projects looked at employee use of social media for misbehaviour and resistance. His more recent research looks at hidden disabilities in the workplace and he is currently working on a range of in-work poverty projects. James is the Research Ethics Officer for the School of Management & Languages.

John Sanders is an Associate Professor in Management in the School of Management and Languages at Heriot-Watt University. He teaches strategic management courses to both undergraduate and post-graduate students. In addition, he teaches a small business management course to final year undergraduate students. Strategic fit within a university setting was the subject of his PhD. His past research efforts have focused on Internet portals, website quality, social networks and the market reach of rural small firms in Scotland.

Katherine Sang is an Associate Professor of Management in the Department of Business Management. Using feminist theory, her research examines how gender inequality is maintained in male dominated professions, including the creative industries and academia. In addition. Kate is researching gender and in-work poverty and supervising PhDs exploring organisational culture, gender and behaviour change. She is the Postgraduate Research Coordinator for Business Management, as well as serving on the University Undergraduate Studies Committee and Equality and Diversity Advisory

Group. She chairs the Feminist and Women's Studies Association UK & Ireland, and coordinates (along with Dr Rebecca Finkel) Scottish Feminist Academics.

Rafał Sitko is a Ph.D. student in Business and Management at Heriot-Watt University with research interests primarily in diversity management and inclusion. His work focuses on explaining intersections of privilege and oppression in a workplace and their effects on migrants' work experience. Rafał received an MSc in International Human Resource Management and Employment Relations from Queen Mary, University of London (2012) and a BA in Psychology and Management (2011) from University of Bradford. During student exchange programs Rafal also studied Employment Relations at Hosei University in Tokyo (2010) and Business Administration at Vrije Universiteit in Amsterdam (2009).

Babak Taheri is Programme Director for the suite of MSc Marketing Management Programmes in the School of Management and Languages, Heriot-Watt University. His main research interests are in the areas of the application of multivariate methods in management, consumer behaviour, heritage marketing management, and experiential marketing. Prior to joining Heriot-Watt University, he was Lecturer in Durham University and a teaching fellow in Strathclyde Business School. His recent work has appeared in *Tourism Management, International Journal of Hospitality Management, Journal of Marketing Management, Consumption, Markets & Culture* and *Advances in Consumer Research*. He is also Deputy Chair of heritage marketing special interest group in the Academy of Marketing, UK.

Vera Tens is currently a PhD student in the Department of Business Management at Heriot-Watt University, Edinburgh. She has an engineering degree from a German university specialising in wood science and technology. She worked in the German timber industry for several years before coming to Edinburgh to do an MBA at Edinburgh Napier University. Before joining Heriot-Watt's PhD programme she worked for a family-owned Scottish company, which raised the interest in doing a PhD in the field of family firms. Her current research interest is future family generations in SMEs, using a stakeholder theory perspective.

Alastair Watson is an Assistant Professor with the School of Management and Languages, Heriot-Watt University Dubai where his primary research interest is the commitment and motivation of staff in the UK hospitality industry, with a contextual application of Goffman's theory of Total

Institutions. Alastair's work is driven by his active industry experience as a senior operational manager and recruiter for a branded organisation. Other projects include spirituality and commitment, and further understanding people's desire, as opposed to their need, to work.

Nikolaos Valantasis Kanelloo is a PhD student in the School of Management and Languages at Heriot-Watt University, Edinburgh. His research draws upon contemporary developments in operations management, and the value creation within business networks. He currently researches the formation of ports' operations strategy in the era of servitisation with a particular focus on UK container ports and the emerging trend of Port-centric-logistics. Nikolaos received an MSc in Logistics and Supply Chain Management from Heriot-Watt University (with distinction) and a BA in Economic and Regional Development from the Panteion University, Athens.

Lakshman Wimalasena is an Assistant Professor of Management, in the School of Management and Languages, Heriot-Watt University and obtained his PhD in Management also from Herito-Watt University. He is a graduate in human resource management (HRM) and also holds an MBA (with merit) and a postgraduate diploma in social research methods (with distinction). His main research interests are meaning of work (MoW), agential reflexivity and habitus. His doctoral study explores the MoW within a postcolonial society – Sri Lanka. This study which develops a new integrated framework to the study of MoW, also extends the applicability of realist reflexive theory and contributes to the ongoing debate 'can reflexivity and habitus work in tandem'.

Preface

After many years of working with undergraduate, postgraduate and research students we recognise only too well the struggles that they often experience wrestling with the somewhat strange and seemingly obtuse language used to describe research philosophy. We once experienced similar difficulties and empathise with the confusion and lack of confidence that flows from being unclear whether you have really understood terms such as *methodology*, *ontology* or *epistemology*. We set out to produce a text that dealt with two problems. The first was to provide something that guides novice researchers through the whole process from identifying a topic to the writing up of findings via engagement with the literature and a brief overview of both qualitative and quantitative techniques. The second problem we wanted to tackle related to what we often refer to as 'the ologies'. Here we wanted to offer a structured approach to familiarising yourself with the terminology and to demonstrate how a nested set of descriptions builds towards a coherent, comprehensive and consistent articulation of your research paradigm.

We are indebted to our colleagues for their help in delivering on the first of these two problems in the first edition of the book. This was achieved at a pace which seemed frankly ridiculous but which produced a remarkably coherent guide for novice researchers. Despite positive feedback on many aspects of the first edition from both students and colleagues, we were however convinced that we could improve in relation to 'the ologies'.

For this reason, the second edition features some relatively minor changes to many chapters and a complete rewrite of our account of research philosophy. Central to the revised text is the methods map (see Chapter 4), which sets out a logical process for researchers to articulate their position in relation to five key aspects of their research philosophy. We have road tested this approach with many colleagues and students to ensure that it is clear and concise. In addition, we have developed a free app to accompany the book and this enables novice researcher to quickly develop a comprehensive justification of their particular research design in an interactive way. We would acknowledge that the methods map makes some simplifications and would suggest that for all but the most sophisticated of purposes, this is entirely appropriate. Indeed, if you are well enough versed in the philosophical nuances of knowledge explored in the method map then you are probably not part of our intended audience since you already possess the skills, confidence and capacity to articulate and defend the underpinning philosophical assumptions of your research. For everyone else, we hope that the second edition of *Research Methods for Business and Management* helps demystify the dreaded 'ologies'.

Introduction to the Second Edition

Outside the academic community, the terms *thesis* and *dissertation* are inter-changeable. At Heriot-Watt and other universities in the United Kingdom, the term thesis is usually associated with a PhD (doctoral degree), while dissertation is the more common term for a substantial project submitted as part of a taught masters degree (e.g. MSc) or an undergraduate degree (e.g. MA, BSc, BBA etc.).

Often thinking about, rather even than writing, your dissertation is the most stressful part of your degree. It does not need to be. Doing your dissertation is not unrelated to the rest of the writing you have done during your time at university. Many of the skills you already possess can be applied to the dissertation writing process. Identifying the purpose of your project, expressing originality and significance, setting appropriate goals, and maintaining strong organization will help you to develop a high quality dissertation.

Regardless of the information given in this book the most important advice is to engage with your supervisors! Be sure to speak with them throughout the process of writing your dissertation. Be clear about goals and deadlines. When you meet, have questions prepared and make sure you understand their directions. Be proactive about solving problems, rather than withdrawing. Take notes and use the time wisely.

Dissertations have always played a significant role in the awarding of a degree. Originally universities were established with advanced degrees being offered in the vocations of medicine, law, and theology. Over time, the universities have adapted to accommodate changing economic and social structures and demand for skills. Indeed, Whitehead (1932, p. 138f) in an essay welcoming the opening of the Harvard Business School observed,

"The universities are schools of education and schools of research. But the primary reason for their existence is not to be found either in the mere knowledge conveyed to the students or in the mere opportunities for research afforded to the members of the faculty... The justification for a university is that it preserves the connection between knowledge and the zest for life, by uniting the young and the old in the imaginative consideration of learning..."

When the Harvard Business School began, the university was the learning environment and some compromise had been reached between the idealist liberal vision and what Newman (1907, p. 156) called "the disciples of a low utilitarianism". John Paul II (2000, p. 3) elaborates the mission of a university and states that it is the duty of academics and researchers to make "universities 'cultural laboratories' in which theology, philosophy, human sciences and natural sciences may engage in constructive dialogue" and observes that in universities "there is an increased tendency to reduce the horizon of knowledge to what can be measured and to ignore any question touching on the ultimate meaning of reality." There is considerable scope within a university business school for a genuine plurality of views and disagreement leading to constructive dialogue and contributing to the enhancement of scholarship.

Once, science, engineering and technology, medicine, the law, and divinity were firmly established and a balance between the vocational and the liberal was pursued. Today, some courses may need to recapture some of the values and characteristics of the traditional higher vocations, however, unfortunately, this is not always possible, so often contract trumps covenant in a wide range of contemporary occupations. Far from the demise of the middle class career predicted by some, professionalism and flexibility are highly desirable general features of *graduateness*; learning to learn and the formation of capacities in general should take precedence over the acquisition of specific content. Imagination and creativeness must complement flexibility and cold hard knowledge as preparation for a world of rapid and continuous change; it's a question of balance.

In many sectors of our society, science is seen as being little short of infallible; anything else must be dismissed as fancy. Even in business journals there is the tendency to trust the so-called hard facts of statistically analysed quantitative data rather than the interpretive results that qualitative analysis tends to produce. However, the physicist Richard Feynman warned his students that when they did research, and before publishing their results, they should think of every possible way in which they might be wrong; whilst another physicist, Alan Lightman, explains the vital importance of this self-questioning approach: "In science, as in other activities, there is a tendency to find what we're looking for" (Lightman, 1996, p. 104. Feynman's comment is found on p106).

The ability to take an imaginative leap, beyond accepted scientific dogma and the entrenched views of academic colleagues, disciplinary boundaries, or even apparent common sense, has been at the heart of a significant number of scientific or technological advances in the last few hundred years. For example, throughout most of the 20th century, in medical circles the conventional wisdom was gastric juice caused ulcers, until a pioneering doctor infected himself with a bacterium thus proving that conventional wisdom was incorrect and wining the Nobel Prize for medicine (Van Der Weyden, Armstrong, & Gregory, 2005). In universities today, ethical approval processes might challenge the wisdom, or at least the legal probity, of infecting yourself or indeed others. Nevertheless, the undercurrent in any study of research methods is the slow realisation that everything that we 'know', even in domains that appear to be based on objective fact or cold hard logic can be questioned. As the physicist Max Planck said, "New ideas are not generated by deduction, but by an artistically creative imagination ... Science, like the humanities, like literature, is an affair of the imagination"(McFague, 1982, p. 72).

Kevin O'Gorman & Robert MacIntosh

References

John Paul II. (2000). Jubilee Of University Professors: Address Of John Paul II to University Professors of All Nations. Retrieved 06/07/14, from http://www.vatican.va/holy_father/john_paul_ii/speeches/documents/hf_jp-ii_spe_20000909_jubilteachers_en.html

Lightman, A. (1996). *Dance for Two*. London: Bloomsbury.

McFague, S. (1982). *Metaphorical Theology: Models of God in Religious Language*. London: SCM Press.

Van Der Weyden, M. B., Armstrong, R. M., & Gregory, A. T. (2005). The 2005 Nobel Prize in Physiology or Medicine. Medical Journal of Australia, 183(11/12), 612-614.

Whitehead, A. N. (1932). *Aims of Education and Other Essays*. London: Williams & Norgate.

1 The Nature of Research

Robert MacIntosh and Nigel Caldwell

Depending on your viewpoint, management and organization studies as a discipline is either as old as civilisation itself or in its infancy. Whilst it is true that we have been organizing and managing in social groups since our earliest days as hunter-gatherers, the formal study of management only emerged at the start of the last century with the seminal work of people like Henry Fayol and Frederick Taylor. Management itself is therefore an emerging profession and, in the period since these pioneering figures gained attention for their work, management has become one of the most studied phenomena of our times. Each year throughout the world, millions of people choose to study management at university or college.

In the latter stages of their programme of study, these individuals are usually required to complete a research project, dissertation or thesis. For our purposes, we will refer to any such extended piece of research-based work as a research project in the remainder of this chapter. To prepare and submit a research project, you must first conduct a piece of original research. This can be a daunting prospect and is often seen as a rite of passage during your studies. A research project typically represents the longest piece of writing that you'll have had to tackle to date. Many people find it challenging and there are common issues that most students experience as they work on their project. This book offers structured and clear advice for those at the start of the journey from a blank page to a completed research project.

We begin by thinking about the nature of management education more broadly before turning our attention to management research and the more specific challenges of conducting a research project in business, organization or management. Management implies coordination and it is possible to think of the management of time, resources and people. Mary Parker Follett's definition of management as the art of getting things done through others draws particular attention to the need to interact with others.

Henry Mintzberg argues that it is highly problematic to teach people to manage, claiming that "pretending to create managers out of people who have never managed is a sham" (2004). Yet this problem is not restricted to management since one could equally ask whether it is possible to teach someone how to become a writer or an artist. Nevertheless, management has begun to develop as a profession. Bodies such as the Chartered Management Institute offer qualifications, accreditation and chartered status in much the same way that professional bodies in engineering, medicine or accountancy have done for decades.

The evolution of management as a profession has seen an accompanying body of theory develop to shed light on how and why management occurs. Schools of Business and/or Management are commonplace in many colleges or universities and, as social scientists, those studying managers and/or management tend to recognise that they are dealing with something that is subtle, multi-faceted and very context-dependent. Given the vast range of organizational, geographic and cultural settings where management occurs, it seems obvious that what works well in one circumstance, may not work at all in another. As management researchers then, we are challenged to move beyond so called "folk theories" (Oaksford and Chater, 1998, p.166).

Broadly speaking there are two ways of thinking about management research, each of which takes a different starting point and focuses on a different primary audience. One view holds that the purpose of management research is to understand the problems facing managers. Therefore the starting point is to engage with managers and their experiences in such a way that, as researchers, we can develop insights that will enable managers to carry out their roles more effectively. Any findings from the research should be targeted at managers since the primary objective is to improve the practice of management. Consider the ways in which medical schools interact with hospitals and other healthcare providers. There is a close relationship and it is relatively uncontroversial to suggest that most medical research is aimed at providing better treatment for patients through new drugs, procedures, etc. Strange though it may seem, this view does not hold universally in management research.

Rather, a counter view exists, which holds that the starting point for any new research is the body of theory already generated about management and organizations. Here management is seen as an interesting, perhaps even important, phenomenon that merits attention. The primary audience however, comprises other academics engaged in the study of management. Knowledge, insights and theory represent suitable ends in themselves and the practice of management is a secondary concern. As the university sector has expanded, more and more business schools have been created with many thousands of academics hired to teach and to research management. One of the consequences of this expansion has been that hundreds of new journals have been developed and the academic profession is sometimes accused of lacking engagement with the community of practicing managers in the wider world. In this chapter we will investigate these different views of management research before setting out the structure of the rest of the book.

Management as a discipline

The American academic Jeffery Pfeffer believes that those disciplines or fields of study where there is broad agreement about the nature and purpose of research tend to do better than those disciplines which are contested. He suggests that "consensually shared beliefs about the nature of knowledge and methods in a field … guide decisions on grant allocations and publication" (Pfeffer, 1993, p. 605). Hence, whilst management research has grown hugely over the last few decades with new business and management departments springing up in universities across the globe, conflicting views about the nature of management research aren't helpful. In fact, there is a long-running debate amongst the management research community about where to focus energy and attention. Over the years, scholars have worried about "the complex and sometimes problematic relationship between management practice and the practice of management research" (MacLean et al., 2002). Periodically, senior scholars write about this relationship (see for example Smith and Robey, 1973; Kelemen and Bansal, 2002). Susman and Evered (1978, p. 582) even suggested that we face a crisis, the principal symptom of which "is that as our research methods have become more sophisticated, they have also become increasingly less useful for solving the practical problems that organizational members face.". Donald Hambrick, the then president of the world's largest management research community (the Academy of Management) used his Presidential address to ask what it would be like if management research mattered to those in managerial positions (see Hambrick and Abrahamson, 1995). In the decades since he asked this provocative question, almost half the Presidential Addresses to the Academy of Management have dealt with this or a related theme.

Part of the problem is that management itself is something of a magpie subject, borrowing ideas and traditions from a range of root disciplines including but not limited to anthropology, sociology, psychology, economics and engineering. Earlier we examined the ways in which medical schools relate to healthcare institutions. Two management scholars, David Tranfield and Ken Starkey argue that we should conceptualise management research as being like medical research (1998). Management research, they suggest, should be a process where new scientific discoveries are converted into practices that have the explicit intention of helping managers understand what works, in what circumstances and why. Schools of business and/or management should be uniquely well positioned to do this since they sit at the interface of social science, other disciplines and the wider business community.

Returning to Jeffery Pfeffer's concern, the problem is that one scholar pursuing management as applied psychology may not even be able to agree on the definition of terms with a colleague studying management as applied sociology. If the academic researchers talk past each other, what hope is there for them when communicating with practicing managers? In practical terms, the business school community has responded by disseminating ideas via two related but distinct channels. Academic research tends to appear in peer reviewed journals where it is expressed in technical language intended for an audience of other academic researchers. There are many hundreds of these outlets ranging from the highly prestigious to others that are a much less reliable source of good research. This is discussed in some detail in Chapter 3. Alongside these academic journals, the same research findings are often written in a different, more accessible format, to appeal to practicing managers. Outlets like *Management Today*, the *Harvard Business Review*, the *Financial Times* or the *Economist* often present new management ideas in a much more readable format. Perhaps the most effective means of distributing ideas about management has historically been in the form of books where sales in the tens of thousands are not uncommon for best-selling texts.

So where does this leave us? Management research is a booming industry beset by structural problems. There is little agreement on the nature and boundaries of management research. There are multiple root disciplines within the management research community and, despite calls for multi-disciplinary research, scholars face difficulties in engaging with each other. Further, the more sophisticated our theoretical and methodological approaches become, the harder we find it to make an impact on the practice of those in managerial jobs. Perhaps for this reason, practicing managers tend to read the work of gurus, who are often not academics but consultants. These are significant challenges and should not be underestimated.

Developing an appreciation of these difficulties is a useful first step on the journey to producing your own piece of management research.

Knowledge production

Research is essentially about the production of new knowledge. In Chapter 2 we discuss where ideas for new research projects come from but first, we set the scene by introducing a distinction between two different approaches to knowledge production. Michael Gibbons and his colleagues (see Gibbons et al. 1994), argue that recent decades have seen the emergence of a new approach to research, which he calls 'mode 2 knowledge production'. To place this in context, it is first necessary to explain that mode 1 represents the traditional, and some would say, ancient approach to discovery.

Think of those historical figures that made breakthrough discoveries. Whether it is Galileo's radical suggestion that the earth moved around the sun (which incidentally earned him a conviction for heresy and a life under house arrest) or Newton's 'discovery' of gravity (though one suspects that gravity was 'there' all along), new insights produced new theory. In Gibbons' terminology, the traditional approach to research is theory led. We begin by reviewing our understanding of a particular phenomenon and design a piece of research that is intended to push our understanding further by scientifically confirming our theoretical hunch. There are few better examples than the use of the Large Hadron Collider at CERN to confirm the existence of the so called Higgs Boson. Peter Higgs had speculated on what was only a theoretical possibility in 1964. It took huge capital investment to create the apparatus required to prove his theoretical insight. The joint award of the Nobel Prize to Higgs and François Englert in 2013 represented the culmination of a long, theory-led journey.

In the Renaissance period, there were far fewer universities than today, and many of our great thinkers were polymaths who might span biology, astronomy, physics and chemistry. As universities became more common-place and the opportunity to study specific disciplines became the norm, we began to produce specialists. One unintended consequence of this, particularly in the natural sciences, is that we began to see the emergence of a scientific method, which placed heavy emphasis on theory and experimental design. In Chapter 5 we return to problematize the idea that there is a single 'scientific' approach to research. For the time being, it is sufficient to draw attention to the observation that traditional, or mode 1, approaches to research have their starting point located firmly in theory.

Turning our attention then to mode 2, we can see that although it was originally an outgrowth from its traditional counterpart (mode 1), it is becoming increasingly distinctive.

> *our view is that while Mode 2 may not be replacing Mode 1, Mode 2 is different from Mode 1 – in nearly every respect … it is not being institutionalised primarily within university structures … (it) involves the close interaction of many actors throughout the process of knowledge production …(it) makes use of a wider range of criteria in judging quality control. Overall, the process of knowledge production is becoming more reflexive and affects at the deepest levels what shall count as 'good science.'*
>
> *(Gibbons et al, 1994, vii)*

Thus the traditional, theory-led, mode 1 approach to the development of research projects is now being joined by a second approach to research, which has five main points of distinction.

First, knowledge produced in mode 2 style projects is *produced in the context of application*. This emphasises the problem-solving nature of mode 2 in that knowledge production is organised around a particular real-world problem where a firm or industry is struggling to achieve particular outcomes. The imperative to be practically useful, rather than theoretic ally curious, is the dominant consideration in framing a new research project and therefore the starting point is that research is produced under 'continuous negotiation' (Gibbons et al 1994, p.3) with practicing managers.

Second, mode 2 research is *transdisciplinary* since the practical problem that forms the focus of the research may best be addressed by a particular combination of skills, expertise and theories drawn from more than one discipline. This forces an interesting return to the more eclectic mix of disciplines and theories, which featured in the Renaissance period but which fell out of favour as scientific specialisation became the norm. In the particular case of management and organizational research, phenomena such as decision making are part psychology, part sociology, part economics. The suggestion that a combination of these disciplines offers the best hope of addressing the practical problem seems obvious but introduces the challenge of not talking past each other, which Pfeffer highlights (see previous section). The particular mix of disciplines required may not be clear at the outset and mode 2 research is therefore characterised as "problem solving capability on the move" (Gibbons et al., 1994, p. 5).

Third, mode 2 research is more **reflexive** than its mode 1 counterpart. This is the only way to offset the tendency to talk past each other. Multidisciplinary teams of experts and practitioners are drawn together around a particular problem and they then need to engage in open communication, continually approaching the research from the standpoint of the other participants as part of the ongoing process of negotiation. In mode 1 research, teams of specialists with a common viewpoint, common methods and common theories can survive without the need to engage in a highly reflexive dialogue about the nature of the problem at hand.

Fourth, in mode 2 research, the composition of the research team is more heterogeneous and more organizationally diverse. That is to say that the research will not exclusively occur within the traditional boundaries of the university sector. Increasingly firms like Google, Apple and Microsoft spend vast sums of money on research and development and in many areas may be ahead of the development curve relative to their academic peers. That said, mode 2 research tends to feature collaboration between industry and academia, creating problem solving teams made up of a diverse set of individuals and experiences.

The fifth and final difference between mode 2 research and its more traditional mode 1 counterpart is that there are a wider **range of quality controls** in play. The quality of knowledge produced in a mode 2 project is judged by a substantially broader community of interest, e.g. both academic peers and practicing managers. Traditional mode 1 research would typically be evaluated by academic peer review of the type whose highest accolade would be the Nobel prize. In mode 2 research, such academically oriented assessments of quality would sit alongside a diverse set of other consideration including issues such as the practicality, ethics and the financial viability of any proposed solution to the problem under investigation.

Knowledge produced in the context of application
Transdisciplinarity
Heterogeneity and organisational diversity
Social accountability and reflexivity
Diverse range of quality controls

Table 1.1: The five features of mode 2 knowledge production

Whilst your own research project is unlikely to be considered for a Nobel prize, at least in the short term, it is worth considering the research tradition within which your work will sit. Is the project that you are considering led by the observation of a practical difficulty facing an organization or industry? Or is your project founded more directly on a theoretical difficulty or problem that you wish to test? Both styles of research are valid but both will eventually be assessed in order to confirm that you have successfully completed your research project.

Assessing the quality of research

All research is produced with an audience in mind and that audience will form a judgement about the merits and limitations of the work. One such audience is the group of academic peers who are also working in the same field. Assessments of quality for this audience typically happen through peer review. The following two quotes give some insight into the peer review process:

Individuals needing to judge the quality of a research article, but unable to judge its merit directly for any number of reasons, rely on the journal in which the article is published to serve as an indicator of quality.

(Extejt and Smith, 1990, p.539).

Extejt and Smith's observation suggests the need to be discerning about both what you read and where you read it. But if the academic quality is associated with the quality of the journal it is published in, then how is journal quality itself assessed? Chapter 3 introduces the process by which you can review academic research papers and offers further commentary on ways to understand the relative status of journals. Some outlets are very prestigious, only publishing work of the highest quality; others are less discerning. In the most demanding outlets, articles are typically subjected to anonymous review by two or three academic experts, often over two or three cycles of review. Only the strongest work survives to appear in print. Rejection rates in excess of 90% are not uncommon in top tier journals. Understandably this process is prone to frustration:

We do understand that, in view of the misanthropic psychopaths you have on your editorial board, you need to keep sending them papers, for if they weren't reviewing manuscripts they'd probably be out mugging old ladies or clubbing baby seals to death.

(Baumeister, 1996)

Academia today is made up of various disciplines and sub disciplines as discussed earlier in this chapter. In management research these specialisms include strategy, marketing, human resources, and many others. Each of these topic areas in turn is comprised of sub-disciplines. Marketing is a broad area of work with distinct research groups in branding, consumer behaviour, digital marketing, ethics and sustainability, business to business marketing, etc. By definition, each sub-community of scholars is interested in a related but distinct set of questions, often pursued using similar sets of methods working within well-established traditions. As a result, each particular specialism tends to have its own journals, sometimes associated with specific professional bodies. The editorial teams of these journals will themselves vary in quality with the very best scholars typically being attached to the most prestigious outlets. As distinct from these specialist outlets, there are general management journals such as the *Academy of Management Journal* or the *British Journal of Management* that will publish research from any management discipline.

For academics then, it is a particular community of scholars that will judge the quality of an individual piece of research, through assessing its worthiness for publication. Authors submit their paper to a journal having prepared it in a form, which is intended to retain their anonymity for fear that famous scholars are treated differently than novices. The intention is to be egalitarian and focus on the quality of the work. The reality is that it can be difficult to disguise the work of very well known scholars. Academic quality is then managed by the process of journal editors asking experts in the field (or one very close to it) to read and assess the submitted paper. These reviewers or referees are also anonymous in the process and their views will be fed back to the author(s) in the form of a detailed report from reviewer 1, 2 or 3. The higher the standing (and ranking) of the journal, the more rigorous the review process. Some of the top journals in business and management research have a lead time of 2-4 years for publication as each round of writing and reviewing can take 6-12 months. Day (2011) dates peer review back to the late 17th century when it was introduced at the Royal Society of London, a body associated with the founding of scientific study through the then trail blazing practice of observation, experimentation and dissemination. It is of course, one part academic screening and one part social negotiation. A very well-known scholar in the field of organization studies was congratulated at a recent conference for successfully publishing in the world's highest ranked management journal, in response s/he said "don't congratulate me, I didn't write the article, the reviewers did." What this somewhat flippant remark highlights is that the reviewers have power in the peer review process and authors are being coerced to foreground some aspects of their work whilst relegating what they may see as their big idea to the background, or worse still, to the cutting room floor.

Reading journal articles you will quickly become familiar with the idea of academics having a hierarchy or ranking of the journals they use to build their articles. For example, Roehrich, Lewis, & George (2014, p. 111) report that their work is "[b]ased on published reviews and journal ranking lists from the UK Association of Business Schools and Web of Science rankings […] we selected peer-reviewed journals, because they exhibit high disciplinary standing and can be considered validated knowledge". Peer review as a method of validating knowledge "ensured that the publications included had been subject to assurance systems for academic quality and rigor" (Lockett et al., 2006). These approaches to so-called systematic reviewing of the literature are covered in greater detail in Chapter 3.

Peer review underpins journal quality but there are other measures – firstly high rejection rates; top-tier journals usually accept less than 10% of submissions (Day, 2011). Much like Groucho Marx's comic aphorism that he would not want to be a member of any club that would accept him; academics are suspicious of journals that are too lenient in their editorial policy and have low rejection rates. As discussed in Chapter 3, surveys of academics in business and management are used to gauge the relative esteem of different journals. When such survey results are published, critics argue that a new, and entirely self-indulgent field is born, namely the ranking and reviewing of journal rankings. Another common indicator of quality is the number of times a particular paper is referred to by other academics. Later in the book we discuss ways of citing existing research and, in published research, this creates what is called a citation index. Such indexes can be used to measure the impact or popularity of individual articles, of individual researchers and of journals. Journal citation analysis is a useful guide to the evolution of one discipline relative to another. Sharplin and Mabry (1985) used citation analysis to identify the 10 most cited journals in management research. The top two journals they identified back in 1985 (the *Academy of Management Journal* and *Administrative Science Quarterly*) remain close to the top of any ranking produced today. Citation analysis is itself a useful way of understanding the development of lines of work within a given body of theory (see for example, the analysis of a particular literature in the strategy field conducted by Peteraf and her colleagues, 2013).

1

Assessing your research project

Having introduced the idea that academic work is subject to assessment through peer-assessment and publication or citation data, we now return to the more pressing concern of judging the quality of your own research project. It should be no surprise that the quality of the research literature that you choose to read, cite and critique will have a major influence on the kind of impression that your own research project will form in the eyes of your supervisor and examiners. Appendix 2 sets out some guidance on the ways in which research projects are marked, offering an overview of the process, the use of grade descriptors and marking guides. These can usually be found in course programme handbooks or other similar documentation. It is worth investing the time to become familiar with the way in which your own research project will be assessed.

Conclusions

In this first chapter we have introduced the subject of management and explored ways of thinking about the nature of research. This should help you to see the difference between traditional, theory-led approaches to research and more contemporary, problem-centred and multidisciplinary approaches. We have also offered an insight into the ways in which peer-reviewed research papers are assessed. Since it is these peer-reviewed papers that will form the basis of your eventual literature review, it is helpful to understand the process that researchers go through in order to see their work in print. The journey from performing the idea to publishing it can be long, convoluted and socially complex, since editors and reviewers will have played a part in shaping the eventual papers that you will be reading. Having set the scene, you are now ready to work your way through the remainder of the book gathering skills, techniques and insights as you go.

Chapter 2 helps with the dilemma of choosing a suitable research project by looking at the source of ideas and how to develop a tightly defined project specification. In Chapter 3 you'll discover the techniques required to produce a literature review and how best to approach this time consuming but critical task. A structured approach to the so-called philosophy of knowledge is offered in Chapter 4 and this will arm you with the insights required to choose which type of research you will undertake and with the vocabulary to locate your choice amongst the wider set of available research traditions using what we call the Method Map. Individual research techniques can be operationalised in very different ways within different research traditions and Chapter 4 is therefore of central importance in producing an informed description of your own research methods. The themes raised in Chapter 4 then permeate much of what follows later in the book. The case study is one of the more commonly used approaches in management research but can be conducted in a range of different ways. Chapter 5 illustrates the range and types of data that might be used in a research project and uses case studies to illustrate how differently types of data can be used. Guidance is offered on where to find the data for your research project, and you are encouraged to choose between primary data, secondary data or a mixture of the two. With the advent of social media and web-based communication, research projects can now draw on the full range of data sources from historical data sources such as archives and to social media, e-mail and other choices. These are covered in Chapter 6. The next four chapters (7 to 10) then cover gathering and analysing qualitative and quantitative data. Reading these four chapters will enable you to choose a specific data type and analytical process for your research project. In particular, choosing and articulating a way of analysing the data that you have gathered is vital and yet, is one of the most common failings when assessing research projects. Chapter 11 deals with the increasingly common requirement to secure ethical approval for your research project. Advice will be available from your own university or college but what is offered here is an overview of ethics in the context of research projects. Finally, Chapter 12 offers advice on the process of writing up your research project.

The book also contains three appendices which cover the process of managing a research project, how research projects are assessed in academic environments, and typical layouts and word counts per section for a range of common types of research projects.

Whilst you may feel anxious about the prospect of conducting a research project, the advice and examples used in this book will help you to break a large piece of work down into a set of interrelated tasks in a way that will also allow you to bring them back together into a coherent whole.

Good luck.

References

Baumeister, R.F. (1996) quoted in Bedian, AG (1996). Thoughts on making and remaking of the management discipline. *Journal of Management Inquiry*, **12**, 311-318

Day, N.E. (2011). The silent majority: Manuscript rejection and its impact on scholars, *Academy of Management Learning & Education*, **10** (4), 704–718

Extejt, M.M., Smith, J.E. (1990). The behavioral sciences and management: An evaluation of relevant journals. *Journal of Management*. **16**(3), 539-551

Gibbons, M., Limoges, C., Nowotny, H., Schwartzman, S. (1994). *The New Production of Knowledge: The Dynamics of Science and Research in Contemporary Societies*, Sage, London

Hambrick, D.C., Abrahamson, E. (1995). What if the Academy actually mattered? *Academy of Management Journal* **38**(5), 1427-1441.

Kelemen, M., Bansal, P. (2002). The conventions of management research and their relevance to management practice. *British Journal of Management*. **13**(2), 97-109.

Lockett, A., Moon, J., & Visser, W. (2006). Corporate social responsibility in management research: focus, nature, salience and sources of influence. *Journal of Management Studies*, **43**, 115-136

MacLean, D., MacIntosh, R., & Grant, S. (2002). Mode 2 management research. *British Journal of Management*. **13**(3), 189-207.

Mintzberg, H. (2004) *Managers not MBAs: a hard look at the soft practice of managing and management development*. Berrett-Koehler: San Francisco.

Oaksford, M. & Chater, N. (1998). *Rationality in an Uncertain World*. Psychology Press: Hove, England.

Peteraf, M., Di Stefano, G. and Verona, G. (2013) The elephant in the room of dynamic capabilities: Bringing two diverging conversations together, *Strategic Management Journal*, **34**(12): 1389-1410.

Pfeffer, J. (1993). Barriers to the advance of organizational science: Paradigm development as a dependent variable. *The Academy of Management Review*, **18**(4), 599-620

Roehrich, Lewis, & George (2014, p. 111) Sharplin, A.D., & Mabry, R.H. (1985). The relative importance of journals used in management research. *Human Relations*, **38**(2), 139-149

Smith, R.D., & Robey, D. (1973). Research and applications in operations management: Discussion of a paradox. *Academy of Management Journal.* **16**(4), 647-657.

Susman, G.I., & Evered, R.D. (1978). An assessment of the scientific merits of action research. *Administrative Science Quarterly.* **23**(4), 582-603

Tranfield, D., & Starkey, K. (1998). The nature, social organization and promotion of management research: towards policy. *British Journal of Management,* **9**, 341-353

2 The Key is in the Reading: Finding a Project

Andrew MacLaren and Emma Hill

"When you have eliminated the impossible, whatever remains, however improbable, must be the truth?"

Sherlock Holmes, *The Sign of Four* (Conan Doyle, 1890, p.111).

Arthur Conan Doyle's Sherlock Holmes has an infamous method of creative reasoning that generates the ideas with which he solves the unsolvable. Ideas can be ground-breaking and positive but can be equally destructive if they are not understood, framed and appropriately applied. Luckily for his clients (and unluckily for the criminals), Sherlock Holmes is not only a master-generator of ideas, but has supreme control of his 'mind palace' in which his ideas are framed, judged and contextualised. The following chapter leads you through where ideas come from, how they can be moulded to attend to a problem space, how they are framed appropriately and ultimately how they can underpin a solid and realistic research proposal.

One of your first challenges will be to come up with an idea for your research project. Ideas do not exist on their own: they have a past and a potential future; stakeholders and context. Ideas emerge when an opinion is challenged or a perspective is offered; they are both socially dynamic and socially dependent, and have roots in and grow from a particular context. Ideas are always part of a theoretical network and come with a heritage of theoretical and philosophical assumptions: Newton's theory of gravity may have fallen from the sky in apple form, but it was supported and developed by his knowledge of his discipline; Archimedes' 'eureka!' moment may have come as he displaced the water from his bath, but it was informed by the scientific and ontological principles of his time. In your research, your idea will come from (literal or figurative) conversation, and it will also interject in conversation – your job will be to navigate these discursive networks and present a well-informed account of your journeys and discoveries there.

In this chapter you will be steered towards understanding your ideas in the context of academia so that, even if you thought your idea was a 'eureka!' style moment, you will also be able to give it roots in extant and firmly-founded scholarship. In Management studies, ideas are valued for their 'innovation', (Bartunek et al., 2006, p.9), their relevance (Rynes et al., 2001) and their introduction of the new (Alvesson and Sandberg, 2011, p.247), and are understood as discipline-shapers (Vermeulen, 2005, p.978). Broadly and philosophically speaking, in Western culture from antiquity to present day, the focus of the 'idea' has shifted. It might be observed that whilst *how* an idea is created has changed, *what* an idea does has not (Lovejoy, 2009; Dupre, 2004, Cline Horowitz, 2005; Megill and Zhang, 2013, p.340-345). The idea – or the idea of the idea – nonetheless endures; for whether through critique, development or invention, ideas promise a progression of knowledge and longevity of their field.

The first section of this chapter relates to grounding your ideas in the literature. In research, your idea must be developed relative to the existing literature on the subject as, whether you like it or not, it is that same literature-base that led you to come up with the idea in the first place.

Research v re-search: Where might ideas come from?

A research project requires that your idea is contextualised within a particular scholarly tradition and within an existing academic conversation. Your idea will likely fall into one of two categories: either it will target a perceived research black hole about which little has been written, or it will attempt to correct, advance or redirect existing concepts. Either way, your idea gains a scholarly past, present, and future that represents a valuable connection to a wider literature. Before proceeding with your research you should be able to identify and clearly state your position relative to your academic peers.

■ Everything comes back to the literature

The key is in the reading; there are two reasons for this. First and foremost your conclusions and the 'contribution' of your study/dissertation/project/ thesis will be measured relative to the literature it discusses, thus for academic research, individual ideas mean little without being contextualised in a particular literature. Second, ideas that are not developed at least in part through consultation with the literature tend to be broader in scope and lacking nuance and complexity. Nuance and complexity are essential to an academic contribution. If you fail to understand this subtlety from reading the existing literature, then your idea will struggle to do full justice to your study from the beginning.

2

■ What does the literature tell us?

The body of literature to which you will be referring consists of a range of different types of study: qualitative/quantitative; inductive/deductive; conceptual/empirical. Other chapters in this book should help you make sense of these and other descriptors of research. Your aim is to understand the features of prior contributions to the literature, with which you are engaging in order to determine what it is exactly they are telling you, and how this is taking you closer towards an idea. A piece of published research that you consult in the pursuit of ideas will have core characteristics. It will most often have:

- ■ A contextual literature that it references in the generation of its own particular idea
- ■ A broader body of theory that underpins that literature
- ■ A form of contextual literature relating to, commonly in management, a specific industry
- ■ An articulated methodological approach

Think back to Sherlock Holmes: there is some detective work to be done here. Look for the clues that tell you what area of literature this study belongs to and in which field it is looking to contribute. The clues are in the language and terminology used within the writing but you will also find clues that support your detective work elsewhere in a peer-reviewed journal article. The title of the journal in which the article is published will give you clues as to the sort of home-based literature to which the study will be contributing. The *Academy of Management Review* publishes scholarly articles that review concepts and literature which could directly impact on business and the way it is conducted. However, the title *Consumption, Markets and Culture* tells us that there is perhaps a broader sociological interest in this journal and thus the literature used will relate more to theories from sociology. This is one clue we can get as to the sort of literature you might see being referenced in an individual article. The other considerable source of clues about an article is its reference list. The list of references will present the field of enquiry that an article is hoping to make a contribution to as it must use the existing literature in the field to form its ideas, just the same as you are having to do in the formation of our own ideas.

Learning to recognise the constituent parts of published research and interpret the messages that they communicate to us is necessary for forming a strong idea of your own. For example, if you can recognise that there has been a large amount of *conceptual* work into the consideration of the use of Wi-Fi in customer relationship marketing in the retail sector in the UK, then you will see that there is a space in which you may be able to contribute *empirical* research to this area.

Creating a space for your idea

It is important to be clear about the space in which you locate your idea and your research. Because of the characteristics already described (qualitative/ quantitative, inductive/deductive, conceptual/empirical) it can be a challenging task to squarely define the space in which you wish to locate your study. That space is likely to be complex and require a degree of understanding of the literature in order to appreciate it fully. The clearer you can make your idea, the more effectively you can defend it as a space representing an opportunity for contributing to the literature. In turn, this will appeal to your audience (i.e. your supervisor(s) and others who will read and mark your dissertation) because it demonstrates that you are working with a viable idea. That space can be defined relating to the aforementioned types of characteristics; for example, there may be little empirical enquiry into an area, in which case there is a space in which your ideas may contribute to the prevailing discourse. Alternatively, there may be an apparent assumption within the literature that has not been interrogated for its counter-theory, for example a body of literature may imply that 'all storytelling in organisations is used as a force for good'. In this case, your idea may be to explore the potential for destructive stories that do harm in organisations.

Of course, if you are reading widely and diversely, then you may identify different research spaces which clash with each other. It is best to keep a record of your reading so that you remain on top of your literature. It is surprising how quickly one article or paper blends into another when you are reading a large volume of material, and you will need to be able to justify why you have decided to investigate your chosen research path at the expense of other avenues. Table 2.1 suggests how you might systematically approach each article, such that you can both manage and analyse content and record any ideas that arise from your analysis.

Table 2.1: Identifying your research gap

	Existing scholarship	Research space	Moving forward...
Prompt questions	What does the article say? What assumptions has it made to say these things? What methods has it used to research its conclusions?	Where is the gap in this article? Which assumptions or methods has it excluded to reach its conclusions? Which of these excluded elements might be used productively in context?	Of the excluded elements you have identified, which are relevant to your research? What might you do with these elements?
Notes	1. 2. 3	1. 2. 3.	1. 2. 3.

Exercise 2.1

Ideas for research must have theory, context and data. Can you name yours? Choose an article you have read recently and create your own version of the table above. Identify a possible research gap and suggest what you might do with it next.

Who cares? How to make your ideas 'interesting'

Davis's canonical article, 'That's Interesting', shook up management scholarship in the 1970s by making the point that research need not be 'true' to be interesting (Davis, 1971). Davis's assertion is one of those ideas that seem so apparent that he could be accused of stating the obvious. However, in a discipline such as management studies, in which scholarship ranges from the strictly positivist to the devotedly interpretivist, and in which ontology is determined by where you situate yourself on this positivist/interpretivist spectrum, 'truth' is a much-contested and malleable commodity. Yet if you can show your positivist colleague why your interpretivist idea is interesting, your research will have currency across the discipline regardless of whether it is considered 'true' or not. If you are able to go further and get the attention of those outside the discipline or the academy, then your idea has really started to develop some significance.

Since the 1970s, management scholarship has (ironically) been very interested in ways in which research might be made 'interesting' (cf. Bartunek et al., 2006). This scholarship makes a variety of contributions, ranging from *what* might be considered interesting to *how* you might make it of interest. As interest is an individual thing, we will leave *what* you find of interest to you, however, in the following section we suggest *how* you might make your ideas interesting to others.

■ Developing a value proposition for your idea

The key to generating and holding your audience's interest in your idea is your ability to state it as a value proposition. If you are able to demonstrate that your idea is of value and that on delivery this value will be experienced, then your audience will be persuaded to invest (at least their time and attention) in your research. Of course, the willingness of your audience to invest depends on good value management: you must be able to persuade your audience of your chosen assets' potential, and you must be able to demonstrate why your chosen methods will bring the best returns. What this means for your research is that you need to be on top of your idea so that you can clearly state:

1 What it will contribute

2 How it will do this

3 (Most importantly) why this matters

Your identification of your 'research space' from section 1.3 will help you develop your answers to these three questions. You can then break your idea down into the first two questions: *what* will it contribute? and *how* does it contribute? These two questions can then be divided into four subsets:

■ *What* does your idea contribute to the **field**? *How* does it contribute **contextually?**

■ *What* does your idea contribute to the **academy** in its widest sense? *How* does it contribute **theoretically?**

■ Does it contribute **methodologically?** How does it contribute to **practice?**

■ *What* does your idea contribute to **wider society**? *How* does it contribute **publicly?**

Your knowledge of the literature will give you a good understanding of the scholarly context so that you can judge what elements of these subsets your audience might find interesting, or might be persuaded to find interesting. Once you have settled on *what* your idea will contribute and *how* it will make this contribution, you can begin to consider *why* this contribution matters (why is it important?). This final step will consolidate your idea's value as it will enable you to state whether you intend to make a contextual, theoretical or methodological contribution – or a combination of two or all three.

In Table 2.2 we have mapped out the value-proposition-creating process. As we have previously discussed the paper, we have used Davis (1971) as an example of how an idea can be broken down, evaluated and valued. The 'why does this matter?' column is the overall objective of the process as this indicates how your idea is valuable, why it might be interesting and who might be interested in it.

Table 2.2: Creating a value proposition for your idea

Idea	What does it contribute...	How does it contribute...	Why does this matter?
Example Davis (1971), 'That's Interesting'	**...to the field?** A study of the 'interesting' factor	**...contextually?** By highlighting the unexplored concept of 'interesting' in management scholarship	Contribution to knowledge. Understanding 'interesting' could improve quality and lead to wider readership or industry links
Davis (1971)	**...to the academy?** A logical analysis on subjective subject matter	**...theoretically?** Shows how the analysis of synthetic statements can support a positivist outlook	Provides a theoretical structure which supports an unusual combination conducive to new conclusions
Davis (1971)	**...to practice?** A method which combines positivist ontology and interpretivist subject matter	**...methodologically?** Shows how the analysis of synthetic statements is useful to management scholarship	That this novel methodology can provide new results
Davis (1971)	**...to wider society?** Provides 11 models of how writing can be 'interesting'	**...publicly?** These models are transferrable to other disciplines and industry	Wider recognition of the discipline and possible new links to industry

◼ Who cares? 'Selling' your idea

Having established why your idea matters, you now need to consider who your idea might matter to. Your research space will provide you with clues to your audience – if, for instance, you have chosen to pursue a theoretical research gap, your audience is likely to be a particular kind of scholar; whereas if you have chosen a contextual, socially-orientated research gap, your research might matter to policy-makers or industry. Although your research project is intrinsically academic, your writing should take into account your target audience, for this will determine assumptions you make about your readership's knowledge-base, the direction in which you angle your research question and your rhetoric, tone and style.

Your tone and style will vary depending on the type of project; and it is important to similarly adapt your rhetoric (how you 'sell' your idea). Is your project controversial? Will your rhetoric be proportionally confrontational or is a little more care and attention required? Is your project exploratory? Do you need to inject a sense of discovery into your writing? Is your project theoretical? Do you intend to stay technical or open out your language so that it is accessible to all? Your rhetorical stance is a performance – one designed to amuse and persuade – and one that will ultimately determine whether your reader considers your idea interesting.

Management research and ideas

In the following section, we deconstruct Maclean, Harvey and Chia's (2012) paper to provide an example of idea generation and justification in practice. We will show how the authors state their idea, place their idea in a scholarly context and frame their idea in theoretical terms. We will also discuss the ways in which the authors justify or 'sell' their idea – both in terms of content and contribution, and in terms of language and rhetoric. We intend that our discussion of this paper acts as a concrete guide to our arguments in this chapter.

◼ Responding to a call

The opportunity spaces within fields of enquiry are typically myriad, one simply must be suitably versed in the language of the field and the history of its development to recognise when there is an implicit call, among the contemporary published authors, for a contribution to be made to a specific space. This section deconstructs elements of an exemplar journal article that is world class in its findings yet clearly articulated and simple in its definition of the research space it attends to. Maclean, Harvey, and Chia (2012, p. 18) state:

> *"The article responds to the call for more research into sensemaking processes within narratives (Brown & Jones, 1998; Sonenshein, 2007), from the perspective of business leaders."*

The nuance of this research space is developed further as the literature review commences, citing multiple, established authors in the field and plainly laying-out where there is a current deficit of understanding:

> *"While the role of narratives and narrativization is generally recognized as crucial to a fuller understanding of organizational phenomena… storytelling by elite actors remains under-explored in the organization studies literature." (Maclean et al., 2012, p. 18)*

If we scrutinize the authors who are cited when this space is articulated, then we gain confirmation of the home-based literature being related to "the organization studies literature" (Maclean et al., 2012, p. 18). The authors being cited have published their work in journals such as: *Academy of Management Review, Human Relations, Journal of Management Studies, Organization, and Organization Studies.* These journals are concerned with the area of literature the authors present as being the field they are looking to contribute to, so we can trust that the articulated idea space is founded in an understanding of the literature.

■ Explore the contribution

After exploring the articulation of a research space and opportunity for a contribution, it is worthwhile checking to see exactly how that contribution is presented at the end of the paper. Any project needs to present well-supported and justifiable conclusions and comparing the research space stated at the outset of the study with the conclusions at the end will help you to understand how well the idea has been developed and defended.

In this exemplar article we see the idea being framed and justified following the execution of the study. The first line presents the broad contribution that most closely relates to the initial research space articulated at the beginning of the article: "This article makes a contribution to the study of storytelling and sensemaking by elite organizational actors, both of which remain under-researched." It then develops the nuances of the original idea by discussing specific contributions to the literature and even more specifically to the theory that underpins the literature:

> *"It contributes to the literature on legitimacy by providing a more nuanced understanding of business leaders' attempts to (re)frame their accounts of their own success. Our contribution to theory is twofold. First, we have responded to calls for more research on sensemaking processes in narratives (Brown et al., 2008; Sonenshein, 2007); identifying and explicating the three processes – locating, meaning-making and becoming – elicited from the stories told by business elites within life-history narratives." (Maclean et al., 2012, p. 36)*

■ Frame the limitations

An idea is not a neutral prospect. It will have its supporters and detractors and deemed 'good' or 'bad' based on your readers' ideas of what is supportable, 'right' or 'true'. Once you have decided on your topic, your job is not necessarily to prove why your idea is true, but how your idea might be true, and why this matters. If you can state the interest of your idea and generate this interest in your readers, then veracity and value statements to an extent will become irrelevant. More than their approval, you will now have your readers' attentions – as you have given them something they will want to discuss and engage with.

The next section will discuss assumptions and how to ensure these are informed assumptions that you can frame them in the same way you framed your idea in the first place. Thus the idea space is defined as much by what was not explored as what was. Therefore, an awareness of limitations and assumptions will strengthen your original idea and make your proposed contribution easier to defend:

> *"The limitations of the present research include the relatively small size of the sample of life-history interviews analysed, and the focus on business elites of a single country at a particular point in time. Temporally and spatially comparative studies might provide a useful means of evaluating and building upon the ideas presented here. We do not suggest that the sensemaking processes we have identified are exhaustive, nor that the legitimating constructions employed in their narratives are the only ones that might be used, and plainly, there is a need to examine further the ways in which*

storytelling and sensemaking inform organizational processes (Brown et al., 2008), which, for reasons of space and focus, this article has touched on only tangentially." (Maclean et al., 2012, p. 36).

Ideas within management research tend to co-inhabit theoretical and practical spheres. It is vital that your idea shows sensitivity to its own practical limitations, whilst remembering that its existence in the first place is couched firmly in the literature. In the above extract you can see the value of the research conducted being defended yet the limitations are clear and prevent the study from overreaching in its intended contribution – the idea is being framed, this is discussed in the next section.

Don't reinvent the wheel: Do something modest, delimited and realistic

Every year in every Business School and Management department around the world students meet with their supervisors for the first time. Within the first few minutes, an ambitious and broad ranging research topic will be announced – "I will be analysing the global marketing strategy of Apple from conception to present day" – and a few minutes later its scope and feasibility will be gently challenged by the supervisor: "I see... How will you access the senior officers of a global firm?" And as the student begins to think about the parameters of their research, their supervisors muse over the difficulties of actually achieving such a project: "... I mean, is this person mad? Global?? Across all of time?! Maybe, if we had a time travel machine this idea might be possible..."

A research assignment is a two-headed beast – it presents the opportunity for you to spend time investigating something in which you are genuinely interested, but it also contains many caveats and requirements which you must take into account in order to complete it successfully. Here we offer some suggestions for keeping both heads contented.

■ Demonstrating research ability

When you are tasked with carrying-out a research project like a dissertation, as part of a university degree, you are being asked to demonstrate your ability to design, administer and analyse a study. You are not being marked on how much impact you have on the way we understand the world, you are being marked on how you managed the project and delivered justifiable and well-supported results. World-renowned academics, Nobel laureates and mad scientists alike rarely set out to change the world; they embarked on studies that were carefully designed and managed and, most importantly, focussed on a specific, delimited problem space, the significance of which only became apparent when it was considered in its wider context and *after its completion*. The point here is that your research should be no different: aim to find out a little about a huge thing and you will end up with an unmanageable number of questions, a great amount of uncertainty and the need to make several (unfounded) assumptions to present your conclusion. Conversely, aim to find out a lot about a tiny problem and you will end up with answered questions, little uncertainty and the need to make only a limited amount of (informed) assumptions. The latter would represent justifiable and well-supported results.

When approaching your research assignment, first consider how you might arrange an unorganised mass of data into something which has theoretical, methodological and contextual meaning. If you ensure that you systematically address these core requirements of the assignment, the rest will begin to become clear.

How to make it achievable?

Your project brief should give you a good general idea of what is required from your research. As we discussed earlier in this chapter, identifying a research space means that you should also be able to generate some research aims. Compare your research aims with your research brief – do they seem to be an even fit, or do the demands of one outweigh the demands of the other? The project brief will have been written to help you control the limits of your research and ambition, so you will find it advantageous to try and stick to it as closely as possible. A little ambition for your research is no bad thing, but it pays to temper ambition with some practicality as you are otherwise likely to only become distracted from the requirements of the assignment, and have your criticality warped by an unexpected agenda. Research impact, no matter how well-intended, is reliant as much upon good luck and serendipity as it is upon your plans for it.

Your research assignment will have clearly defined parameters, whether in terms of a word count, page limit, or presentation length. You will have completed shorter assignments before, so these should give you a relative indication of how much reading is required for this longer project, how long your data collection might take and how long it might take you to write it. However, bear in mind also that this is a project of a slightly different kind – both in its length and in the sense that it must carry idea cohesion across its various sections – so it requires more planning than the projects you have completed before. Make sure you give yourself enough time to write it up properly – there is little point in having collected fascinating data if you have no time to adequately present and analyse it. If you are someone who works best only with a deadline looming, then ask your supervisor to set you a series of mini-deadlines, and prevail upon yourself to meet them. Make sure you give yourself time to fall in and out of love with your topic, data and writing. Most importantly, schedule some time away from your project, as a little space and a few episodes of your favourite TV programme can work wonders when you're finding it difficult to make progress.

■ Make sure you like it

Your research project is likely to be the longest piece of writing you complete during your degree. It is also likely to be the one feature of your degree you will be most frequently asked about in a post-degree environment. In order to maintain the stamina required to complete your research project and to engagingly talk about your research in a post-degree environment, it greatly helps if your topic is something you enjoy, or in which you have an interest. You can choose your topic strategically so that it is of relevance to your plans post-degree, or you can choose your topic because it addresses that thing that has always fascinated you, but remember that this is one time in your adult career when you have the chance to devote time to something you are interested in. Take the opportunity to be selfish.

Make your ideas fit: Writing a research proposal

You've got an idea and you've framed it. You've read relevant literature and can locate your idea in a broader tradition (see Chapter 3). You've grasped the theory and your methodology is ready to go (see Chapter 4). Congratulations! You are now ready to write your research proposal. It may seem as if an awful lot of preparation has gone into only getting this far – but persevere. A well-researched, structured and written research proposal can act as an essential guide to your entire project – and putting the time in now to set-out your work will greatly help you in the long run. Below, we offer some advice about how to put one together.

◼ Build the skeleton

Writing a research proposal is about structure (see Appendix 3). This is a snapshot of your overall project and it allows you to consider how it will link together as a whole and what obstacles may stand in your way. This helps you prepare and plan before you become concerned with the fine details of writing and thinking through the inevitable daily challenges that come your way as you progress through the process.

Exercise 2.2

fill-in the blanks of a research proposal structure

Title	
Aim	
Objectives	
Literature Theory Context Research Space	
Research Question	
Methodology Research Philosophy Method Data Collection Data Analysis	
Contribution and Limitations	

◼ Make it hang together as one

As you go through, develop a 'meta-narrative' that introduces each chapter and provides continuity when you reach the end of a chapter or section. No reader will understand the project as well as you do and therefore you must remember to act as their guide through the structure of the research as well as communicating the specific content. A way to ensure that every element of your work is communicating the same message is to remind yourself of the answer to the following seven questions, try answering them while you develop your idea:

1 What is the research about?

2 Why is it important?

3 What research conversation will your work contribute to?

4 Who are the key voices in that conversation and what are their big ideas?

5 What are my research questions?

6 Is it theory building or theory testing?

and where appropriate

7 What is the dependent variable?

8 What is the unit of analysis?

■ Flesh it out

Now for the fun part. Once you have the 'technical' elements complete, you are ready to create that linchpin of *interest* we discussed earlier. No matter how innovative your theory or how technical your methodology, there are two key bits of content that will make your proposal come alive: examples and evidence. These two elements will not only provide context for your project, but will give a real flavour of the kind of research you intend to do. Before you start writing, consider whether there is an example that is really representative of the problem you are trying to solve, or whether there is an anecdote that contextually demonstrates the point you wish to make. Once you have these, the *social* aspect of your research will be clear, which, if nothing else, is the foundational *interest* of the social science discipline.

Directed further reading

■ Read Davis's (1971) 'That's Interesting'. Which of his models do you think best applies to the way you have generated your idea? Are there ways to generate ideas which Davis's models do not cover? What are the limitations of his approach and how might these inform yours?

■ Read Maclean, M., Harvey, C., & Chia, R. (2012). Sensemaking, storytelling and the legitimization of elite business careers. *Human relations*, **65**(1), 17-40. This was our exemplar paper and is an extremely interesting read both to give a good example of ideas being developed and worked-through, but also as a great example of elite research at the highest level.

References

Alvesson, M. and J. Sandberg (2011), 'Generating research questions through problematization', *Academy of Management Journal.* **39** (2). 247-271.

Bartunek, J.M., S.L. Rynes and R. Duane Ireland (2006), 'What makes management research interesting and why does it matter?', *Academy of Management Journal.* **49** (1). 9-15.

Brown, A. D., & Jones, M. R. (1998). Doomed to failure: Narratives of inevitability and conspiracy in a failed IS project. *Organization Studies,* **19**(1), 73-88.

Cline Horowitz, M. (2005), 'Historiography', *A New Dictionary of the History of Ideas.* MI: Thomson Gale.

Conan Doyle, A. (1890) *The Sign of Four,* London: Spencer Blackett

Davis, M. (1971), That's interesting! Towards a phenomenology of sociology and a sociology of phenomenology, *Phil.Soc.Sci* **1**. 309-344.

Dupre, L. (2004), Introduction, *Enlightenment and the Intellectual Foundations of Modern Culture.* New Haven: Yale University Press.

Lovejoy, A.O. (2009), *The Great Chain of Being: A Study in the History of an Idea.* NJ: Transaction Publishers.

Maclean, M., Harvey, C., & Chia, R. (2012). Sensemaking, storytelling and the legitimization of elite business careers. *Human relations,* **65**(1), 17-40.

Megill, A. and X. Zhang (2013), Questions on the history of ideas and its neighbours, *Rethinking History.* **17** (3). 333-353.

Rynes, S., J. Bartunek and R.L. Daft (2001), Across the great divide: knowledge creation and transfer between practitioners and academics, *Academy of Management Journal.* **44** (1). 340-355.

Sonenshein, S. (2007). The role of construction, intuition, and justification in responding to ethical issues at work: The sensemaking-intuition model. *Academy of Management Review,* **32**(4), 1022-1040.

Vermeulen, F. (2005), 'On rigour and relevance: fostering dialectic progress in management research', *Academy of Management Journal.* **48** (6). 978-982.

3 The Literature Review

Norin Arshed and Mike Danson

Being able to establish what is known about a subject area, and by association what is not yet known, is an important skill for students, researchers and practicing managers alike. In academic circles this is referred to as reviewing literature, and allows you to understand the current state in a subject area, to relate this to the ongoing research, and to identify gaps in this knowledge. A literature review may resolve a debate, establish the need for additional research, and define a topic of inquiry. This chapter concentrates on establishing and understanding the purpose of the literature review and the steps involved in undertaking a comprehensive literature review.

The purpose of the literature review

The purpose of a literature review is simple: it is to educate oneself in the topic area and to understand the literature before shaping an argument or justification. A literature review is "an important chapter in the thesis, where its purpose is to provide the background to and justification for the research undertaken" (Bruce, 1994, p. 218). The writer "extracts and synthesises the main points, issues, findings and research methods which emerge from a critical review of the readings" (Nunan, 1992, p. 217) to build a "coherent argument which leads to the description of a proposed study" (Rudestam and Newton, 2007, p. 63). Over the years, numerous types of literature reviews have emerged, but the four main types are traditional or narrative, systematic, meta-analysis and meta-synthesis. The primary purpose of a traditional or narrative literature review is to analyse and summarise a body of literature. This is achieved by presenting a comprehensive background of the literature within the interested topic to highlight new research streams, identify gaps or recognise inconsistencies. This type of literature review can help in refining, focussing and shaping research questions as well as developing theoretical and conceptual frameworks (Coughlan et al., 2007). The systematic literature review in contrast undertakes a more rigorous approach to reviewing the literature, perhaps because this type of review is often used to answer highly structured and specific research questions. The meta-analysis literature review involves taking the findings from the chosen literature and analysing these findings by using standardised statistical procedures (Coughlan et al., 2007). Polit and Beck (2006) argue that meta-analysis methods help in drawing conclusions and detecting patterns and relationships between findings. They also discuss meta-synthesis, a non-statistical procedure, which evaluates and analyses findings from qualitative studies and aims to build on previous conceptualisations and interpretations.

Of the four approaches described above, the two dominant styles of literature review are the traditional or narrative literature review and the systematic literature review. Therefore it is important to distinguish the traditional literature review (which usually adopts a critical approach) from the systematic literature review (which aims to identify all the literature in the topic area to ensure that no existing understanding or knowledge is missed). The systematic literature review has been long used in healthcare literature (Ernst and Pittler, 2001) and is a "method of making sense of large bodies of information, and a means to contributing to the answers to questions about what works and what does not" (Petticrew and Roberts, 2006, p. 2). The traditional social science and business management literature review is useful in identifying gaps in knowledge whereas the systematic review concentrates on promoting research knowledge. Jesson et al. (2011, p. 11) provide a continuum of the different approaches to both of these literature reviews (Figure 3.1).

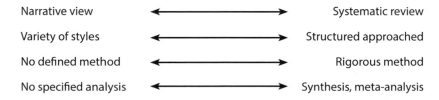

Figure 3.1: A continuum of literature review approaches

Our aim is to provide guidance on undertaking a traditional literature review, concentrating on the context of doing a more traditional and critical literature review rather than a systematic literature review. Literature reviews are important for numerous reasons. First, by undertaking a literature review, the information gathered from credible articles or studies that are of relevance, important and valid can be summarised into a document (for example, a thesis or a dissertation). This can then allow for the rationale or reason for a study to emerge, which may include a justification for a specific research approach (McGhee et al., 2007). Second, it provides a starting point for researchers where they are required to identify and understand what has been written about a particular area. That will usually mean reading all the relevant texts and then going through each to summarise, evaluate, critically review, synthesise and compare these research studies in their chosen area. Third, by carrying out a literature review it not only highlights the gaps in knowledge but it means that students, researchers and managers alike are not replicating or repeating previous work – it identifies discrepancies, knowledge gaps and inconsistencies in the literature. Finally, it can support "clarity in thinking about concepts and possible theory development" (Henwood and Pidgeon, 2006, p. 350). The purpose of a literature review is to follow a process as illustrated in Figure 3.2.

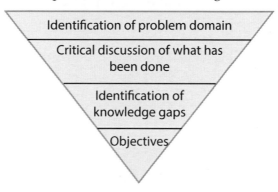

Figure 3.2: The purpose of the literature review. Source: Maier (2013, p. 4)

Often business students will find that there are many subject areas, themes, strands, theories, etc. that overlap with one another. For example, in marketing studies, 'opportunity' and 'creativity' are both themes that are essential for marketers to understand because this is how they develop marketing plans. However, 'opportunity' and 'creativity' themes are also discussed in the entrepreneurship field where 'opportunity' and 'creativity' are based on seeking gaps in the market and developing a business plan to address the gap. Both share many fundamental concepts but depending on what field of research that you undertake or follow, the language and labels used may differ slightly. It is imperative that your literature review is clear and consistent over such issues. Therefore, if you choose to look at the themes 'opportunity' and 'creativity' within the entrepreneurship field, you would have to ensure that the scope of your research remained within the field of interest.

Ideally the literature review will be able to answer the following questions.

1 What do you know about the research area?

2 What are the relationships between key ideas, dynamics and variables?

3 What are the current theories, trends and themes?

4 What are the inconsistencies, implications and shortcomings of previous studies?

5 What needs further investigation because evidence is lacking, inconclusive, contradictory and/or limited?

6 What methodological approaches have been taken and why? Are the methodological approaches justified?

7 Why does this area of research need to be studied further?

8 What contribution will your work make to the current debate?

Given these questions, the initial literature review will reveal areas requiring further research and will help to formulate your research question(s). However, literature reviews are not without their problems. If a literature review is not undertaken with a comprehensive and focussed search of the existing literature, the literature review is potentially weak. The literature review could be too narrow, too general with little structure, include obsolete citations, and searches may be of little value if they are primarily taken from websites, textbooks, press articles and so forth. The issue for you is not to review or cite as many authors as possible, but rather to *synthesise* and make an adequate argument for the purposes of the chosen research. By synthesising, you are required to critique the existing literature: to think, read and write critically in a manner which is consistent and supports and justifies your argument in your chosen area of interest.

Selecting a topic

Selecting a topic can be overwhelming. As a first step, the selection of a topic should be based on your interest and understanding of that domain. But many students ask "how do I choose which topic to review?" This may seem like a daunting task but your main ideas for studying or researching come from your own interests. Reading journals and papers, attending conferences and workshops, having discussions with your peers and academics will all help in refining the topic of interest. For example, if you are interested in entrepreneurship, is there a specific element of this wide-ranging topic which is of interest, such as social entrepreneurship, enterprise policy, business growth or entrepreneurial diversity? Identifying what exactly is of interest and asking why this is the case can help you reflect on your own motivations and can help refine the topic of your study (Hendy and Farley, 1998).

Ideally, once there is an idea of the initial topic, it is useful to do an outline search. It has been argued that a "well-thought and planned outline will assist in searching for necessary types of information and sources, save time while writing, and allow for a clearer and stronger argument for readers" (Denney and Tewksbury, 2013, p. 224). The outline is simply a guide of what an individual intends to discuss, and how (Denney and Tewksbury, 2013). This involves choosing a general (but interesting topic) to study. The reason to choose a general topic is to ensure that as much information as possible can be gathered before specifying the area to concentrate on; you will funnel down from a broad area and start to focus in on a more specific area (see Figure 3.2). If a narrow area of interest is chosen to begin with, then this reduces the information collected for the undertaking of a literature review. It is best to start general and hone in on the topic once an overview of the literature review is developed and understood. Once you begin to 'get to grips' with the general reading, the topic area starts to become refined and this is where modifications, revisions and refocussing of areas emerge. Throughout the literature review iterations of ideas, arguments and justifications take shape. This is not to be seen as a hindrance – rather it contributes to the scope and strength of the current study because sub-themes and sub-topics begin to emerge and will set the parameters. Furthermore, aims and objectives become more focused and clear.

Searching the literature review

Once the area of research has been chosen and outlined, searching the literature to clarify thoughts, ideas, arguments and justifications requires much more effort. However, it should be noted that even a well-executed literature review is rarely an all-encompassing and inclusive piece of work.

The literature review should start broad but the keywords should assist in identifying specific areas that would be of interest within a given time period. A first step to searching the mass databases for information about the chosen subject area is to begin the search with keywords from the outline. Pick keywords that are relevant and appropriate to the subject.

As a business and management student, you have access to a wide-ranging number of databases, these databases often primarily hold academic journal articles and papers. The best place for searching literature for business and management students is the library. There are many such sources but the most commonly used business databases are set out in Table 3.1.

Table 3.1: Business databases

Database	Database information
ABI/INFORM Complete/Proquest	Full-text business periodicals and news sources.
Emerald Journals	Provides abstracts and full text articles in the subject areas of marketing, general management, human resources, training and education, quality, economics, information management, library and information studies, operations, engineering, production and property.
Business Source Premier	The most popular business research database, featuring the full text for more than 2,200 journals.
JSTOR	Primarily articles in the humanities and social sciences.
OmniFile Full Text Select (EBSCO)	Journal areas include arts, biology, business, current affairs, education, humanities, information science, law, literature and social sciences.

When searching the literature it is useful to ensure the following:

- The parameters of your search
- The key words and search terms you intend to use
- The database and search engines you wish to use
- The criteria you intend to use to select the relevant and useful studies from all the items you find (Saunders et al., 2009).

This allows the research question to focus on the area of interest and refines the literature search into a more manageable task. However, students should be careful as to what sources they use to undertake their search for their literature review. It is important that whilst undertaking a literature review, credible, peer reviewed and relevant sources are used. Berg (2009, p. 389) lists the potential sources and their relative value in the order of:

1 Scholarly empirical articles, dissertations, and books (not textbooks and academic books).

2 Scholar, non-empirical articles and essays.

3 Textbooks, encyclopaedias, and dictionaries.

4 Trade journal articles.

5 Nationally and internationally recognised and credible newsmagazines.

3

Useful tip

At the initial stage you will have many questions about a literature review. Questions like: What is a literature review? What does one look like? What is included? What is needed?

The *International Journal of Management Reviews* (IJMR) is a high quality journal which publishes literature reviews. This is an excellent journal for you to access and source in supporting you to understand the literature review process.

Table 3.2. gives guidance as to how credible the article/source could be.

Table 3.2: Academic sources checklist

Academic sources checklist	Yes	No
Is the article peer reviewed? Is the journal which the article appears in listed in the ABS[1] rankings? What impact factor does the journal have?		
Is there a reference list/bibliography, where the citations are made throughout the text?		
Who is the author? What is the job title of the authors? Are they linked to a university, a research institute, or possibly government?		
Is the text written in formal language? Are the academic arguments and justifications apparent? Who is the author of the website?		
If you are using a website, is there an author and a copyright date? Is the URL readily available?		
Is the article dated within the last ten years? If it is more than ten years what has been said about this particular study? Who says it? Why do they say it?		

1   The Association of Business School (ABS) is the body which represents the UK's Business Schools and independent Management Colleges and sets the agenda for business and management education in the UK (www.associationofbusinessschools.org/). The ABS publishes the *Academic Journal Quality Guide* which is a reliable indicator of the overall quality of research published in particular academic journals.

Not only should you be searching within the databases but it is a good idea to read the reference lists of recently published journal articles to lead you to further literature. This is known as 'backward' searching (Paulus et al., 2014). Often the journal articles are available for immediate download (via digital copies), if not, your library has access to hard copies or they can arrange for an inter-library loan – this is a library system in place in many higher education institutions. The inter-library loan system refers to sharing sources with other institutions because it is not possible for universities to have every journal and article available to them. Furthermore, Google Scholar is often a very useful starting point to begin searches and is often linked to the university's own database (if on campus). This is known as 'forward' searching (Paulus et al., 2014).

Useful tip

By using Google Scholar, you can search for the most recent articles, citations and works of authors and this can save time and avoid having to trawl through individual databases.

Furthermore there are a number of useful resources that can be accessed for undertaking a literature review; the library catalogue with the databases is only one of many. Official websites (i.e. commissioned research reports), online repositories (i.e. theses, working papers etc.), and bibliographic databases (i.e. citations), books etc. are all also worthwhile for searching information related to the topic of your interest.

Reading and reviewing the literature

As soon as you begin reading and reviewing the literature, take notes of the ideas, themes and concepts that you see developing. These ideas, themes and concepts will quickly become useful as you begin to develop a structure for the literature review. It is important to take notes because it allows you to identify and understand the main points of what you read, helps you recall information, and allows you to make connections across studies (Jesson et al., 2011). It might be useful to follow a framework in order to undertake a comprehensive literature review (in particular for empirical studies):

1 Area of interest; literature cited; gap addressed; theoretical framework; research questions/hypotheses

2 Paradigm of researcher(s)

3 Design (including the research approach, the sampling strategy, demographics of participants, data collection instruments, procedures and limitations)

4 Data analysis strategy (the use of software, for example, SPSS (see Chapter 9) for quantitative data or NVivo for qualitative data (see Chapter 8)

5 Results and/or discussion

6 Conclusions and

7 Your own evaluation (including strengths and weaknesses and ideas for your own research area) (Merten, 2009).

By following a framework this enables you to synthesise your literature to identify some main ideas, themes and trends and will enable and assist you in answering the research question. For analysing individual works the following questions should be addressed to ensure a concise and comprehensive literature review is formed:

■ What is the argument? Is it logically developed? Is it well defended?

■ What kind of research is presented? What are the methods used? Do they allow the author to address your research question effectively? Is each argument or point based on relevant research? If not, why?

■ What theoretical approach does the author adopt? Does it allow the researcher to make convincing points and draw credible conclusions? Are the author's biases and presuppositions openly presented, or do you have to identify them indirectly? If so, why?

■ Overall, how convincing is the argument? Are the conclusions relevant to the field of study? (University of Ottawa, 2007).

To ensure that the argument is sound, Hart (1998) argues that the literature review has the following:

■ **Structure**: use a reliable structure that is explicit.

■ **Definition**: define the terms you will use carefully using clear examples.

■ **Reasons**: provide the reason for anything you have included as support.

■ **Assumptions**: substantiate your assumptions. Do not leave them implicit. Use only reliable assumptions that are free from value judgements or are based on valid reasoning.

■ **Fallacies**: avoid fallacies, such as generalisations, abstraction and misplaced concreteness.

■ **Evidence**: use only reliable documented evidence in the public domain that is legitimate and relevant and not trivial.

■ **Authority**: avoid appeals to authority, convention and tradition.

Critiquing the literature

When you begin to analyse and synthesise the literature it is useful to understand that you are not merely summarising what you have read. Rather you are linking the studies together and making a useful argument given your research question. The following steps enable you to constructively and critically approach the evaluations.

1 It is useful to look for patterns in the literature. For example, what are the commonalities between the studies? What are the recurring theories?

2 Compare and contrast the studies and try and recognise what makes the studies different.

3 Explore the methodological approaches of the studies included in your literature review. The methodological approach may be useful in assisting you with your own research question but the weaknesses may be apparent and could be used to build on or contribute to previous studies given your own research question.

4 Understand whether the findings of the studies within your literature review are of any relevance and whether they are consistent across the board.

5 Synthesising the findings will allow you to understand the empirical and theoretical arguments for addressing the gaps (if there are any).

If you are addressing theory, there are two ways to undertake this in your literature review. First, including theory in the literature review could potentially highlight why the theory has been discussed in previous studies and the use of the particular theory may also apply to the research undertaken by the initial literature. Second, it could be argued that a new theory should be used and the literature review should focus on the shortcomings of the other theories. Table 3.3 highlights the questions that should be answered when evaluating the literature review article by article.

Table 3.3: How to evaluate articles

How to evaluate the literature article by article	Yes	No
Content - Is the article easy to understand?		
Does it use good arguments?		
Is evidence given for any claims made?		
Does the article make clear any limitations?		
Is the writing biased?		
Context in discipline - Is this one of the key articles in the discipline?		
Does the writer agree with other writers?		
Does the writer disagree with other writers?		
Methodology - Is the methodology appropriate for the study?		
Is enough information given for another researcher to replicate the study?		
Was the sample size adequate?		
Author - Is this a reputable, academic author?		
Does the writer refer to other literature to support some of their claims?		
Relevance - Is the research recent?		
Is the purpose of the research similar to your own?		
Was the study conducted under similar circumstances to your own subject?		
Can you draw on the research for your own work?		

Source: Adapted from Roberts and Taylor (2002).

Literature reviews are not simply descriptive summaries of what has been read and who has written what – you are required to critically analyse the articles. By critically analysing the articles, the argument is strengthened with a justification. Browne and Keeley (2004) highlight words that can be applied to critical writing which may be of use to you when undertaking the literature review (Table 3.4).

Useful tip

See Blackburn, R. and Kovalainen, A. (2009). Researching small firms and entrepreneurship: Past, present and future. *International Journal of Management Reviews* **11** (2): 127–148. This article provides a debate on the agendas, methodologies and methods used in the field of small business and entrepreneurship.

Table 3.4: Forming critical sentences using signalling words

As a consequence of x then y
Consequently…
Hence…
Therefore,…
Thus…
In short…
In effect…/It follows that…
This indicates that…
This suggests that…
It should be clear now that…
This points to the conclusion…
This means that…
Finally,…

You should note that when you are critically writing the literature review you should indicate your own position when comparing and contrasting different theories, concepts, arguments and terminology. Include only relevant references to underpin the arguments which form the fundamentals of your research; balance your argument (with both its merits and limitations) and synthesise and reformulate arguments from a couple of sources to construct a new or more developed argument (Ridely, 2012).

Useful tip

Do not use 'me, myself or I' when arguing and justifying claims, theories, arguments etc. Always write as an observer. For example, you can write 'The research', 'This study' etc.

Writing the literature review

Once a topic has been selected, literature searched, reading and reviewing undertaken and the literature critically analysed it is time to begin writing the literature review. There are crucial characteristics of a well-written literature review:

1 An introduction that provides an overview of the focus and objectives of the reviews, along with a statement of the research.

2 A set of themes that categorise, review and are used to develop the research topic (e.g. sources that support a particular position, those opposed, and those offering alternative views).

3 Explanations and evaluation of conclusions reached by key sources, and justifications of how they converge and diverge from the conclusions reached from other sources.

4 Conclusions, reasonable speculations, and gaps that emerge after considering the sources as a whole (Zorn and Campbell, 2006).

It is crucial therefore that the literature review is structured, with an introduction, a body and a conclusion and should be centred on an argument about the literature that has been reviewed. The literature should have a very clear and precise introduction. One which outlines and articulates the focus of the literature review – the research objectives or questions should guide the literature review and this should be apparent in your introduction. From this, the themes, headings and sub-sections should all convey and link back to the research question. For example, the overall arching research question could be 'how is enterprise policy formulated in the UK?' This can be used to guide the literature review and a set of key themes from the body of literature can subsequently serve as headings for the literature review. Given the example research question, the key themes could include (a) defining policy and enterprise policy (including the foundations and historical background of enterprise policy in the UK) (b) the increasing importance of enterprise policy (the arguments for and against such a policy) (c) the instruments involved in enterprise policy and (d) the key actors involved in the policy process and (for example, information on the formulation of policy). Within the main themes it is important that you focus on the arguments and fundamental conclusions by explaining and evaluating the key literature. The job here is not to be descriptive or summarise what you have read, it is to show that you can write concisely, explain and build arguments given the common or conflicting conclusions reached by others. The conclusion within the literature review should effectively answer or address the research aim set out in the introduction. This concluding review should summarise the answers to the research question with justifiable sources and identify the gaps in knowledge: the gaps identified in the literature review can provide a justification for future research calls or recommendations. Furthermore, within the body of the literature review, an argument of the research area should be apparent. This transparency and explicitness should be justified with the literature review.

Given the structure, the write-up stage of the literature review is iterative (Figure 3.3). It is important that whilst writing, you audit and edit at the same time to refine, correct and perfect your literature review.

Figure 3.3: The iterative process of writing. Source: Machi and McEvoy (2009, p. 130).

Useful tip

To keep the logical flow of the argument and connecting the dots, phrases such as 'similarly' or 'in addition' or 'in contrast' should elaborate, and substantiate the topic in question (Zorn and Campbell, 2006).

When writing, synthesising and linking each sentence it is important for a logical flowing argument as well as keeping the argument within the research question. The initial sentence should make a clear point, with the following sentence in the paragraph connecting the dots. It is useful to understand how to use verb tenses usefully. Some examples that you should be aware of are outlined below.

The present tense is used for relating what other authors say and for discussing the literature, theoretical concepts, methods, etc.:

"In her article on enterprise policy, Smith specifies that ...."

The present tense is also applied when you present your observations on the literature:

"However, on the important question of policy formulation, Smith's argument is weak."

Moreover, the use of the past tense is used for recounting events, results found, etc.

> *"Smith and Jones conducted a longitudinal study over a five-year period. They determined that it was not possible to recreate the same process for formulating enterprise policy."*

Try to avoid making sweeping generalisations such as "Most researchers agree", "It is obvious", "Many think" etc. This raises questions from the reader – what researchers? Obvious to whom? Who thinks that? (Olloff, 2013). Always ensure that all the sources used are cited appropriately. Each idea, argument, justification, and school of thought must be cited and supported with the relevant references. This allows the reader to be assured of the credible sources used and have an understanding of the preceding knowledge from reading the literature review. It also highlights prior research undertaken in the area, highlighting the topic of interest in 'joining a conversation' with other work in the topic area. Often citations and quotes will be inserted, but ensure that when using quotes, the exact citation is inserted and quotes should be used in moderation – just enough to allow for credibility and clarity when making a point or defining a word, term or phrase. Also ensure that the correct method of citing is applied to the literature review. This differs from institution to institution. For example, some institutions use Harvard, others may use APA 6th.

Pitfalls of literature reviews

There are several common errors made by students whilst undertaking their literature reviews. The first mistake is to cite only references supporting your arguments, and advocating a particular school of thought or scholar. A literature review objectively states all arguments, based on the research. Second, if citations are only made to support one side of an argument, then a stream of literature (the opposing argument) is missed, not giving the whole picture as it were. Third, not synthesising and critically writing the argument is often a grave error. A literature review is not about 'what she said' or 'what he said', analysing, synthesising and criticising the literature respectably and academically is what is required. Fourth, using unreliable (and often outdated) sources is not acceptable. Sources such as magazines (e.g. Vogue), populist newspapers and TV channels (e.g. The Sun in the UK or Fox News), and websites (e.g. Wikipedia) are not suitable. Academic, peer-reviewed and reputable sources are required for undertaking a literature review. A literature review requires legitimacy to ensure that it is taken seriously. Finally, literature reviews often fail to analyse the data. For example, reporting the findings in a descriptive manner are not enough, rather you should enable the reader to engage with the findings throughout your literature review by analysing and synthesising research findings which contribute to the literature review.

For the literature review to be seen as a legitimate and timely piece of work, ensure that you do not violate academic standards by undertaking any of the following: falsification (misrepresenting the work of others), fabrication (presenting speculation as if they were facts), sloppiness (not providing the correct citations), nepotism (citing references of colleagues that are not directly related to your work) and plagiarism (the acts of knowingly using another person's work and passing it off as your own) (Hart, 1998).

Hart's checklist of dos and don'ts for literature reviews

Hart (1998, p. 219) outlines a number of major dos and don'ts for undertaking a literature review. It is good to bear these in mind before you start.

Dos...

- Identify and discuss the relevant key landmark studies on the topic;

- Include as much up-to-date material as possible;

- Check the details, such as how names are spelled, what year the article was published;

- Try to be reflexive;

- Critically evaluate the material and show your analyses;

- Use extracts, illustrations and examples to justify your analyses and argument;

- Be analytical, evaluative and critical and show this in your review;

- Manage the information that your review produces, have a system for records management;

- Make your review worth reading by making yourself clear, systematic and coherent, and explain why the topic is interesting.

Don't...

- Omit classic works and landmarks or discuss core ideas without proper reference;

- Discuss outdated or only old materials;

- Misspell names or get date of publications wrong;

- Use concepts to impress or without definition;

- Produce a list of items, even if annotated – a list is not a review;

- Use jargon and discriminatory language to justify a parochial standpoint;

- Accept any position at face value or believe everything that is written;

- Only produce a description of the content of what you have read;

- Drown in information by not keeping control and an accurate record of materials;

- Make silly mistakes, for example, 'polity' instead of 'policy';

- Be boring by using hackneyed jargon, pretentious language and only description.

Further reading

Denney, A.S. and Tewksbury, R. (2013). How to Write a Literature Review. *Journal of Criminal Justice Education* 24(2), 218-234.

Machi L. A. and McEvoy, B. T. (2009). *The Literature Review*. Thousand Oaks, CA: Sage.

Ridley, D. (2012). *The Literature Review: A step-by step guide for students* (2nd ed.). London: Sage.

For business and social science students the *International Journal of Management Reviews* is a high quality journal which publishes literature reviews. The journal covers all the main management sub-disciplines including, for example, HRM, OB, International & Strategic Management, Operations Management, Management Sciences, Information Systems & Technology Management, Accounting & Finance, and Marketing. You can find the journal at the following link: http://onlinelibrary.wiley.com/journal/10.1111/(ISSN)1468-2370

References

Berg, B. L. (2009). *Qualitative research methods for the social sciences* (7[th]ed.). Boston, MA: Allyn & Bacon.

Browne, M. N. and Keeley, S. M. (2004). *Asking the right questions: A guide to critical thinking* (7[th]ed.). London: Pearson Prentice Hall.

Bruce, C. S. (1994). Research students' early experience of the dissertation literature review. *Studies in Higher Education*, **19**(2): 217-229.

Coughlan, M., Cronin, P. and Ryan, F. (2007). Step-by-step guide to critiquing research. Part 1: quantitative research. *British Journal of Nursing* 16 (11): 658–63.

Denney, A. S. and Tewksbury, R. (2013). How to Write a Literature Review. *Journal of Criminal Justice Education* **24**(2): 218-234.

Ernst, E. and Pittler, M. H. (2001). Assessment of therapeutic safety in systematic reviews: literature review. *British Medical Journal* **323**(7312): 546-547.

Hart, C. (1998). *Doing a literature review: Releasing the social science research imagination.* London: Sage.

Henwood, K. and Pidgeon, N. (2006). Grounded Theory. In G.M. Breakwell, S. Hammond, C. Fife-Shaw & J.A Smith (Eds.), *Research methods in psychology* (3rd ed., pp. 342-365). Thousand Oaks, CA: Sage.

Jesson, J. K., Matheson, L. and Lacey, F. M. (2011). *Doing Your Literature review: Traditional and Systematic Techniques.* London: Sage.

McGhee, G., Marland, G. R. and Atkinson, J. (2007). Grounded theory research: Literature reviewing and reflexivity. *Journal of Advanced Nursing* **60**(3): 334-342.

Nunan, D. (1992). *Research Methods in Language Learning.* Cambridge: Cambridge University Press.

Olloff, J. (2013). *How to write a literature review: Workbook in six steps.* Farmington: Sparrow Media Group.

Paulus, T. M., Lester, J. N. and Dempster, P. G. (2014). *Digital Tools for Qualitative Research.* London: Sage.

Petticrew, M. and Roberts, H. (2006). *Systematic Reviews in the Social Sciences: A practical guide.* Oxford: Blackwell.

Polit, D. and Beck, C. (2006). *Essentials of Nursing Research: Methods, Appraisal and Utilization* (6th ed.). Philadelphia: Lippincott Williams and Wilkins.

Ridley, D. (2012). *The Literature Review: A Step-By-Step Guide for Students.* London: Sage.

Roberts, K. L. and Taylor, B. J. (2002). *Nursing research processes: An Australian perspective.* South Melbourne: Nelson.

Rudestam, K. E. and Newton R. R. (2007). *Surviving you Dissertation: A Comprehensive Guide to Content and Process* (3rd ed.). Thousand Oaks, CA: Publications Inc.

Saunders, M., Lewis, P. and Thornhill, A. (2009). *Research methods for business students* (5th ed.). Italy: FT Prentice Hall.

University of Ottawa (2007). Academic Writing Help Centre – http://www.sass.uottawa.ca/writing [accessed 28 March 2014].

Zorn, T. and Campbell, N. (2006). Improving the writing of literature reviews through a literature integration exercise. *Business Communication Quarterly* **69**(2): 172-183.

3

4 Mapping Research Methods

Kevin O'Gorman and Robert MacIntosh

For no apparent reason, research philosophy tends to send dissertation students into a mild panic. The befuddlement caused by a range of new terminology relating to the philosophy of knowledge is unnecessary when all that you are trying to achieve is some clarity over the status of any knowledge claims you make in your study. Business and Management sits within the broader context of the social sciences, and this chapter offers a guide to the standard philosophical positions required to specify the particular form of research you plan to undertake. Collectively, these positions will define what we refer to as a research paradigm (see Figure 4.1: Methods Map). For us, a comprehensive articulation of a research design draws together five layers of interlocking choices that you, the researcher, should make when specifying how you plan to execute your research. There is no single 'right' way to undertake research, but there are distinct traditions, each of which tends to operate with its own, internally consistent, set of choices.

The Methods Map in Figure 4.1 offers a clear and structured approach that will ensure that you can identify each of the choices you are making in selecting your research design for your project. The process of developing a research design begins with the location of your proposed work within a particular research paradigm. Certain methods of data gathering and analysis tend to follow from certain paradigms, although it is important to notice that these implied pathways are not fixed. What is truly important is your ability to recognise and justify the interlocking choices which represent your own research design. Later chapters will deconstruct and explain the subsequent stages of the Map, namely those choices relating to both data gathering and data analysis. The sections that follow in this chapter relate to the starting point of the Methods Map, labelled 'Research Paradigm.' We

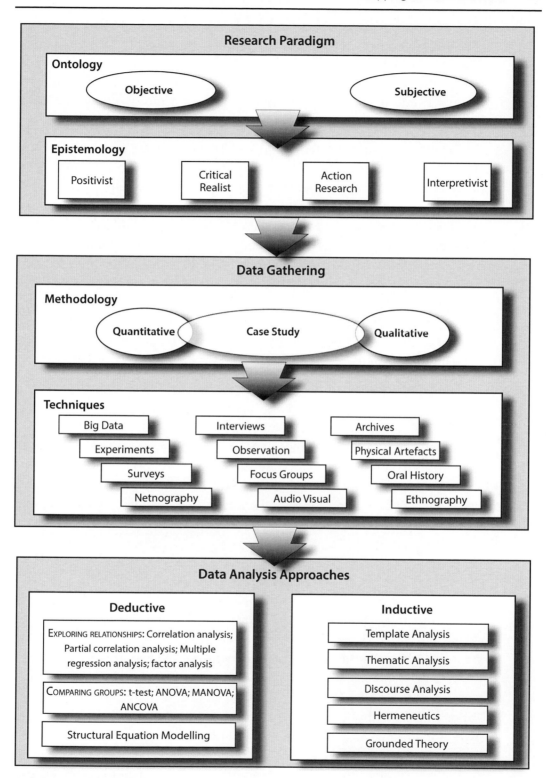

Figure 4.1: Methods Map

shall first consider the reasons for articulating a research philosophy, before exploring objective and subjective ontologies, and the epistemological positions known as positivism, critical realism, action research and interpretivism. In passing, we will also look at rhetoric (the study of persuasive language) and axiology (the study of value) as a means of rounding out your understanding of some key phrases and concepts.

Whilst these concepts emanate from philosophy, it is not necessary to have studied philosophy in order to make sense of the terminology. In essence, the purpose of setting out your research philosophy is to help signal to other researchers those claims you might make in your findings, and the basis on which you would make such claims. However, it is highly likely that the same broad research question or objective could have been approached using a very different style of research. All that you are required to do is demonstrate that you engaged in a conscientious selection and defence of what you deemed to be the most suitable approach, given your chosen topic. Historically, certain paradigms may have been used for certain topics and methods, yet it would be foolhardy to dismiss the potential for innovation to be found in combining ideas and mixing methods.

Some of the ideas that follow may at first seem challenging and difficult to work with. As a health warning, we would acknowledge that we have made some simplifying assumptions in the approach that we have set out. Those well versed in the philosophy of knowledge may take issue with some aspects of our presentation here. However, we are confident that the structured approach we are proposing will suffice for the vast majority of individuals tasked with articulating a methods statement. Let's first look at why this is important.

Articulating a research philosophy

When undertaking any research project it is considered good practice to clearly outline the basis for claiming to know what we know. Kuhn (1971) set in place the tradition that once a paradigm is chosen it is advisable for the researcher to remain within it. For the purposes of this discussion, a paradigm, as defined by Harré (1987, p. 3), is considered to be "a combination of a metaphysical theory about the nature of the objects in a certain field of interest and a consequential method which is tailor-made to acquire knowledge of those objects." At the philosophical level it could be perceived as dualistic if the researcher were to argue simultaneously that they believe that social reality is separate and external, whilst maintaining that reality is merely a construction of the mind. Hussey and Hussey (1997) emphasise the importance of researchers recognising and understanding their philosophical orientations within the paradigm adopted for a specific project.

In 1781 Immanuel Kant published his *Critique of Pure Reason* (1780/1998) and caused a revolution in philosophy. Kant argued that there are ways of knowing about the world other than through direct observation, and that people use these all the time. This proposition provided the platform for the launch of many of the ideas associated with research philosophy. Kant's view proposes considering not how our representations may necessarily conform to objects as such, but rather how objects may necessarily conform to our representations.

Prior to this, objects were considered in isolation, separate, and unchangeable. Kant theorised that things could be considered as objects of experience: *phenomena*, rather than things in themselves (specified negatively as unknown beyond our experience): *noumena*. Therefore, if human faculties of representation are used to study these phenomena, *a priori* conceptualisations can be envisaged. An 'a priori' judgement is based on theory and argument rather than verified by experiment. For example, if we had only ever had the experience of sitting in chairs before and we saw a stool for the first time, rather than categorise it as unknown, we could conceptualise *a priori* that it would be possible to sit on a stool just like we do on a chair. Kant also showed how flawless logic can prove the existence of God and at the same time prove that there is no God at all; illustrating that opposing philosophies can be equally logical and at the same time contradictory and incomplete: a salient warning to any emergent researcher defending their philosophical stance.

The roots of research method

Gorgias, a fifth century Sophist, is remembered for his provocative aphorisms. The most notable is his treatise *On What is Not*:

> *"Firstly ... nothing exists;*
>
> *secondly ... even if anything exists, it is incomprehensible by man;*
>
> *thirdly .., even if anything is comprehensible, it is guaranteed to be inexpressible and incommunicable to one's neighbour"*

(Gorgias 500 BC, quoted in Arist. De Melisso Xenophane Gorgia *980a: 19–20)*

Gorgias' treatise *On What is Not* is just a rhetorical parody of philological and rhetorical philosophical doctrines. The aphorism deals with ontology, epistemology and introduces the problem of rhetoric and language in a world where communication was shifting from the spoken to the written word. Plato (Phaedrus) in 320 BC argued that writing would deteriorate memory, wreak havoc on logical constructions, and create an artificial reality. Yet despite being written 2500 years ago, Gorgias' writing neatly summarises the central concepts of this chapter. Before exploring some philosophical concepts (first relating to ontology), Table 4.1 gives the meaning of some commonly used terms:

Table 4.1: Some commonly used terms. Adapted from O'Gorman (2008)

Term	Meaning
Axiology	The branch of philosophy dealing with values, as those of ethics, aesthetics, or religion.
Deduction	*a priori* argument: deriving a proof or using evidence to test a hypotheses.
Epistemology	The branch of metaphysics that deals with the nature of knowledge, its presuppositions and foundations, and its extent and validity. • The study of knowledge • Theories of what constitutes knowledge and understanding of phenomena • How we explain ourselves as knowers, how we arrive at our beliefs
Induction	*a posteriori* argument, deriving knowledge from empirical investigation.
Metaphysics	The branch of philosophy concerned with the ultimate nature of existence.
Ontology	The branch of metaphysics that deals with the nature of being and of reality.
Methodology	The study and application of methods.
Paradigm	Theoretical framework, within which research is conducted.
Philosophy	The academic discipline concerned with making explicit the nature and significance of ordinary and scientific beliefs, and with investigating the intelligibility of concepts by means of rational argument concerning their presuppositions, implications, and interrelationships; in particular, the rational investigation of the nature and structure of reality (metaphysics), the resources and limits of knowledge (epistemology), the principles and import of moral judgment (ethics), and the relationship between language and reality (semantics).
Reflexivity	Critical self-awareness and examination of beliefs and knowledge-claims. • Need for conscious, reflexive thinking about our own thinking, and critique our pre-understandings, and their effect on our research
Rhetoric	The art or study of using language effectively and persuasively. • In particular the style of speaking or writing, especially the language of a particular subject as used in the dissertation process

Ontology

As the Methods Map shows, the first stage in formulating your research design is to articulate your ontology. In the most basic sense this means that you must articulate whether you see the world as objective or subjective. We'll define both terms in a moment but first let's look at ontology. The term ontology is rarely used beyond academic institutions and it can be difficult to know how to use it confidently. As with much specialist terminology, a brief look at the linguistic components that form the word can help to unlock a more practical meaning. If you can understand and use the word 'biology' (where 'bios' means life) then you can do the same with ontology and epistemology. Biology is the study of life since the suffix ('-logy') is derived from 'logos', which in this context can be taken to mean the 'study of.' The word 'Ontos,' which provides the root 'onto-', at its most basic means 'being' or 'reality'. Therefore ontology is the study of being or reality. In lay terms it may be considered as how we view reality.

Outside of science fiction and fantasy novels, we might think of there being only one reality, in which we live, breathe, and die. Yet the afore-mentioned fictions are often inspired by the thought experiments through which philosophers and theorists question our understanding of reality. The most well-known of these is the brain-in-a-vat scenario, whereby a scientist stimulates a disembodied brain with such precision as to simulate an entirely realistic participation in what we call reality. Does the brain experience reality, or is the experience of the scientist somehow more real? In more contemporary terms, popular stories such as the Narnia novels or the Matrix film series are based on the premise of stepping into a different reality. In ontological terms, the philosophical notion of solipsism asserts that since we cannot know other minds, the world and those other minds do not exist. Similarly, a nihilist ontology contends that knowledge is impossible, and that there is no such thing as reality. A rather more mundane example of an altered reality relates to illness or pain: do we experience the world in the same way when we are suffering? For example, if you were asked to remove a hot dish from an oven, you would instinctively look to put a protective glove on your hand to perform this task. You would do this because you would expect to feel pain in your hand if you attempted to remove the dish without protection. The pain would be caused by your nervous system reacting to the heat of the dish so as to protect the skin from being burned. If you were to remove the hot dish with an unprotected hand the pain you would suffer as your skin burned would subconsciously be associated with the dish itself: the dish is painful. However ontologically we can understand that the dish itself is simply hot and the body's reaction to the heat is to suffer pain. Therefore, the interaction between the two things (hand and dish) has 'created' or precipitated pain to be felt, but we can ask ourselves: is the pain real? Can it be objectively measured? If it is just our body trying to send a message to our conscious brain that lifting the hot dish with unprotected hands is a bad idea, then surely we can override this message and lift the dish anyway? Pain is possibly the most visceral sensation we experience as human beings but the important word to remember here, as with Husserl's work on phenomenology, is *experience*. The theoretical reality of pain, as simply a sensory message to our brains to protect us from harm, versus our experiential reality of pain, as something that is unpleasant and negative, presents the different ways in which ontology can be considered. Despite knowing that viruses don't *intend* to cause their hosts any pain, don't we sometimes feel a grudge against the natural world when we get ill? Can suffering even exist without being experienced?

As shown by the Methods Map, ontological assumptions can be broadly divided into two fundamental configurations: objective and subjective. Although these terms are far more commonly used, it may be helpful to develop clear distinctions relating to their use in the context of research. An **objective** perspective might be thought of as looking at reality as made up of solid **objects** that can be measured and tested, and which exist even when we are not directly perceiving or experiencing them. In particular, an objective perspective would allow that something as simple as measuring your height would result in the same answer, regardless of who does the measuring. In more complex settings, we might aspire that our objectivity allows us to make the judgements necessary to decide upon the guilt of a defendant in a court of law. In contrast, a **subjective** perspective looks at reality as made up of the perceptions and interactions of living **subjects**. For instance, our response to a particular piece of music varies such that we might find something delightful whilst our friends find the same piece entirely unlistenable.

Having established these basic definitions, we can return to the process of researching organizational settings. For instance, take the claim that happier workers are more productive. We might hold the belief that the lives of others continue independently of our perceptions, and so we can measure and test their actions and reactions whilst maintaining our role as detached observers. This belief, typical of enquiries into the physical sciences, would be described as an **objective** ontology. An objective ontology thus assumes that reality exists independently of our comprehension of it, and that it is possible to establish and explain universal principles and facts through robust, replicable methods. At this point, you may find yourself agreeing that this seems rather obvious and sensible. Alternatively, you may feel a sense of discomfort at what you perceive to be an oversimplification of the myriad factors that might influence happiness, productivity, motivation, duty or fear, each of which may be influencing how productive an individual worker is in a given circumstance on a given day.

In contrast to an objective stance, a **subjective** ontology assumes that our perceptions are what shape reality, and this is a belief expressed in large sections (though not all) of the social sciences. A subjective ontology sees facts as culturally and historically located, and therefore subject to the variable behaviours, attitudes, experiences, and interpretations – what we call the subjectivity – of both the observer and the observed. This is sometimes known as a relativist ontology, although this is arguably misleading, as one can appreciate the power of subjectivity without necessarily being a moral or cultural relativist. Subjective ontology approaches reality as multiple in the sense that each individual experiences their place and time in the world in a different way. For example, the subjectivity of an African-American woman in 1960s Mississippi is likely to be entirely different from that of a Native American Indian male in the same time and place (although both are likely to have their experiences shaped by severe oppression). You may already notice a problem with the subjective approach, namely that it seems to require a certain objectivity to make a universal claim for a subjective ontology. This is not a problem that we shall attempt to solve here. A simpler criticism of an entirely subjective ontology would be to say that there *are* things in the world with observable characteristics, without which they would be something else. For instance, zinc, or ethanol. A subjective approach might counter this by saying that these characteristics are only observable relative to a particular vocabulary, set of assumptions, and people who subscribe to them; that scientific knowledge is widely accepted as true does not mean that it is universally accepted.

Questions of objective and subjective ontologies continue to fuel philosophical debate, perhaps because they are largely irresolvable. Our perceptions of ourselves and of others *are* mutually influential. Like it or not, when interacting with other people we are constantly making subconscious comparisons and judgements, to ascertain our position within that interaction. We may change the way in which we act if we know that we are investigating something, or indeed our actions are being investigated. At the same time, it seems there *is* an observable reality that exists outside of human interactions, the properties of which can be measured and predicted. As such, it should be understood that objective and subjective ontologies are not mutually exclusive, and many researchers delineate their positions in relation to these poles, somewhere between the two.

If this leaves you uncertain as to which way of studying reality is the most appropriate for your research, then take some comfort from the fact that this is a healthy sign that you are engaging with an exploration of the underlying philosophy of your research. At the beginning of any project (and often towards the end!) this uncertainty is entirely warranted, and very much desirable. Ontological questions require careful and continuous answering, and there will always be a valid argument against any position you select. The one certainty is that considerations of how the researcher and the act of researching might unwittingly impact upon that being researched must be expressed, in order for the study to demonstrate an appropriate depth of investigation. In academic research (particularly within the social sciences) asserting our ontological position is crucial, since this sets out the basis on which we view reality. All that we can really hope for is a general consensus within the parameters deemed acceptable by a given community, and it is therefore important to recognise that the somewhat manufactured and exaggerated opposition between objective and subjective ontologies acts as a catalyst for critical thinking.

Following the Methods Map from our considerations of ontology, we now encounter and must make decisions about our epistemology.

Epistemology

Epistemology concerns the way in which we obtain valid knowledge. The Methods Map illustrates four epistemological positions: positivist, critical realist, action research, and interpretivist. Although there are others, articulating your epistemological position in relation to these four allows you to define your own ideas about the way in which we decide what constitutes reliable knowledge. For instance, if you are asked for the time, and guess it correctly without a watch, is this reliable knowledge? Or should this guess be verified somehow? Would hearing a time announcement on the radio represent confirmation, or would you be unsettled to know that digital transmission of radio signals introduces a small delay? The importance placed on the verified accuracy of the time would depend upon the context in which you need confirmation, e.g. you may want to catch a connecting flight, announce the turning of a new calendar year on live television or you may want to measure the heartbeat of a newborn baby.

The term epistemology can be deconstructed in a similar way to ontology. '*Episteme*' means knowledge and therefore, epistemology is the study of knowledge. By being clear about the way in which we might obtain valid knowledge we are in turn being clear about the nature of any knowledge claim that we might make. For instance, the observation that happier workers tend to be more productive is a form of knowledge claim. In everyday life we might engage in a debate as to the validity of such a claim, citing other factors that might influence happiness, productivity, or the relationship between the two. However, as researchers, we are required to draw connections between the assumptions we hold about reality (ontology) and the ways in which we might develop valid knowledge (epistemology).

Again referring to the Methods Map we can see a 'positivist' epistemology on one side, opposed to an 'interpretivist' epistemology on the other. These are placed in similar opposition to objective and subjective ontologies, as representing two different ways of thinking about knowledge. As implied by the vertical flow of the Map, an objective ontology is typically aligned with what is called a positivist (sometimes 'foundationalist') epistemological approach to knowledge, while subjectivity tends to be driven by an interpretivist (sometimes 'constructivist', although there are differences) epistemology. Again, these are specialist terms that can seem difficult to grasp, but a useful shorthand is to think of **positivists positing** and explaining principles, and **interpretivists interpreting** and understanding relationships. As we progress, it will be become clear that a research study expressing an objective ontology with a positivist epistemological approach might naturally be aligned with a quantitative methodology, whilst a study expressing a subjective ontology with an interpretivist approach tends to be aligned with a qualitative methodology.

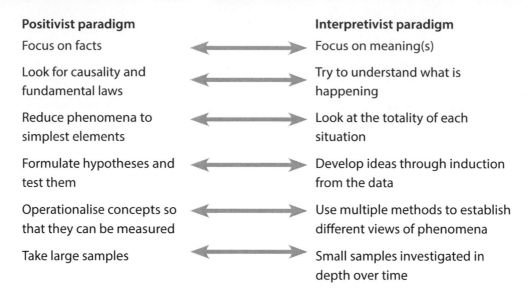

Positivist paradigm		Interpretivist paradigm
Focus on facts	⟷	Focus on meaning(s)
Look for causality and fundamental laws	⟷	Try to understand what is happening
Reduce phenomena to simplest elements	⟷	Look at the totality of each situation
Formulate hypotheses and test them	⟷	Develop ideas through induction from the data
Operationalise concepts so that they can be measured	⟷	Use multiple methods to establish different views of phenomena
Take large samples	⟷	Small samples investigated in depth over time

Figure 4.2: Epistemologies with Positive and Interpretivist influence

There now follows a presentation of four different epistemologies in social science research: *Positivism, Critical Realism, Action Research* and *Interpretivism.* There are many others being applied within social sciences research, however, particularly when it comes to undergraduate and postgraduate research, a solid understanding of these epistemologies is necessary to make an informed decision about the approach you will take.

▪ Positivism

Positivism is most commonly associated with the natural sciences, but there are advocates who suggest that social science would benefit from adopting the same basic assumptions (see Donaldson, 1996). Three assertions are associated with positivism:

- ▪ Methodological procedures of natural science may be directly adapted to the study of human social actions;

- ▪ The outcomes of research in the social sciences will take the form of causal laws; and

- ▪ The results of social research are value-free.

Comte (1830/1853) first used the term positivism; he had envisaged that sociology was to be the apex of positivism. This view is summarised in Giddens (1974, p. 1) as "the science of man completed the historical evolution of the hierarchy of the scientific disciplines, and for the first time made possible an adequate understanding of that evolution". Durkheim (1895/1964) was to defend Comte's (1830/1853) traditional version of positivism, which accentuated the supremacy of logic and scientific knowledge as the paradigm of all valid knowledge; the solution to the major practical problems facing mankind. Durkheim (1895/1964) understood sociology to be the objective study of 'social facts'; and that social facts were to be considered as things. However positivism was used in a derogatory sense by the Frankfurt School (typical examples can be seen in Horkheimer and Adorno (1944/1988), Marcuse (1967), Adorno (1969)), in the 1960s, to describe the assertions of Popper (1957) that science offers the best method in the pursuit of objective knowledge. Popper (1957) describes the scientific method as the "method of bold conjectures (hypotheses) and ingenious and severe attempts to refute them (falsification)" (cited in Checkland 1999, p. 57). Popper (1957) argues that sociologists must adopt the procedural rules, standards and intellectual conventions of science and embrace the point that there are no such things as 'truth' other than conjectural, relative truth.

The popularity of positivism in business research is probably because the data used is highly specific and precise. Babbie (1998) argues the place for positivism in social research and points out the interacting links between positivism and phenomenology by noting that "every observation is qualitative at the outset" (Babbie, 1998, p. 36), whilst observing the reason "qualitative data seem richer in meaning is partly a function of ambiguity" (Babbie, 1998, p. 37). In social science, unlike physical sciences, paradigms cannot be true or false, as ways of looking; they can only be more or less useful.

■ Critical realism

Critical realism is a relatively recently articulated epistemological position, derived from both objective and subjective ontologies, and chiefly espoused by Roy Bhaskar (1978; 1989; 1993). Critical realists assume that there *is* a reality that exists independently of human perceptions, but that our access to this reality is always limited and skewed *by* those perceptions. Our perceptions are both physically limited (e.g. we can't see into the past or future) and ideologically limited (e.g. we are biased by personal experiences). Although the critical realist makes assumptions about the world in order to produce knowledge from observations grounded in reality, it is accepted that these assumptions only create a temporary reality, which may well take on a different appearance from another perspective. Put simply, this position is 'realist' in believing in an external reality, but 'critical' of our ability to access and measure it.

Building on this, critical realists hold that although it is not possible to objectively verify universal characteristics of reality, humans nevertheless behave as if this were possible. We interpret and act upon situations as though causal relationships (e.g. **if** I drop this **then** it will fall) exist independently of our perceptions and actions. This view assumes that the power of perceptions can and does shape the world, but at the same time sees the effect of that shaping as the construction of often reliable and measurable circumstances. For example, when I strike a match, I assume that the flame will not be so large as to engulf and ignite the rest of the box. Furthermore, even when performing the same action with the unshakeable belief that the striking of a single match *would* ignite the box, this wouldn't happen unless an unusual set of physical conditions were met to make it so. Our perceptions inform and guide our decision-making, yet many scientific theories have physical consequences independent of human experience.

This layering of reality is expressed by critical realists as **stratification**, which is a principal feature of this perspective, although there is arguably some ambiguity in the application of the term. Briefly, stratified reality consists of a hierarchy of overlapping layers, with lower (or deeper, invisible) levels causing effects at higher (more easily perceived) levels. We might consider this as the distinction between what we can see happening, the events leading up to this, and the various forces that may or may not come into play at a given moment. This uniquely structured interaction of layers produces a particular outcome that cannot be reduced to its constituent parts, but nevertheless can be observed at the higher levels of stratification.

This becomes more complicated when we start to think about social reality, such as the case of happy workers. Phenomena such as happiness are subject to similarly layered distinctions based on what we assume to be reality, and again tempered by our limited ability to perceive what is occurring. Critical realists are particularly interested in the differences and interactions between the individual and society, and between individual actions and social structures. Although this is not the space to fully explore the stratification of reality, nor the 'emergent' powers stemming from its layers, it might be helpful to consider the stratification of this small section of the chapter. We (the author and imagined reader) acknowledge that there *is* something called 'critical realism' in the real world, but we can only gain access to this through language. We can read the words on these pages without having access to the process of writing, the chemical properties of ink, the historical chance and measurement that led to the printed word, or to the discussions that preceded the decision to write. The way in which we read these words is likely to be altered if, for instance, we have had an unfortunate prior experience with a spontaneously combusting box of matches. Such idiosyncratic elements of human experience and biography come together to create a perspective on critical realism that is completely individual, yet refers to something that certainly seems to exist.

Even if this all seems quite remarkably *un*realistic in its apprehension of what we understand as reality, it is hoped that this brief summation of critical realism will both prompt further investigation and generate searching questions about the nature of one's philosophical inquiries.

■ ## Action research

Far from being a single approach, Action Research is an umbrella term used to cover a wide range of styles of research unified by a shared emphasis on effecting change to the situation being studied. One of the most commonly used definitions of action research is that it involves working with organizational members on matters of genuine concern to them and over which they have a genuine need to take action (Eden and Huxham, 2001). It is therefore a highly applied and engaged form of research which sees managers and researchers collaborate to foster change.

Kurt Lewin introduced the term in 1946 to denote a new approach to social research that combined generation of theory with changing a social system through the researcher acting on or in the social system. He suggested that action research was concerned with two rather different questions "the study of general laws and the diagnosis of a specific situation" (Lewin, 1946: 36). Lewin's early Action Research projects concerned critical social problems, like racism and anti-Semitism, since he believed traditional science was failing to make an adequate response to such problems. Sadly, Lewin only wrote 22 pages on the topic of Action Research (Peters and Robinson, 1984), and died suddenly in 1947, aged 57 years old. Nevertheless, Action Research evolved in two related but distinct traditions. In the US, with the help of Douglas McGregor, Lewin set up the Center for Group Dynamics at

4

MIT and then at the University of Michigan. Working with Lewin's guidance Cook, Chein and Harding outlined four varieties of action research – diagnostic, participant, empirical and experimental. (see Cunningham, 1993:15). In the UK, a group of war-time researchers who later formed the Tavistock Institute of Human Relations in London, developed their own variant of Action Research using a steering committee to develop a strategy for carrying out the research and implementing the findings in a particular context. Researchers would gather background data, perform analysis and implement changes, often in the first instance using a test area of the organization.

Today there are a number of variants of Action Research in use (see Reason and Bradbury, 2001 for a comprehensive overview). Some approaches to Action Research use "survey feedback" where systematic feedback of data from, for example, a company-wide employee attitude survey would be used to bring about change through group discussion and involvement. However, Action Research is more commonly associated with qualitative data. Indeed, MacIntosh and Bonnet (2007 p. 321) note:

"Qualitative research is sometimes styled as the poor cousin of 'real science'… if this is the case, action research is the poor cousin's downtrodden neighbour".

The validity of Action Research is often challenged precisely because it places heavy emphasis on developing a deep understanding of one specific setting, thus critics claim it has a limited capacity to develop generalizable knowledge. Despite its popularity as a method, only a handful of empirical publications in the most prestigious journals feature Action Research in their method statements. Researchers considering Action Research therefore face two challenges. First, they must find a host organization willing to (a) participate in the research and (b) committed to taking action on the basis of the research conducted. Second, they may face greater difficulty in publishing their findings in mainstream peer-reviewed journals.

■ Interpretivism

Interpretivism is often considered the generic paradigm of the social sciences and was developed in reaction to the dominance of positivism in the 19th and 20th centuries. Interpretivism identifies that there are fundamental differences between the natural and human sciences and these distinctions stemmed from the different aims – explanation versus understanding.

Weber (1924), a key proponent of this paradigm, argued that the social sciences seek to 'understand' social phenomena in terms of 'meaningful' categories of human experience and therefore, the 'causal-functional' approach of the natural sciences is not applicable in social inquiry. Weber (1924) recognised the nature of 'subjectivity' in studying humans, and noted that whilst physical systems cannot react to predictions made about them, social systems can. He pointed out that the 'self-consciousness' of human beings and the 'freedom of choice', which that consciousness entails, implies that an observer can never obtain an up-to-date account of the subject's state of mind, which would be correct for the agent to accept. Hence in the interpretivist tradition, the social scientist can only reveal 'trends' rather than 'laws'.

Weber's interpretive social science, based on the 'attribution of meaning', is closely related to Husserl's (1950/1964) work on phenomenology. The basic premise of the interpretivist paradigm is that unlike the physical sciences, which deal with objects external to the researcher, the social sciences deal with action and behaviour generated from within the human mind. There is a clear interrelationship between investigators and the investigated, researcher and the researched. Verification of what actually exists in the social and human world depends on the researcher's interpretation; the researchers' beliefs regarding the metaphysical realm could influence their interpretation of the physical realm.

In essence, the interpretive paradigm takes into account the multiple realities which are inevitably revealed by the perspectives of different individual(s), the context of the phenomenon under investigation, the contextual understanding and interpretation of the collected data and the nature and depth of the researcher's involvement. Broadly speaking, *interpretivism* allows the focus to be fixed on *understanding* what is happening in a given context rather than just *measuring* it (Patton, 1990; Klein & Myers, 1999).

A note on (research) paradigms

St Anselm, the 11th century philosopher and Archbishop of Canterbury, wrote, "I do not seek to understand so that I may believe, but I believe so that I may understand" (Anselm *Proslogion* 154-5). St Anselm asserts that nothing is achieved or ascertained by merely speculating from the sidelines; a certain level of committed involvement is necessary. Indeed, different research vantage points would yield different types of understanding, whilst accentuating these diverse perspectives does not negate the existence of an external reality. Hammersley (1992) referred to 'subtle realism'; the acceptance that the social world does exist independently of individual subjective understanding, although highlighting that the social world is regulated by normative expectations and shared understandings. The theory of the independent existence of the social world was established by Aristotle (circa 350BC) when he argued that something exists apart from the concrete thing:

> *"If, on the one hand, there is nothing apart from individual beings, and the individuals are infinite in number, how is it possible to get knowledge of the infinite individuals? For all things that we know, we know in so far as they have some unity and identity, and in so far as some attribute belongs to them universally. But if this is necessary, and there must be something apart from the individuals, it will be necessary that something exists apart from the concrete thing" (Aristotle Metaphysics 999a 25 – 28).*

At the ontological level, the scientific method has been questioned with observations that there are many more social processes at play than are usually acknowledged in the development of new scientific 'facts' (Latour and Woolgar, 1986). Also, developments in chaos theory and quantum physics have led to an increasing number of studies questioning whether the natural world is as stable and law-like as had been previously supposed (see for example Prigogine and Stengers, 1984). Businesses, events, organisations, and even individuals do not, in themselves, possess meaning; meaning is conferred on them by and via interaction. Interpretivism seeks to observe the general trends and perceptions of a social phenomenon. Fundamentally, qualitative methods are useful for unravelling and understanding what lies behind any phenomenon about which little is known. Management is a practice rather than a science and even proponents of the unity of science (such as Popper (1957) who assumes that facts can be gathered in the social sciences in much the same way as in natural sciences) have unfortunately devoted little attention to the particular problems of social science.

Recognition also needs to be given to the importance of being as objective and neutral as possible in the interpretation and presentation of the research. Current thinking would consider it essential for a research project to be framed within one philosophical paradigm, and to remain within it: the philosophical paradigm and the basic research assumptions must be compatible and clearly understood. Whilst mixed methods are increasingly popular, we would contend that mixed philosophies are likely to be a recipe for confusion. In summary, the research assumptions which relate to the philosophical paradigm are:

- Ontological issue (nature of reality);
- Epistemological issue (relationship of the researcher to that being researched);
- Rhetorical issue (language selection in research); and
- Axiological issue (role of values in a study).

We shall now turn to the effective use of language, before considering the role of values in your research.

4

Rhetoric or the use of language in a dissertation

Rhetoric is the art or study of using language effectively and persuasively, and within the context of the research process it normally applies to the particular style of speaking or writing, especially the language of a particular subject. This section briefly explores two aspects of rhetoric which are central to the dissertation and underpinned by your research philosophy: metadiscourse and authorial voice. You are more familiar with this subject than you think. For a start we all use rhetoric every day to serve our agendas in conversation with friends and family, at university or at work. A *rhetorical question* is a question used in a context where the question in itself drives a particular agenda without needing answered, for example if someone asked you if you liked ice cream, your likely response would be *yes* but instead of simply saying yes, you might choose to drive a persuasive rhetorical agenda by responding with the rhetorical question, "Do fish live in water!?!". By responding in the form of a rhetorical question you are enforcing the idea that someone shouldn't have to ask if you like ice cream because *everyone* likes ice cream.

Metadiscourse is a term for words used by an author to mark the direction and purpose of a text. It refers to all those devices which you use to organise the text for the reader and can include textual as well as interpersonal functions. It includes use of language, first person pronouns, and evaluative expressions. When you are writing your dissertation you should consider the reader looking over your shoulder. You write to meet the reader's needs at the time, and you must always consider your hypothetical reader when writing. In the case of this book the reader is multifaceted: students who are taught by the authors and other students; colleagues who also engage their own students; the wider academic community who have an interest in the subject; and there is always the possibility of other readers looking at the content as an example of how to write a text book. In writing a dissertation you must address your reader who is probably your marker too, whilst proving you are making a contribution and demonstrating yourself as a competent member of the academic discipline.

How you use aspects of metadiscourse will also help shape your authorial voice – the way in which you write to differentiate yourself from other authors. This does not mean that as an author you have to write the same way all the time, just as different social occasions require different dress codes, different texts require different writing styles. A reflective essay would require a strong personal voice whereas a report or an exam would require a more formal tone. This view of authorial voice also has close parallels with a major tenet of post-structuralist thought. According to Foucault (1981) people have, by their very nature, multiple instead of unitary personalities or subjectivities. The Russian literary and linguistics scholar Bakhtin (1986) proposed the notion of *heteroglossia*, (from the Greek meaning many tongues). All language is made up of words, phrases, and ideas in effect borrowed from other authors and infused with their intentions; an author's voice is inevitably multiple, intertextual, and appropriate to the situation. Most academic writers develop an autobiographical self, the identity they bring with them to their writing.

The underpinning philosophy that informs the research design that you adopt for your study will shape how you write your dissertation. If you adopt an interpretivist stance then you might be more inclined to write in a personal voice, using personal pronouns (if considered appropriate by your supervisor) and the tone could highlight the evolving decision making which took place during the research process. Whereas if you were positivist in your approach, your writing might more naturally take a more formal tone, based on set definitions and with a rather impersonal voice. As has been implicitly mentioned in this chapter, language itself is a construction that we use to communicate our work and our ideas. Within the area you are studying there will be prevailing assumptions relating to the meaning of words and phrases and their appropriate uses. With the same precision that you would seek to spell and arrange words appropriately, you must endeavour to be aware of the *meaning* of the language you use to the particular literature space to which your dissertation will belong. For example, you may intend to interview for your dissertation business owners who could legitimately be described interchangeably as *entrepreneurs, leaders and managers*. However, each of these three terms has a vast area of literature that inform their meanings, and thus by using all three your metadiscourse would be weakened, thereby jeopardising the strength and validity of your conclusions. Your writing style and language choices will influence your marker, and should be appropriate to your academic community. Finally, and most importantly, it should be readable. This might seem like an obvious thing to say but how often have we read academic papers that are full of incomprehensible words and groaning under a writing style so impenetrable that the text is rendered unreadable. Writing should use language that is accessible to as many people as possible.

Axiological considerations

Axiology is the philosophical study of value, often seen as the collective term for ethics and aesthetics; the two branches of philosophy that depend on notions of value. This is distinct from Research Ethics which should inform your data collection. Values here inform the bias, which you as an individual bring to the research project. We all have biases; it is how we deal with them or at the very least acknowledge them that is important.

One of the defining features of contemporary industrial society is post-modernity and the development of reflexivity or self-consciousness. Simply put, reflexivity is that stage beyond reflection: reflecting back on oneself. Reflexive modernity or postmodernity, and the vagaries of the post-modern condition are virtually unavoidable in contemporary research within the social sciences, which include business management. Personal subjective experiences are often central to the choice of research path, and should not go unacknowledged.

In social science research we deal with human interaction and feelings, not the cold hard facts normally studied in the natural sciences and engineering. This can present individuals in sensitive and demanding situations, such as the complex dynamics studied in Alexander et al. (2012), where the subjective interpretation of the concept of bullying is dealt with among organisational teams. In his address to the universities, Pope John Paul II (2000, p.3) states that it is the duty of academics and researchers to make "universities 'cultural laboratories' in which theology, philosophy, human sciences and natural sciences may engage in constructive dialogue" and observes that in universities "there is an increased tendency to reduce the horizon of knowledge to what can be measured and to ignore any question touching on the ultimate meaning of reality."

In the research process a positivist axiological approach would be a value-free and unbiased process, whereas interpretivism could be more value-laden and biased. That said we might also keep in mind the words of Benedict XVI (2005, p.2) when he observes that today "we are building a dictatorship of relativism that does not recognize anything as definitive and whose ultimate goal consists solely of one's own ego and desires." Now, it seems likely that Benedict had his own bias when he said that, after all he was a Cardinal at the time, and he made that speech to the other Cardinals the day before he was elected Pope. Most texts are value-laden and have inherent bias.

Assumption	Question	Positivism	Critical Realism	Action Research	Interpretivist
Ontological	What is the nature of reality?	Reality is singular, set apart from the researcher	Reality is stratified and engaged with by the researcher	Reality is knowable through interaction with the specifics of a given situation	Reality is multiple and interpreted by the researcher
Epistemo-logical	How do we obtain knowledge of that reality?	Researcher is independent from that being researched	Interdependent but analytically distinct nature of society, culture (structure) and individual (agency)	Researcher interacts with what is being researched with the express intention of changing the situation	Researcher interacts with that being researched
Rhetorical	How is language used in the research?	Formal based on set definitions; impersonal voice	Formal as well as considers first and third person voice	Tends toward the first person voice	Informal evolving decisions; personal voice
Axiological	What is the role of values?	Value-free and unbiased	Considers the influence of values as experience	The values of the researcher are imposed through the overt attempt to effect a particular kind of change	Value-laden and biased

Figure 4.3: Research assumptions and positivistic and interpretivist paradigms. Adapted from O'Gorman (2008)

Once you have formed your research paradigm, a further set of choices can be made relating to the approach that you take to gathering your data. As illustrated by the Methods Map, this involves the selection of a general methodology, and specific techniques. Chapter 5 looks at case studies, and Chapter 6 explores different sources of data. Chapter 7 offers a discussion of qualitative data gathering techniques, while Chapter 8 looks at quantitative data gathering techniques. Again, following the Map, you will then come to select an appropriate approach to data analysis. These approaches are broadly categorised as deductive, which typically works to analyse quantitative data, and inductive, which tends to be used to analyse qualitative data. Chapters 8 and 10 provide the accompanying discussions on analysing qualitative and quantitative data respectively.

Only since the era of the Enlightenment, and the rise of rationalism – with its rigid view of a nature governed by intractable rules – has the written word been straitjacketed by very clear ideas of just what is and is not physically possible. Imagination and a refusal to take things at face value play a big part in scientific understanding, research and discovery. For instance the King James Bible, first published in 1611, refers several times to the unicorn, while dragons were often hunted in the Dark Ages. The ability to take an imaginative leap beyond accepted scientific dogma and the entrenched views of academic colleagues, disciplinary boundaries or even apparent common sense has been at the heart of a significant number of scientific or technological advances in the last few hundred years. For example, throughout most of the 20th century, the conventional wisdom was that peptic ulcers were caused by gastric juice. Only by a pioneering doctor infecting himself with a bacterium (Helicobacter pylori) could he prove that conventional wisdom was incorrect and win the Nobel Prize for medicine. This is true even for advances that seem to be based on objective fact or cold hard logic, as the physicist Max Planck said: "New ideas are not generated by deduction, but by an artistically creative imagination ... Science, like the humanities, like literature, is an affair of the imagination" (McFague 1982, p.75). After all, as Shakespeare's Hamlet tells Horatio "There are more things in heaven and earth, than are dreamt of in your philosophy" (Hamlet Act 1 Scene v).

References

Classical sources

Anselm, St., *Proslogion , with, A reply on behalf of the fool by Gaunilo; and The author's reply to Gaunilo translated, with an introduction and philosophical commentary*, by M. J. Charlesworth. Clarendon Press Oxford (1965).

Aristotle, *Metaphysics, Oeconomica, and Magna Moralia*. Loeb Classical Library, Volume 17. Heinemann 1968.

Modern sources

Adorno, T. W. (1969). *Der Positivismusstreit in der deutschen Soziologie*. Berlin: Luchterhand.

Alexander, M., MacLaren, A., O'Gorman, K., & Taheri, B. (2012). "He just didn't seem to understand the banter": Bullying or simply establishing social cohesion? *Tourism Management*, **33**(5), 1245-1255.

Babbie, E. (1998). *The Practice of Social Research*. Belmont, CA.: Wadsworth.

Bakhtin, Mikhail (1986). *Speech Genres and Other Late Essays*. C. Emerson and M. Holquist (Eds.). Austin: University of Texas Press.

Bhaskar, R. (1978). On the possibility of social scientific knowledge and the limits of naturalism. *Journal for the Theory of Social Behaviour*, **8**(1), 1-28.

Bhaskar, R. (1989). *Reclaiming Reality: A Critical Introduction to Contemporary Philosophy*: Verso.

Bhaskar, R. (1993). *Dialectic: The Pulse of Freedom*: Verso.

Checkland, P. (1999). *Systems Thinking, Systems Practice*. New York: Wiley.

Comte, A. (1830/1853). *Cours De Philosophie Positive*. London: John Chapman.

Cunningham, J.B. (1993) *Action Research and Organizational Development*, Praeger, Westport, CT.

Donaldson, L. (1996) *For Positivist Organization Theory: proving the hard* core SAGE: London

Durkheim, E. (1895/1964). *Les Règles de la Méthode Sociologique*. New York: The Free Press of Glenco.

Eden, C. and Huxham, C. (2001) The Negotiation of Purpose in Multi-Organizational Collaborative Groups, *Journal of Management Studies*, **38**(3), 373-391

Foucault, M. (1981). The Order of Discourse. In R. Young (Ed.), *Untying the Text: a post-structuralist reader* (pp. 47-78). London: Routledge & Kegan Paul.

Giddens, A. (Ed.). (1974). *Positivism and Sociology*. London: Heinemann.

Hammersley, M. (1992). *What's Wrong with Ethnography?* London: Routledge.

Harré, R. (1987). *Enlarging the Paradigm. New Ideas in Psychology*, **5**(1), 3-12.

Horkheimer, M., & Adorno, T. W. (1944/1988). *Dialektik der Aufklärung: philosophische Fragmente*. Frankfurt am Main: Fischer Taschenbuch.

Husserl, E. (1950/1964). *Die Idee der Phänomenologie. The Idea of Phenomenology*. The Hague: Nijhoff.

Hussey, J., & Hussey, R. (1997). *Business Research, A Practical Guide for Undergraduate and Postgraduate Students*. London: Macmillan Business.

Kant, I. (1780/1998). *Kritik der Reinen Vernunft. Critique of Pure Reason* (P. Guyer & A. W. Wood, Trans.). Cambridge: Cambridge University Press.

Klein, H. K., & Myers, M. D. (1999). A set of principles for conducting and evaluating interpretive field studies in information systems. *MIS Quarterly*, **23**(1), 67-93.

Kuhn, T. S. (1971). *The Structure of Scientific Revolutions*. Chicago: University of Chicago Press.

Latour, B. and Woolgar, S. (1986*) Laboratory Life: the construction of scientific facts*, Princeton University Press: New Jersey

Lewin, K. (1946) Action research and minority problems, *Journal of Social Issues*, **2**, 34-46.

MacIntosh, R. and Bonnet, M. (2007) International Perspectives on Action Research: introduction to the special issue, *Management Research News*, **30**(5), 321-324

Marcuse, H. (1967). *Der Eindimensionale Mensch: Studien zur Ideologie der fortgeschrittenen Industriegesellschaft*. Berlin: Luchterhand.

McFague, S. (1982) *Metaphorical Theology: Models of God in Religious Language* SCM Press, London.

O'Gorman, K. D. (2008). *The Essence of Hospitality from the Texts of Classical Antiquity: The development of a hermeneutical helix to identify the philosophy of the phenomenon of hospitality*. University of Strathclyde, Glasgow.

Patton, M. Q. (1990). *Qualitative Evaluation and Research Methods*. London: SAGE.

4

Peters, M., & Robinson, V. (1984). The origins and status of action research. *The Journal of Applied Behavioral Science*, **20**(2), 113-124.

Popper, K. R. (1957). The Unity of Method. In J. Bynner & M. Stribley (Eds.), *Social Research: Principles and Procedures* (pp. 17-24). Essex: Longman and The Open University Press.

Prigogine, I. and I. Stengers (1984) *Order out of Chaos: Man's New Dialogue with Nature*. New York: Bantram

Reason, P. and Bradbury, H. (eds) (2001) *Handbook of Action Research: Participative Inquiry and Practice*, Sage Publications, London.

Weber, M. (1924*). Gesammelte Aufsätze zur Soziologie und Sozialpolitik*. Tübingen: J.C.B. Mohr.

5 Case Studies and Data

Angeliki Papachroni and Sean Lochrie

The backbone of every research project is the collection of data that a researcher has identified as worthy of analysis. Interviews, survey questionnaires, publically available information and audio-visual material are all potential sources of data to a researcher. However, collecting data can be a daunting experience, either because you have too little data or because what looked like a rich dataset has turned into a nightmarish sense of data-overload. It is therefore helpful to spend time thinking about where you will look for data. Evaluating data sources will save valuable time and resources but also tends to lead to better analysis and more robust results. What constitutes good practice when collecting data is very much dependent on the research tradition within which your project is placed. How do different research traditions define and use data? For those scholars whose work you are engaging with closely, where did they source data? This chapter is our first look at the 'Data Gathering' area of the Methods Map. The sections that follow will help you evaluate data quality, consider ways in which different sources of data be combined and will provide practical advice on data collection. Additionally, a great part of this chapter is dedicated to case studies as an example of a methodology that can be based on different types of data. By following the advice offered here, you will be able to collect data that are relevant to your research methodology and build high quality insights.

Data in different research traditions

Elsewhere in this book, we have established that research is a broad term which covers a range of different views of what constitutes knowledge and whether social realities are fixed or constructed. Each of these traditions has developed accepted practices in terms the nature of data and approaches to both data collection and data analysis. For the moment, we would simply assert that what is considered 'data' within the different epistemological traditions varies widely. On the one hand, the natural sciences are often based on a view (*positivism*) which assumes an objective world that exists independent of the researcher; one that is based on universal laws of human nature and social reality (Patton and Appelbaum, 2003). From within this worldview, research designs, for example, that seek to verify hypotheses using statistical generalizations seem entirely reasonable (Guba and Lincoln, 1994). As a result, management research within such a tradition would feature data gathered in the form of large-scale surveys, questionnaires and other methods shown in the Methods Map that entail the quantification of a phenomenon, e.g. examining the amount, intensity or frequency of something (Valsiner, 2000, Ketokivi and Choi, 2014). Wherever possible, data within this epistemological tradition are gathered in specific ways that are intended to allow generalizations across populations.

At the other end of the epistemological spectrum, other research traditions begin with the premise that for a researcher to understand complex social phenomenon, they should consider the subjective experiences of participants (Sandberg, 2000), which Weber defines as 'verstehen' (Weber, 1964). This view of research highlights the socially constructed nature of our experience where, in simple terms, our perceptions are shaped by our own past experiences, the views of influential others, etc. So-called social constructionism (Luscher et al., 2006, Berger and Luckmann, 1966) is a well-established research tradition in its own right, but is very different from the kinds of scientific, factual and objective orientation of a positivistic research tradition. Researchers using qualitative data in the form of narrative (text) such as interview transcripts, observations and documents could then perform their analysis under either tradition (Patton, 2002), with interview data being regarded as objective or subjective according to the research tradition being used. More constructionist epistemological traditions aim to uncover the complexity of everyday life through 'thick descriptions': accounts of personal experiences, views, emotions, processes, etc. (Suter, 2011). Research is significantly influenced by how a researcher views the world, mandating significant value be placed upon ensuring rigorous data collection and analysis processes (Suter, 2011), whatever the research approach.

Table 5.1: Types of data and research traditions

<table>
<tr><th colspan="3">Types of data</th></tr>
<tr>
<td></td>
<td>Primary
Original data, generated for the specific purposes of a research project</td>
<td>Secondary*
All available data that are 'out there' for a researcher to collect and analyse.</td>
</tr>
<tr>
<td>Positivism</td>
<td>"Quantitative Data" surveys, questionnaires, web-based surveys</td>
<td>Publically available surveys, census reports, public databases & reports, archival records, computer based databases,</td>
</tr>
<tr>
<td>Interpretivism</td>
<td>"Qualitative data" Interview transcripts, observation notes, field notes, photos, video material</td>
<td>Publically available documents, company reports, public speeches & interviews, journal articles, books, archival records</td>
</tr>
</table>

Research Tradition (row label spanning Positivism and Interpretivism)

* Secondary data can be used both as the only sources of data (see for example historiometric studies) or as complementary sources of data to primary data for triangulation purposes.

Primary and secondary data

Primary data is original data generated for the specific purposes of a research project. This can include transcripts from interviews that you have conducted yourself, or questionnaires from a survey which you have organized for your research (Bryman and Bell, 2007). When starting a research project there are many sources from which you can draw your data such as interview transcripts, documents, audio-visual material or publically available data from newspapers and websites (Baxter and Jack, 2008). In essence every source of information that is relevant to your research question is a potential form of data (Bryman and Bell, 2007). In general data can be numeric, textual, visual or a combination of the above (Blaxter, Hughes & Tight, 2001). The following list covers the main types of primary data each researcher can choose from:

- questionnaires
- surveys / web-based surveys
- transcripts of interviews
- field notes from focus groups
- observations

5

- charts, maps, tables or diagrams
- documents, reports, etc.
- photos
- diaries

Which of these types of data you choose will depend upon the wider methodology and philosophical orientation that you are adopting as a researcher, as well as the purpose and nature of the research projects you are conducting. As described earlier, an empirically-oriented research drawing from the interpretivist or social constructionist tradition would likely be aiming to understand the underlying processes of a phenomenon, as experienced by social actors themselves. Such a research strategy is likely to rely upon qualitative primary data (such as interviews, documents and observations). For example in a longitudinal case study research of Singapore Airlines, Heracleous and Wirtz (2014) collected qualitative data (observations and in depth interviews) as their primary source of data in order to explore the airline's strategic processes for sustainable competitive advantage over time. In this context, primary qualitative data (personal accounts from employees as well as observational data from the researchers) collected over a period of 10 years, uncovered subtle insights about the underlying processes within the organization and how these processes shaped the company's strategy.

On the other hand, the method map shows that a researcher following a positivist tradition would most likely gather primary data in the form of quantitative surveys, questionnaires or perhaps databases. Following such a research approach, Schneider, Ehrhart, Mayer, Saltz, & Niles-Jolly (2005) examined data occurring from a large survey in 56 supermarket departments. In their quantitative analysis, the researchers tested three hypotheses on the correlation between different organizational processes, customer satisfaction and overall sales. The construction of a conceptual model that hypothesises about linkages, effects and causal mechanisms, and the subsequent gathering of data to test these hypotheses relies on data, yet both the data and the analytical process vary from one research tradition to another. In the examples above we see how different types of primary data (qualitative data such as those occurring from interviews, and observations and quantitative data such as those occurring from large scale surveys) support different types of research. Whereas these distinctions are clear in most cases, it is possible that an individual research project can span some of these boundaries, opening new ways of researching. For example, questionnaires may feature both Likert scale questions and free text sections providing the researcher with both qualitative and quantitative data. Mixed method research designs are increasingly common.

Secondary data is the label used to describe data that is already available 'out there' for a researcher to collect and analyse. This naturally-occurring data may take the form of public reports, newspapers, magazines, websites, books or articles (Blaxter et al., 2001). Other forms of secondary data can also be useful, such as personal documents and official documents, which may be further categorized as private or public (Scott, 1990). What is secondary data to you may have been primary data to another researcher during some earlier study, as is the case with census data for example. Secondary data can act both as a complement to primary data or as the sole source of data for your research project. The following list covers the main types of secondary data that researchers find useful:

- publically available surveys
- public databases & reports (i.e. census reports)
- archival records
- computer based databases
- publically available documents
- company reports
- published speeches & interviews
- journal articles
- books

When used as complement to primary data, analysis of secondary data can provide new insights to existing research. Published interviews with individuals who would be difficult to access, for example CEOs or senior political figures, can be a valuable source of insight, even where the particular set of interview questions or prompts are not an exact match for your requirements. Sometimes, secondary data is preferable to no data. Also, findings from secondary data can modify, confirm or contradict findings from other primary data, leading to more robust research findings. For instance, primary data in the form of interviews with local and/or more junior members of a global organization may be contrasted with secondary data in the form of public interviews with senior members of the organization, regulators, industry commentators, etc.

Furthermore, ready made data sets or archives can be a valuable and cost-efficient source of resources for researchers, and many successful projects use such secondary data as the main source of information for a research project. For example, in their study concerning tactics of competitive action between organizations, Ming-Jer and Miller (1994) tested a number of hypotheses, based on data they selected through published articles appearing in the industry journal *Aviation Daily*. The data set covered a period of eight years. Their sample consisted of 32 major US airlines, and the researchers used published articles to track move and counter-move within an industry, through commentary on issues such as dramatic price cuts. A second example would be the study by Danneels (2011) who collected 20 years of published information on Smith Corona (appearing both in the media and in academic journals), in order to perform a qualitative exploration of the company's transition from mechanical to electronic typewriters, and eventually to word processing. Both of these examples were published in one of the world's most prestigious academic journals, dispelling any concerns that secondary data is in any way less useful than primary data. The choice between primary data, secondary data or some combination of both is driven by two related but distinct concerns. First, relates to the set of pragmatic choices concerned with time pressures, feasibility and access. Second, an assessment of the types of data that are appropriate to the particular research question and analytical methods you intend to pursue.

Case studies

The case study approach is one of the most common ways of students conducting their research project and offers a useful way of demonstrating the different research traditions described above. Case studies often involve the detailed exploration, typically with information accumulated over a phase of time, of phenomena within their context (Dul and Hak, 2008). A case study can be defined as "…an empirical inquiry that investigates a contemporary phenomenon in depth and within its real-life context, especially when… the boundaries between phenomenon and context are not clearly evident" (Yin, 2009, p.18). The fundamental objective is to generate an analysis of the context and processes which enlighten the issue being researched (Gillham, 2001). Therefore, unlike laboratory research, the phenomenon is not divorced from its context but is of appeal as the purpose is to realise how behaviour and processes affect and are affected by context.

Case studies, which can be single or multiple, regularly concentrate on one or more specific entities, for example, organisations, individuals, departments, groups, and processes (Hartley, 2004). They present a valuable approach for use in theory development and testing as they are particularly suitable for addressing 'Why', 'How' and 'What' questions. Good case studies often begin with a predicament that is poorly comprehended and is inadequately explained or traditionally rationalised by numerous conflicting accounts. Therefore, the aim is to comprehend an existent problem and to use the acquired understandings to develop new theoretical outlooks or explanations.

While there is a consistent overview of what a case study aims to achieve, it must be noted that there exist different traditions in the case study literature, which can influence the methodological choices taken by the researcher. On the one hand, cases are presented in the broader tradition of positivist research, as exemplified in Kathleen Eisendhardt's (1989) article on 'Building theories from case study research'. Within this view the use of multiple cases are seen as instrumental in developing theory from the chosen context (Eisendhardt, 1989). Within this perspective, the objective is to advance theory through testable propositions and the pursuit of facts through the process of induction. This approach is best suited to circumstances where there is limited knowledge about a phenomenon or where exiting knowledge is contradictory or unclear (Yin, 2009). Therefore, case study evidence can provide evidence which offers novel insights into the phenomenon being explored. For example, Martin and Eisendhardt (2010) used this approach to examine the key differences between successful and failed cross-divisional projects in multi-business organisations.

This contrasts with the more interpretivist and constructionist approach taken by researchers such as Gioia, Price, Hamilton and Thomas (2010) and Robert Stake (1995) to case studies. In contrast to the more positivist method to case study research, this approach focuses more on apprehending and exhibiting the meaning of those being studied and their understanding of events. It has, therefore, a less structured approach to case study research, in contrast to the more procedural tactic employed by Eisendhardtz (1989). Additionally, unlike the proponents of a more positivist perspective, the use of as single case approach is deemed acceptable, due to its ability to produce a revelatory perspective and opulence of information (Corely and Gioia, 2004). For instance, Corely and Gioia (2004) used an interpretivist single case study approach to investigate organisational identify change in the spin-off of a Fortune 500 company's top functioning organisational unit into an independent company.

■   Research design

Research design refers to the steps which will be embraced to relate the study's questions to the data collection and analysis stages in a coherent way. Primarily, the researcher should consider if their case study will be used for explanatory, exploratory and descriptive research (Creswell, 2007). Table 5.2 describes and offers examples of each.

Table 5.2: Case study types

Type	Description	Example
Exploratory	Usually employed when present literature and knowledge is inadequate. Research questions are often broad and the use of hypotheses is rare. Data collection may be commenced prior to the definition of research questions. They can be deliberately designed to help build theory through inductive methods in order to create hypothesis about new research questions.	Salk, J. E., & Shenkar, O. (2001)
Explanatory	Used when seeking to provide causal explanations – explaining how events occurred. Considered the only appropriate type for theory testing.	Amaya, Ackall, Pingitore, Quiroga, & Terrazas-Ponce, (1997)
Descriptive	Is used to present a rich and comprehensive description of an entity of interest in the context in which it transpired.	Ap, J., & Wong, (2001)

Understanding the case study type will influence the focus on the study's queries. The development of research questions is a significant phase within any manner of academic investigation. For example, Eisenhardt (1989, p. 536) argues that "an initial definition of the research question, in at least broad terms, is important in building theory from case studies." Well-articulated questions will also facilitate in helping to ground the most relevant areas of the researcher's examination.

■   Unit of analysis

The definition of the 'case' (unit of analysis) is an essential requirement. Typically, the case is a bounded entity, for example: an event, a time-period, an organisation, a person, a nation, a policy or even a social interaction. For instance, exploring how innovative knowledge-based structures emerge and get embedded in organizations, Anand, Gardner, and Morris (2007) define their unit of analysis as 'new practice area development efforts' to ensure the focus of their study. Therefore, the case is the central object of the study and is a context-specific decision that is contingent on the research questions and context of the investigation. The definition of the unit of analysis is important as it specifically defines where the case commences and terminates in both spatial and temporal terms (Stake, 1995). This is essential as it enhances the probability that the research, the questions being probed and the data gathered, remain within the parameters of the focus of interest.

5

■   Single or multiple case designs

A single case study

Similar to a solitary experiment, a single case concentrates on a sole focus of study and can be an organisation, an individual, a department, or even a specific process. For example, MacLaren, Young, and Lochrie (2013) used the Fanthorp Inn in Texas to explore commercial hospitality enterprise and its impact on settlement development in the American West during the 1800s; while Butler, Curran, and O'Gorman (2013) conducted a single case study of Glasgow Govan to explore pro-poor tourism in a First World urban setting. The value of this approach resides in its ability to produce precious information about particular research questions due to the comprehensive exploration of its solitary focus.

While multiple case research if often preferred, there are occasions where the decision to adopt a single case approach will be appropriate. First, if the study represents a critical case then a single case is adequate (Hartley, 2004). The rationale revolves around testing a well-formulated theory with a distinct set of propositions, allowing the investigator to verify, develop or dispute the theory. Second, single case studies are also acceptable when the research focuses on a unique or extreme case. Therefore, the justification rests upon the infrequency on the event. Third, a longitudinal investigation can merit the use of a single case. This involves the study of the same case over a specific period(s), using theory to explain how specific conditions alter over time. Finally, a single case may be justified for practical reasons. For example, the researcher may have the opportunity to gain access to a rare and typically restricted research context that may be singular.

Multiple case studies

Conversely, multiple case study research relates to the investigation of several cases. This allows the researcher the ability to analyse within and across settings. Therefore, multiple case studies are more desirable due to the belief that the results derived are more robust and generalizable (Eisenhardt, 1989). For example, Roome and Wijen (2006) used a multiple case study approach to investigate the environmental management practices found in major companies, to address the lack of understanding on how and why stakeholder power and organizational learning interact. Conducting multiple case study research requires careful consideration when selecting cases to investigate. Unlike survey research, this selection is not based on sampling logic but on replication logic. The central reasoning of replication logic is that according to a theory, one would anticipate that the same phenomenon transpires under the exact or comparable circumstances or that the phenomenon diverges if the conditions are modified. Therefore, cases should be selected so they (1) predict similar results for predicable reasons (literal replication); or (2) produce contradictory results for predictable reasons (theoretical replication).

Determining the number of cases to use can be problematic. The decision is the responsibility of the researcher. However, some recommend that cases should be added to the point of redundancy or to the stage of theoretical saturation (Lincoln & Guba, 1985). However, experts on case study design have recommended a more specific range, with Eisenhardt (1989, p. 545) recommending "a number between four and ten … [w]ith fewer than four cases, it is often difficult to generate theory with much complexity; and its empirical grounding is likely to be unconvincing."

Collecting data

Collecting data for research is a challenging and exciting process of 'data mining', as throughout your project you will get closer and closer to the issues that you are researching (Corbin and Strauss, 2007). Upon engaging in a project there are three questions you should ask yourself as a researcher:

- In which context would it be most suitable to explore your research question?

- How easily can you gain access to this setting?

- What type of data would be most suitable for your research?

First and foremost, data collection should strike a balance between what is exciting, new or interesting and what is feasible within the time and resource constrains of a research project. For example, it would be an exciting idea to study the strategic decision making of a high performing multinational organization but one has to think practically: do I have access to this organization? How much time would it take me to negotiate this access? Do I need to travel to get my data? Would I need to sign a confidentiality agreement?

Negotiating access to an organization involves making initial contacts with key decision makers within the company (e.g. the HR director, a Head of a Department, section, etc.). These individuals or groups may act as gatekeepers and might be able to introduce you to fellow members of the organization. If your research design is based on a sample of a few or a single organizational setting you will need to do some background research on the organization(s) in question: financial position/corporate history/ organizational structure or any other issue that is relevant to your research. Using publicly available data from company reports, newspaper articles and similar material is often a useful first step in familiarizing yourself with the research setting in which you will gather data. Such preparation will not only allow you to position yourself better when negotiating access, but is also a crucial step of choosing a setting that is appropriate for your project. When negotiating access with potential organisations and managers, being able to explain the purposes of your research and the type of data you need to collect (interviews, questionnaires, mixture of both? other?) is important. This will also depend on the research method you have chosen to employ. For example, a longitudinal case study methodology is more likely to be based on in-depth interviews than by some form of web-based survey or questionnaire. When negotiating access for conducting your field research you also need to be in position to answer questions of how many people you would need to contact from the organization, how much time is needed for them, and other practical issues of your research design.

These critical and practical issues can be difficult for a novice researcher, but they have a significant impact on the time and effort required to complete the data collection process. It is likely that both the host organization and you, the researcher, will need to have some idea of the scope and scale of your data gathering. Also, when entering the field, a novice researcher is usually keen to collect as much data as possible. However, the researcher should bear in mind that data collection is followed by data analysis; a process that is equally (if not more) demanding and time-consuming. Therefore, when planning and scheduling field research, the researcher needs to take into account the time that they will need to analyse and write up their findings.

Case studies can utilise a number of data collection techniques. Using multiple sources of evidence is essential as it allows for a more comprehensive investigation. Additionally, the validity of the research can be enhanced. For example, evidence for documentation can be used to support evidence gathered from interviews. Table 5.3 highlights the sources which can be used.

Table 5.3: Sources of evidence in case study research

Source of evidence	Examples
Documents	Minutes of meetings, strategic documents, brochures, newsletters, internal documents, press releases, emails and memos, guidelines, annual general reports, media articles.
Archival records	Annual General Reports, company publications, memos, databases, audio and visual media, newspaper articles, books, financial reports, client proposals.
Interviews	Formal, informal, semi-structured, and group interviews.
Direct observation	Observing: meeting, work environments, workshops, presentations, conferences, sites visits.
Participant observation	Actively taking part in organisational activities, for example: meetings and work processes. Engaging with participants throughout the process
Physical artefacts	Photographs, historical ruins, promotional material (adverts or posters), uniforms.
Surveys	Used to collect various form of information: demographics, personal information, work-related data.
Websites	Company websites and corporate intranet

Assessing the quality of secondary data

If you are working with data collected for other purposes, for example a census report, it is imperative that you form a view of the quality and integrity of the original data. The benefits of time efficiency gained by not having to collect your own data must be weighed against the appropriateness of the data for your particular purpose. Large publically available data sets, such as governmental reports, can provide nationally representative data that may simply be impractical to collect from scratch. However, questions remain about the reliability, age and representativeness of such secondary data. Survey datasets like the International Social Survey Programme (ISSP) may enable you to perform cross-cultural analysis on particular themes which may also be infeasible by any other means. Nevertheless, the data may have been collected so long ago that it is no longer valid. Furthermore, information in the report may have been gathered using sampling strategies that don't meet your particular requirements. Hence, whilst secondary data might offer valuable opportunities for seemingly easy ways to perform longitudinal or comparative analysis, some caution is merited.

Not all sources of secondary data should be treated equally. Data from established sources which employ rigorous data collection techniques, such as the UK Data Archive, are a valuable source of insight. On the contrary, popular information databases, such as Wikipedia, may not be founded on the basis of such research rigour and cannot therefore be treated as equally credible data sources. Some useful questions to ask of any potential secondary data source that you may plan to use in your research include:

- Why, when, by whom and for what intended audience was this document produced?

- In cases of statistical data sets, have variables changed over time? If so how? Have the measurements or indicators changed over time?

Scott (1990) also suggests the following criteria for evaluating the quality of secondary data:

- Authenticity (genuine data where the original source can be traced)

- Credibility (data free from error and distortion)

- Representativeness (how typical or untypical are the documents affects the conclusions we draw from them)

- Meaning (data clear to comprehend)

Finally, as secondary data can multiply your data set exponentially, you need to make sure that any secondary data you use is not only of high value, but also of high relevance to your research question. A very broad data set may not only delay your data analysis process but could also blur the focus of your research project.

Data analysis

For case studies, the data analysis procedure is regarded as complex. Typically, published studies offer limited space to deliberate the analysis, making it challenging to grasp how the researcher reached their ultimate conclusions from considerable amounts of gathered information (Miles and Huberman, 1994). Often the data collection and analysis overlap. However, the choice of data analysis will often depends upon the methods used and the philosophical underpinnings of the research (Marschan-Piekkari & Welch, 2011). Commonly, the analysis of quantitative and qualitative data can be segmented into deductive and inductive approaches. For example, more quantitative data collection will require the interpretation and presentation of numerical or systematic information. Conversely, the analysis of qualitative data requires three stages: data reduction; data display; and conclusion drawing and verification. Analysing evidence commonly begins with the coding of data, allowing for themes and categories to be developed (Miles and Huberman, 1994). This is followed by within-case analysis, then by cross-case analysis for multiple case research. Within-case analysis allows the researcher to become deeply accustomed with each case as a separate entity. Through this, detailed reporting can help hasten the cross-case comparisons. Cross-case analysis then explores the parallels and dissimilarities across cases, allowing the researcher to develop theory through their interpretations (Anand et al., 2007).

Verification methods

Within case research there must be the well-defined accounting of the processes and practises used when gathering the data and during its analysis, and that prejudices have been controlled (Guba and Lincoln, 1994). Within a more quantitative approach this reliability is associated with strategies and terms such as validly and reliability (Dul and Hak, 2008). However, within qualitative studies such scientific terminology is often substituted with phrases such as dependability, confirmability, transferability, and credibility (Lincoln & Guba, 1985). Table 6.4 highlights some of the main approaches used to confirm verification.

Table 5.4: Verification methods

Strategy	Description
Triangulation of evidence	The researcher uses at least three sources of evidence to collect data. For example: interviews; observations; surveys; physical artefacts; archival research.
Triangulation of sources	The research uses a wide range of participants, periods of time, or different locations. Permits views and perspectives to be conformed against each other. Produces a deeper picture of the thoughts and behaviours of the contributing participants.
Triangulation of researchers	Can augment the ingenuity of the study. Increases the credibility and validity through multiple perspectives.
Member checking	Participants review drafts of written work or accounts derived from the interview process. Allows them to approve the interpretation of their accounts. This increases the validity of the study's conclusions.
Ensuring honesty or participants	Achieved through: guaranteeing confidentiality, obtaining consent, and not being deceptive. Allows for collected information data to be more reliable.
Replication logic	Cases are selected so that they either predict similar results (literal replication) or predict contrasting results for anticipatable reasons (theoretical). Helps conclusions to become generalizable. Often a tactic embraced within more positivist approaches.
Thick descriptions	The researcher presents a rich and detailed description of the phenomenon being investigated. Narrative and storytelling is essential. Typically, associated with interprevitist case studies.
Maintaining a journal	A record can be kept of the researcher's reflections during the study. Allows the researcher to assess their own subjectivism and why they arrived at specific conclusions.
Database	The organised documentation of the gathered evidence. This permits others to examine the information and allows them to see where conclusions were drawn.
Case study protocol	The creation of a guide to overseen and provide support during the process. Includes: a summary of the research; field procedures; and interview guides. Augments reliability.

5

■ Data triangulation

The triangulation metaphor, taken from navigation and military strategy, refers to the use of "multiple reference points to locate an objects exact position" (Jick, 1979, p.602). In the social sciences, the process of 'triangulation' is an important step within a research project as it allows the researcher to examine a phenomenon from different standpoints (Scandura and Williams, 2000). Regardless of philosophical tradition, the process of reviewing multiple data sources tends to heighten our awareness of warning signs when, for example, one perspective suggests different conclusions than another. Perhaps your secondary data suggests one thing, whilst interview data that you have gathered yourself suggests another. Perhaps, your views when reading one article or interview transcript seems incompatible with what you gather from other data sources. These experiences should be embraced as an opportunity for you, the researcher, to build a plausible and convincing account of the inconsistency. Triangulation, at least in some research traditions, limits the potential for researcher bias and increases the reliability of your findings. As such, it is often seen as adding significantly to the methodological rigour of a research project (Vikström, 2010).

In that context, secondary and primary data need not be viewed as alternative sources of data, as in certain cases they can be quite complementary (i.e. when a qualitative case study research based on interviews is complemented by publically available company reports and historical data that span beyond our field research time frame). Such a combination of primary and secondary sources of data helps the researcher in a process by which insights from certain source are compared and contrasted with those of other. In a four year longitudinal case study of the role of communities of practice, for example, Borzillo et al. (2012) combined primary data (interviews, direct observations) with secondary data (company reports, strategic documents) for a more holistic view of the organizational processes in operation. In another study by Kan and Parry (2004), on leadership within a hospital setting, the authors employed a different set of data sources including non-participant observation, informal/unstructured and formal/semi structured interviews, document analysis, and the Multifactor Leadership Questionnaire (MLQ). Each different source of data provided a new perspective on leadership mechanisms leading to more nuanced findings.

Within some research traditions, the use of multiple data sources facilitates triangulation, which in turn leads to the confirmation of findings.

Whilst in other research traditions, other data sources simply offer an insight into the same phenomenon as experienced from a different perspective.

More broadly, triangulation can be applied not only to the use of multiple data sources (data triangulation) but also to the use of different methodologies (method triangulation) (Bryman and Bryman, 2003). Method triangulation, often referred to as using a mixed-methods research design, can allow you to collect, analyse, and mix both quantitative and qualitative data in a single study or series of studies to both explain and explore specific research questions (Roberts, Mcnulty & Stiles, 2005). Again, this seems an attractive proposition since it can appear to combine the best of both worlds. Yet potential risks stem from the use of different types of data and different methodologies. Triangulation is lauded in some places yet criticized in others for not adequately explaining the process or the fitness of the methods being combined in a specific research design (Bryman and Bryman, 2003). Especially in the cases of mixing different methodologies, some researchers argue that triangulation is methodologically impractical as it requires the researcher to be equally skilled in both qualitative and quantitative techniques, risking diluting the robustness of their findings (Vikström, 2010). However, this risk is mitigated within larger research groups where each individual researcher may have been trained in specific research methodologies. More fundamentally, some styles of research would probleamtize the whole concept of triangulation on ontological or epistemological grounds.

Generalizing findings from case studies

While the case study approach may be appealing, its central disadvantage, often cited by more positivist stances, is its limited ability to offer generalizable conclusions. This uncertainty is heavily prevalent in the application of a single case. Such criticism questions the capacity of a single case study in testing or developing theory successfully and reliably. However, this criticism has been challenged, with authors arguing that generalizability can be obtained through more structured and reliable approaches and through combining evidence from multiple cases (Eisenhardt, 1989; Yin, 2009). Additionally, case studies focus on analytical generalizations. This is where a previously developed theory is employed as a template with which to contrast the outcomes of the case study. Therefore, by comparing the emerging themes and theories with existing literature the researcher can enquire about the parallels and differences, and why these are so.

Case study overview: Advantages and disadvantages

Having set out the types of data that can be gathered during a research project, it is worth bearing in mind that no single research methodology is infallible. Ultimately, what is important is the justification that you give for the linkage between the nature of your topic, the kinds of data required, the types of analysis prevalent within the research tradition of your chosen methods and the kinds of insights, findings or knowledge claims that you can subsequently produce. Consistency matters far more than the individual choices themselves, and whatever you choose to do, you'll be balancing your research question, your time and a number of other resource constraints including access to the types of data that you want. Considering the use of case study is an important process which requires careful thought. Table 5.5 offers an overview of the advantages and disadvantages of the approach, which should be deliberated. While there are some intimidating limitations, case study research can be rewarding, engaging and knowledgeably invigorating. Given their propensity to assist in understanding innovative and first-hand phenomena, case studies offer a fruitful approach for any researcher who is enthusiastic about generating findings that illuminate theory, while being willing to delve into the intricacies of the method.

Table 5.5: Advantages and disadvantages of case research

Advantages	Disadvantages
Useful for exploring novel behaviours or practises and under-researched phenomenon. Therefore, they are ideal for theory building and testing.	Case studies are typically conducted by one individual, so researcher subjectivity can influence the results. Therefore, they have been accused of lacking rigour.
Case studies are holistic and offer an all-encompassing description of real-life situations which is often not captured by other approaches.	Single cases have limited ability to generate generalizable conclusions. A question often posed is, "How can you generalise from a single case?" Yin (2009, p. 15)
Allows the researcher to demonstrate the intricacies of social life, and to explore alternative interpretations and meanings within the evidence.	Can be time-consuming and costly. Access to the focus of study may be problematic if continual contact is required.
Takes advantage of multiple techniques to gather data.	The high quantities of data gathered can be overwhelming.

References

Amaya, M. A., Ackall, G., Pingitore, N., Quiroga, M., & Terrazas-Ponce, B. (1997). Childhood lead poisoning on the US-Mexico Border: A case study in environmental health nursing lead poisoning. *Public Health Nursing,* **14**(6), 353-360.

Anand, N., Gardner, H. K., & Morris, T. (2007). Knowledge-based innovation: emergence and embedding of new practice areas in management consulting firms. *Academy of Management Journal,* **50**(2), 406-428

Ap, J., & Wong, K. K. F. (2001). Case study on tour guiding: Professionalism, issues and problems. *Tourism Management,* **22**(5), 551-563

Baxter, P., & Jack, S. (2008). Qualitative case study methodology: Study design and implementation for novice researchers. *The Qualitative Report,* **13**(4), 544-559.

Berger, P., & Luckmann, T. (1966). *The Social Construction of Reality, A treatise in the sociology of knowledge.* New York: Anchor Books.

Blaxter, L., Hughes, C., & Tight M. (2001). *How to Research.* Buckingham: Open University Press.

Borzillo, S., Schmitt, A., & Antino, M. (2012). Communities of practice: keeping the company agile. *Journal of Business Strategy,* **33**(6), 22-30.

Bryman, A., & Bell, E. (2007). *Business Research Methods.* Oxford: Oxford University Press.

Bryman, A., & Bryman, P. S. R. A. (2003). *Quantity and Quality in Social Research.* New York: Routledge.

Butler, R., Curran, R., and O'Gorman, K. D. (2013), Pro-poor tourism in a first world urban setting: Case study of Glasgow Govan, *International Journal of Tourism Research,* **15**(5), 443-457.

Corbin, J., & Strauss, A. L. (2007). *Basics of Qualitative Research: Grounded theory procedures and techniques.* London: Sage.

Corley, K. G., & Gioia, D. A. (2004). Identity ambiguity and change in the wake of a corporate spin-off. *Administrative Science Quarterly,* **49**(2), 173–208.

Creswell, J. W. (2007). *Qualitative Inquiry and Research Design: Choosing among Five Approaches.* Thousand Oaks: Sage.

Danneels, E. (2011). Trying to become a different type of company: dynamic capability at Smith Corona. *Strategic Management Journal,* **32**(1), 1-31.

Dul, J., & Hak, T. (2008). *Case Study Methodology in Business Research.* London: Elsevier.

5

Eisenhardt, K. M. (1989). Building theories from case study research. *Academy of Management Review*, **14**(4), 532-550.

Gillham, B. (2001). *Case Study Research Methods*. London: Continuum.

Gioia, D. A., Price, K. N., Hamilton, A. L., & Thomas, J. B. (2010). Forging an identity: An insider-outsider study of processes involved in the formation of organizational identity. *Administrative Science Quarterly*, **55**(1), 1–46.

Guba, E. G., & Lincoln, Y. S. (1994). Competing paradigms in qualitative research. In N.K. Denzin & Lincoln, Y. S. eds, *Handbook of Qualitative Research* (pp. 105-117). Thousand Oaks: Sage.

Hartley, J. (2004). Case study research. In C. Cassell & G. Symon (Eds.), *Essential Guide to Qualitative Methods in Organizational Research* (pp. 323-333). London: Sage.

Heracleous, L., & Wirtz, J. (2014). Singapore Airlines: Achieving sustainable advantage through mastering paradox. *The Journal of Applied Behavioral Science*. **50**(2), 150-170

Jick, T. D. (1979). Mixing qualitative and quantitative methods: Triangulation in action. *Administrative Science Quarterly*, **24**(4), 602-611.

Kan, M. M., & Parry, K. W. (2004). Identifying paradox: A grounded theory of leadership in overcoming resistance to change. *Leadership Quarterly*, **15**(4), 467-491.

Ketokivi, M., & Choi, T. (2014). Renaissance of case research as a scientific method. *Journal of Operations Management*, **32**(5), 232-240.

Lincoln, Y. S., & Guba, E. G. (1985). *Naturalistic Inquiry*, London: Sage.

Luscher, L. S., Lewis, M., & Ingram, A. (2006). The social construction of organizational change paradoxes. *Journal of Organizational Change Management*, **19**(4), 491-502.

Maclaren, A., Young, M. E., & Lochrie, S. (2013). Enterprise on the Frontier: Taverns, Inns and Economic Development in the American West, 1800-80. *International Journal of Contemporary Hospitality Management*, **25**(2), 264–281.

Marschan-Piekkari, R., & Welch, C. (2011). *Rethinking the Case Study in International Business and Management Research*. Cheltenham: Edward Elgar.

Martin, J. A., & Eisenhardt, K. M. (2010). Rewiring: Cross-business-unit collaborations in multibusiness organizations. *Academy of Management Journal*, **53**(2), 265-301.

Miles, M. B., & Huberman, A. M. (1994). *Qualitative Data Analysis: An Expanded Sourcebook*. London: Sage.

Ming-Jer, C., & Miller, D. (1994). Competitive attack, retaliation and performance: An expectancy-valence framework. *Strategic Management Journal*, **15**(2), 85-102.

Patton, E., & Appelbaum, S. H. (2003). The case for case studies in management research. *Management Research News*, **26**(5), 60-71.

Patton, M. Q. (2002). *Qualitative Research & Evaluation Methods*. London: Sage.

Roberts, J., Mcnulty, T., & Stiles, P. (2005). Beyond agency conceptions of the work of the non-executive director: Creating accountability in the boardroom. *British Journal of Management*, **16**(S1), S5-S26.

Roome, N., & Wijen, F. (2006). Stakeholder power and organizational learning in corporate environmental management. *Organization Studies*, **27**(2), 235-263.

Salk, J. E., & Shenkar, O. (2001). Social identities in an international joint venture: An exploratory case study. *Organization Science*, **12**(2), 161-178.

Sandberg, J. (2000). Understanding human competence at work: An interpretative approach. *Academy of Management Journal*, **43**(1), 9-25.

Scandura, T. A., & Williams, E. A. (2000). Research methodology in management: Current practices, trends, and implications for future research. *Academy of Management Journal*, **43**(6), 1248-1264.

Schneider, B., Ehrhart, M. G., Mayer, D. M., Saltz, J. L., & Niles-Jolly, K. (2005). Understanding organization-customer links in service settings. *Academy of Management Journal*, **48**(6), 1017-1032.

Scott, J., (1990). *A Matter of Record, Documentary Sources in Social Research*. Cambridge: Polity Press.

Stake, R. E. (1995). *The Art of Case Study Research*. London: Sage Publications.

Suter, N. W. (2011). Introduction to educational research. A critical thinking approach. London: Sage.

Valsiner, J. (2000). Data as representations: contextualizing qualitative and quantitative research strategies. *Social Science Information*, **39**(1), 99-113.

Vikström, L. (2010). Identifying dissonant and complementary data on women through the triangulation of historical sources. *International Journal of Social Research Methodology*, **13**(3), 211-221.

Weber, M. (1964). *The theory of social and economic organization*. New York: Free Press.

Yin, R. K. (2009). *Case Study Research: Design and Methods*. London: Sage

6 From Archives to the Internet

Keith Gori & Rodrigo Perez-Vega

As shown in the Methods Map (see Chapter 4), qualitative data comes in many forms and – though sometimes unjustly characterised as less valuable or robust than its quantitative counterpart – offers penetrating insights that numbers sometimes simply cannot, and allows research into areas where quantitative methods would be unsuitable. Two broad approaches to the collection of qualitative data are addressed here: historical research and the use of the Internet as a social research tool. Other more common social science data collection approaches are reviewed in the following chapter, and methods for the analysis of qualitative data in Chapter 8.

Historical research in business and management

The Business History discipline emerged as a sub-field of Economic History but today occupies its own position, and is increasingly being applied in other sub-fields of business and management, in what has been termed the 'historic turn' (Bucheli and Wadhwani, 2014). Following the first half of the twentieth century in which detailed, narrative accounts of business development dominated the field, it has grown into a much broader, analytically-driven discipline in which the focus and methodological approach of research is the subject of much debate (Amatori and Jones ,2003). The following three sections of this chapter introduce some of the core methodological approaches used in the historical research of business as an introduction to the field. Documentary archival material and oral histories are the two source types most likely to inform an undergraduate business history project and are here dealt with in more detail, but attention is also given to lesser used and non-traditional techniques; often these techniques are best utilised in conjunction with one or more other approaches to add depth to the research. These are listed in the 'Techniques' section of the Methods Map. First, let us briefly consider the merit of using a historical approach to explore business and management, starting with a succinct attempt at defining the role of the business historian.

> *"Business historians study the historical evolution of business systems, entrepreneurs, and firms, as well as their interaction with their political, economic, and social environment. They address issues of central concern to researchers in management studies and business administration, as well as economics, sociology, and other social sciences, and to historians. They employ a range of qualitative and quantitative methodologies, but all share a belief in the importance of understanding change over time."* (Jones and Zeitlin, 2007).

The most important part of this definition comes in the final sentence, the notion of *understanding* change over time. Business history is often reduced to, or seen as merely, a longitudinal account of business and management subject areas; the study of a company, industry, business function or management practice in a historical context through a narrative chronicling of the details in change over time but not the underlying importance of the change or the processes involved. Good business history is much more than this. It is through its analytical strength, supported by methodological rigour, and the insight and understanding of change over time that business history provides strength and utility to wider business and management research. Indeed it should emphasize temporally contextualized *explanations* of business and management phenomena through emphasis of the significance and meaning of evidence from the past. In this manner, business history offers the prospect of new perspectives on the nature of business and management, which challenge assumptions from sub-fields (Amatori and Jones, 2003; Bucheli and Wadhwani, 2014; Jones and Zeitlin, 2007). Having decided to use an historical approach in your project, the next thing to consider is the kind of source material you will draw upon. The most commonly used types of historical sources are documentary sources found in archives and oral history sources. These two source types are discussed in some detail below, before a few lesser used source types are introduced.

6

Exercise 6.1.

Take some time to write some notes on the value of historical research in business and management.

Archival sources

What is an archive?

According to the Oxford English Dictionary, an archive can be defined either as an historical collection or the environment in which they stored and used, and come in a number of forms. Table 6.1 briefly summarises some of the key types, their features and gives examples. Each of these archives may contain similar types of material: official records and documents, correspondence, diaries, information from news sources, photographs, pictures and many more (Brundage, 2013).

Table 6.1: Archive types, with examples

Archive type and description	Examples
Government/state archives. Largely hold material relating to administrative affairs of state. Often they hold information relating to private companies and listings of business/corporate archives (see below).	The National Archives, The National Archives of Scotland, National Archives and Record Administration (USA).
Business/ corporate archives. Hold information detailing the running of a business/corporation.	Most large companies maintain an archive. To check for UK company archives search the National Register of Archive database (www.nationalarchives. gov.uk/nra/default.asp).
Special collections. Usually organised thematically in that they hold material from a wide range of sources but relating to a similar subject, e.g. a particularly industry, social movement, political party etc. Often these archives are located within, or attached to, a university archive.	Scottish Business Archive (University of Glasgow).
University archives. Hold the administrative information of the university, can be very useful for collecting biographical material relating to former students. They also often have affiliated special collections (above).	Heriot-Watt University Archive, Harvard Business School Archive.
Religious archives. Hold material relating to a major faith, denomination or physical place of worship.	Scottish Catholic Archives, St. Paul's Cathedral Archives, Vatican Secret Archives (this also constitutes a state archive).

The type of archive and materials useful as source data is very much dependent on the nature of the project being undertaken. For example, a project looking at marketing changes would be more interested in the final marketing and advertising material produced and any documentation pertaining to the decision behind changes, such as marketing committee minutes, agendas etc. A project more focussed on the impact of those at the top of a large company may be more interested in the correspondence and diaries of senior figures.

The value of archival research

The table below gives a brief analysis of some of the major strengths and difficulties of using archives. It should not be considered exhaustive, and the importance of the varying factors detailed is altered by a number of project-specific factors such as the type of archive used, the material underpinning the research and both the theoretical and contextual elements of the study.

Table 6.2: The major strengths and difficulties of using archives.

Strengths	Difficulties
Detailed description of events: evidence from a variety of sources, often vast quantities.	Time consuming: large amounts of material which require equal attention during collection and analysis
Primary values: the value that the creation of records had to the creator can give information for analysis to the researcher. Secondary values: the 'other' information in records, however consequential, can also provide useful insights for analysis.	Interpreting sources from the past requires sensitivity: we cannot think like people did X-hundred years ago; the significance of semantic terms changes over time (and may have been disputed at the time, e.g. the term 'liberty' considered in the American Revolution compared to twenty-first century USA).
Allows chronology to be established (though this should not be deemed the basis on which analysis is made). Be careful of assuming a causal relationship between events, i.e. just because something happened after something else does not mean it happened because of it…	Archives carry bias and should be questioned. They are imbued with the social and political decisions made to maintain certain things ahead of others. Always question archives and their contents: Why does the collection exist? Why do certain sources appear and not others?

It should be noted that some are linked, and an advantage can often throw up a pit-fall and vice versa. The important lesson is that you must always acknowledge the biases that archival research carries. Wherever possible, acknowledge the drawbacks of using archival sources, and try to harness these as positive things. For a long period archival material was viewed as an objectively truthful source with which to access the past. In more recent decades the inherent bias they carry has been the subject of much literature. For example, Foucault (1969) highlighted that the archive is a structure of power in which only particular sources are stored, limiting what can be said of the subject. Derrida (1998) highlighted that archives limit access to only those deemed worthy. Both serve to highlight the inherent biases and structures of power that archives therefore produce and reproduce, and which limit the knowledge that can be derived from them (Manoff, 2004). The final value that archival research can bring to your project is one of personal enjoyment, providing a stimulating research experience, eloquently described by Farge (2013) as the 'allure' of the archive.

Using an archive

Though archival research may seem daunting, and can be a long, tiring process, there are a number of measures you can take to ensure the process is a fruitful a possible:

1 Know what to look for and where, starting with the literature on your subject. Has your theoretical area been addressed through historical research previously? Which archives have been used to look at the contextual dimension of your research in previous studies? Use archive databases to try and locate a convenient archive for your work.

2 Research the archives you identify. Most archives have comprehensive material available online and you can contact the archivist directly to ask for more information. It is good practice to contact the archive in advance and let them know you wish to use the facilities. Explain your project and your requirements and ask any questions you may have.

3 Making a preliminary visit to the archive is helpful if time allows. You are able to get a feel for the place, understand the requirements of the archive (each often has their own), how the archive functions, is organised, and how to locate and request items.

4 Reconsider your project, specifically the aim and objectives, and think about what sources are going to be most applicable. Make a list of the items you wish to view at the archive, be realistic about how much you can get done in one visit and consider how much time you will have to focus in on the most important sources.

5 When visiting archives be methodical and thorough, making notes on sources and, if permitted, taking pictures for subsequent use. You need to ensure that you keep good records so that you can make best use of them in the analysis of your data (see Chapter 8) and writing up of your dissertation.

By considering all of the information above you will be able to approach archival material in such a way as to add significant value to your project.

Exercise 6.2

Think of a consumer product, business or organization: what types of archival sources might inform research into it and how?

Oral history sources

What is oral history (and what isn't)?

Though the use of oral sources can be traced back as far as 'The Father of History' Herodotus it has developed enormously since the mid-twentieth century as an historical research methodology (Murray 2001). It has come to develop both a popular and a professional academic or archival meaning, and is the subject of ongoing debate and advances in techniques, theoretical consideration, and application.

> *"Oral history is characterised by a structured, systematic planning process, thorough research, careful consideration of copyright, emphasis on depth and detail of information collected, and adherence to strict processing techniques. Oral history, despite the generic use of the term, is a research methodology with a 'precise, bounded meaning' and a process that supports and defines the interview as the collecting step." (Sommer and Quinlan, 2009, p.3)*

The value of oral history

Oral history offers something that other methods of historical research cannot provide – direct contact with individuals involved in the subject of the study. The number of situations in which oral history is possible is smaller than with other historical methods, due to the fact that individuals must be alive and well enough to take part, or an extant oral history collection was created when they were. If oral history is a possible route for your research project to take, then there are a number of advantages it can provide, most often as a complementary method to archival research rather than a complete alternative. By pursuing oral history contributions to your project you can elevate the research, adding multiple layers of depth and meaning to the evidence informing it.

Oral history also holds a significant advantage over archival research in that it is deeply rooted in people, widening the scope of your research from the institutional bias archival sources carry. Oral histories allow for individual reflexivity on the part of the subjects involved: "Oral sources tell us not just what people did, but what they wanted to do, what they believed they were doing, and what they now think they did." (Portelli 2006, p.36). Given the importance of individual subjects in oral history, this technique has often been used to access historical subjects who are not well represented in archival repositories. As such it is seen as a mode of people's history (as opposed to a history of the powerful), and a tool for giving historical agency to non-hegemonic groups (Charlton, 2006; Perks and Thomson, 2006).

Using oral history

There are two routes down which your project may allow you to use oral history: conducting interviews yourself or utilising a collection of extant oral histories to incorporate added depth to your research project. The first is more time-consuming and requires access to both individuals relevant to the research and to resources for conducting and recording interviews. The second is much quicker but the utility of the histories is reduced as you are not able to ask questions tailored to your research or to follow up on points brought out in the interview. The motivation for the original collection – and the impact on the source – must also be considered.

If you decide to undertake an oral history collection process, you need to ensure that you apply appropriate ethical considerations and procedures (see Chapter 11) and are well prepared for the eventualities of interviewing people, especially if you are asking participants to talk about emotional or difficult subjects. You need to prepare well in advance of the interview so that you understand the chronology and context of events involved and are able to follow up with questions during the interview. More information about the technicalities of preparing for and carrying out interviews and the different interviewing approaches can be found in the following chapter and in the list of further reading at the end of this.

■   Other historical sources

Though archival and oral history are the most likely source bases to inform an undergraduate research project there are some other sources worth consideration here. These are often able to provide a richer understanding of your subject and certainly give an interesting dimension to your research derived from 'beyond the text'. Almost anything left by the past can be used as an historical source for analysis and a few common examples are given below with further suggested reading at the end of the chapter.

Material culture

Material culture refers to "the manifestations of culture through material productions", the objects and artefacts people use or have used, the clothes they wear or have worn, the buildings in which they live or have lived and so on (Harvey, 2009, p.6). Using material culture to inform historical research requires a process of description, deduction and speculation which allows the inference of meaning and bridging of the gap between the physical and metaphysical. When studying material culture, it is crucial that any sources be placed in the context of the built and natural environment that surrounded their use (Bryce, O'Gorman, and Baxter, 2013).

Visual sources

The adage "a picture paints a thousand words", though a cliché, holds some value in detailing the rich and vivid depth offered to historically rooted research by visual sources. Paintings, photographs, posters, advertising material are amongst some of the most commonly used.

Audiovisual sources

Radio, film and television – powered by technological advances in recording and viewing equipment – have been extremely powerful in driving much social and cultural change since the late nineteenth century. As such, they provide a great source for historical research, offering a lens through which to analyse not only the source itself but those who made it and those whom it was made for.

Exercise 6.3

Thinking again about the product, business or organization from exercise 6.2: how might oral and other historical sources inform such research?

■ Online archives

Before moving on to discuss the use of the Internet as a social research tool, let's consider the use of the Internet to archive historical material. Increasingly, archives are embracing the Internet as a medium through which to make their contents more widely available, some offering partial contents and others digitising entire collections, opening up archives to more researchers than before and to some extent "democratizing the doing of history" (Bolick, 2006). This makes an historical approach a much more attractive alternative for a short-term research project (such as a dissertation), as it removes the time and cost associated with travelling to many archives, and allows continual access rather than a rush to cram in as much archival work as possible in a short trip. Although easy access of this kind is extremely beneficial, it ought to also be approached critically. If only a portion of an archive's material is available online, then the researcher has to consider the selection decisions that went into this process and the bias this creates in the archive. In cases where only partial collections are available by this medium, a further visit to investigate non-digitised aspects of the collection is advisable.

As online archives are a relatively recent phenomenon there are often wide variations in their usability. Things to consider include: loading speeds, search facilities and other tools such as ability to zoom, crop images, and download documents (Maxwell, 2010). Online archives also remove the element of serendipity that accompanies an archival visit, and which often leads to important and unexpected discoveries. These can come as a result of a conversation with archival staff or other researchers at the archive, or because you chance upon something whilst looking at something else held in the same box or file. Online archival research also tends to take place in the same location as the rest of your work, whereas a trip to the physical archive removes you from your regular routine, often takes you away from distractions such as emails or peers and colleagues with queries, and allows you to fully immerse yourself in archival work in a manner that online access may not.

■ Summary

The above sections outline briefly the considerations surrounding utilising historical sources in your research. Doing so, you open your research project to a vast contextual and theoretical field which may not otherwise be accessible and can add extra depth and meaning to your research. Of course, there are many deeper theoretical issues within this field, and a wealth of scholarship offers perspectives on, for example, how to ensure one's theoretical approach to historical resources is itself historically informed (Maclean, Harvey, & Clegg, 2015). Having considered the use of archives via the Internet, the chapter now moves to look more widely at the Internet as a research tool.

Online research: using the Internet and social media

The focus of this section is on how the Internet and social media can be used to gather both primary and secondary data to answer many (if not all) of your research questions.

■   The Internet

The Internet is a medium of communication that is not new for the majority of the readers of this book, most of whom will have grown up surrounded by it, however Figure 6.1 outlines the relatively short and recent history of the Internet. It shows that Internet has quickly become a very important part of our daily lives, with over a quarter of the population being connected directly and an even higher proportion of users. For instance in the UK 87% of the adult population use the Internet, and 76% of the adult population use it every day (ONS, 2014). This makes the Internet a very powerful and relatively accessible way to conduct both primary and secondary research. To understand the potential of this medium, we will discuss the advantages and disadvantages of using this communication tool when conducting research.

Exercise 6.4

Reflect on your own Internet usage. How many hours do you spend online? Do you check the Internet at the beginning or end of every day. If so, what are you checking and why?

Advantages of using the Internet

The Internet has made empirical research easier. In general terms, the recruitment of participants, the carrying out of observational research, applying self-reported surveys, and doing interviews are accelerated when using the Internet. However, the advantages of the Internet are not limited to making empirical research faster; Internet research allows for the implementation of more complex studies and an understanding of communities that would be otherwise inaccessible.

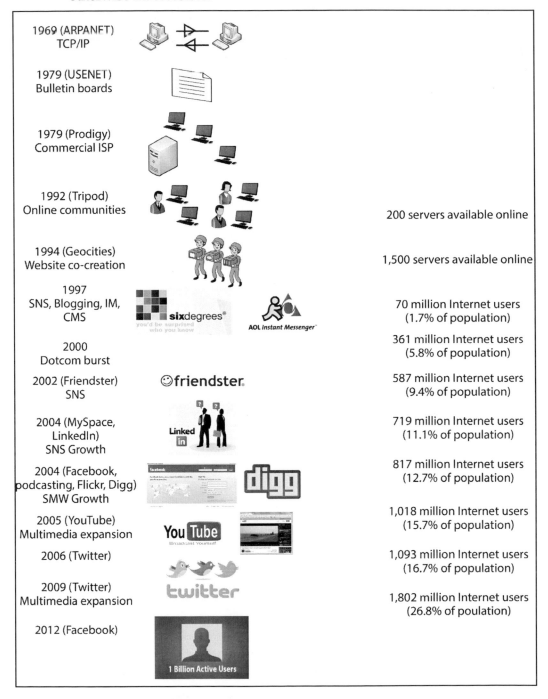

Figure 6.1: A brief history of the Internet

The Internet as a research tool

The Internet makes longitudinal studies more feasible practically as its duality between synchronous and asynchronous interactions allows for the collection of information that otherwise would require substantial resources and effort. For instance, interactions occurring in blogs, review sites or Twitter newsfeeds can be relatively easily captured for further analysis. Much of this information is both free and easily retrievable.

The Internet allows you to reach geographically distant yet highly segmented participants more easily. When conducting studies, you might be interested in reaching people with a specific profile or interest, such as entrepreneurs, or users of a particular brand or product; the Internet allows you to reach them based on those profiles in a more accessible way, via specific websites, forums, online groups or social media platforms.

Challenges of using the Internet

Despite the increasing penetration of the medium, Internet-mediated research has been criticised by many researchers due to the skewed nature of the samples that can be reached through it. Initial criticism was in terms of how representative users could be, as during early stages of Internet adoption, computers and Internet access were seen as a middle and upper class luxury (Stanton, 1998; Szabo and Frenkl, 1996). More recent criticism has claimed that the platforms selected will create a certain degree of skewedness in your sample. Until recently Twitter was a rather obscure social network, a tool for 'geeks' and early adopters of technology. With increasing mainstream media attention and a growth in youngsters migrating to it from established social networks, this platform is proving increasingly popular (Business Insider, 2014). As a result, the selection of platform to conduct your research is likely to influence the profile of your sample and should be considered when designing and writing up your research.

■ Online qualitative methods

There are three main types of online research methods:

1 Active ones where the researcher takes a participative role within the online environment,

2 Passive ones that are mostly informed by observation of information patterns on websites as well as the interactions that occur in this environment and,

3 Ones where the researcher is using the channel uniquely as a recruiting channel in order to gather information online (e.g. online interviews, Internet-based surveys) or to invite them to take part in offline research (Eysenbach and Till, 2001).

These are illustrated alongside other methods in the 'Techniques' section of the Methods Map in Chapter 4.

■ Active research methods

Online focus groups

Internet-mediated communication allows researchers to conduct focus groups via the Internet. Similar to an offline focus group, this method allows for an interaction between participants and a moderator in a semi-structured manner. The advantages of doing focus groups is that group interaction can generate insights which one-to-one interactions (e.g. interviews) cannot. One of the main advantages of Internet-based focus groups is the removal of many geographical barriers, increasing the potential pool of participants. There are also a number of limitations to online focus groups, such as a lack of moderator control and the inability to observe the level of attention of participants.

Online interviews

Interviews are a popular method in qualitative research, and can provide deeper understanding of what participants think and feel regarding a particular topic. Interviews in online environments can be conducted both synchronically and asynchronically. Synchronous interviews are usually conducted with the support of voice and video application. They have the advantage that participants do not have to move in order to attend the interview – particularly valuable if gathering information from participants in a large number of locations. Technology advancement has allowed online interviews to become almost as interactive as face-to-face ones, since most of the software now supports voice and image. However there might be some limitations, particularly when targeting participants that are not technologically savvy. Other issues associated with this type of interviews are technological problems that may unexpectedly arise during the interview. Problems with attention (due to participants doing other things) can also reduce the degree of involvement and rapport that an interviewer can build, and some physical responses (e.g. hand movements, levels of stress) might not come across in online interviews.

Asynchronous interviews are mainly conducted via email, where questions are sent to the participants who are then left to answer in their own time. As a result, participants have more time to reflect on their answer allowing them to develop structured ideas about what s/he wants to communicate. Often a number of questions are sent initially, with further questions sent once answers to the first batch are provided. (Some examples of research via asynchronous interviews are Illingworth, 2001, 2006; Mann and Stewart, 2000). Limitations of this type of interview include the loss of spontaneity and the time that long interviews may take to be completed.

■ Passive research methods

Netnographic research

Similar to ethnographic studies, netnographic studies focus on the understanding of online cultures and communities. The method is defined by Kozinets (1998, p. 366) as "a written account resulting from fieldwork studying the cultures and communities that emerge from on-line, computer mediated, or Internet-based communications, where both the field work and the textual account are methodologically informed by the traditions and techniques of cultural anthropology." Netnographic studies require the researcher to immerse themselves in the environment where the research is conducted in order to understand the nature of the interactions that occur in the online environment, as well as the motivations behind the group dynamics. One of the biggest advantages of doing netnographic research is that finding and joining online communities (e.g. forums, online branded communities) can be relatively simple. There are however some online communities that are closed or private, and to get access to them the researcher should usually get the right credentials or permissions. For instance, research on brand-related communities usually require some knowledge of the brand and the situation for which the community was formed. An understanding of the rules that govern the online community is also important, as lack of compliance can lead to the researcher being excluded from the community or to the participants 'shutting down' from genuine participation.

6

Exercise 6.5

In groups share the names of one Facebook group/online forum each that you often use. Pick two of the groups named and spend some time identifying the dynamic of each group. Are there a small number of regular contributors or many? What other conclusion can you draw from comparing the groups?

Research of forums/blogs

Another type of passive research method is to investigate content that has been already generated in forums and blogs. Hookway (2008) differentiates between unsolicited blogs, that were created organically by the participants before taking part in the research, and solicited ones that are created after the participant agreed to take part in this research. Ethical implications of both will be further discussed later in this section. Either way, research in forums and blogs has the advantage that content is recorded by the participant, which facilitates the collection of data. Another advantage of conducting research in forums and blogs is that there are a vast number of them and they are supported by user-generated content in a wide range of topics. WordPress, which is one of the main platforms used to create blogs, estimates that on a monthly basis over 409 million people view more than 14.4 billion pages of content (WordPress, 2014).

Online environments as a recruiting channel

The Internet can be used as a recruitment channel to find people, before conducting research in a more 'traditional' way. Online communities gather people with similar interests, and therefore can be a very productive way to reach people with certain profile but who are scattered geographically. An example would be the use of specialised web forums to reach consumers interested in a particular type of cheese, or fan forums where the details of the latest film franchise is being actively discussed. If your research context is very specific, online environments as a tool for participants' recruitment could be a better alternative than traditional recruitment methods.

Exercise 6.6

Imagine you are looking for consumers of a very specific branded product. Using Twitter's advanced search (https://twitter.com/search-advanced) to find users of that product based on keywords and location. Design a recruitment strategy on how best to get those consumers to participate in your research project.

Social media

Social media websites (commonly referred just as 'social media') are websites that are gaining increasing interest among both practitioners and, of particular interest here, academic research (see Figure 6.2). The interest in this type of site is nested in the impact that these platforms have had as sources of information and as a means to enable constant interaction with other users. The increased use of social media channels means that, within the field of business management, a greater understanding of the channels and the interactions that occur in them are becoming more relevant, as they are reshaping the way in which consumers interact with brands and organisations (Hoffman and Novak, 2012; Perez-Vega, Waite, and O'Gorman, 2014).

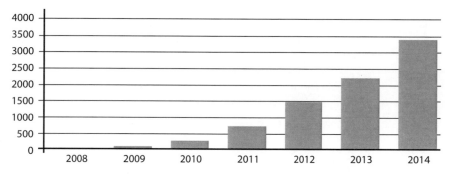

Figure 6.2: Social media in academic research

■ Defining social media websites

We have summarised some definitions of social media in Table 6.1 highlighting that three main characteristics of this type of site emerge:

1 Social media enables *user-generated content* (UGC),

2 The possibility to form *online communities* from which this content can be passed along, and

3 All these interactions occur in an online environment.

From these definitions, you might now realise that in today's online environments more websites than the most commonly mentioned (i.e. Facebook) allow users to generate their own content and form online communities. In plain words, social media allows you to socialise with others and let users be both the consumer and producer of content. However, this broad definition can include many of today's websites. After all, it is possible to socialise not only with your friends on Facebook, but also with other YouTube users in the comments section, with consumers of similar brands and products in online brand communities, and even with complete strangers via Twitter.

Table 6.1: Academics' and practitioners' definitions of social media

Author	Definitions of social media
Mangold & Faulds (2009) *Academic*	Definition linked to a practitioner's concept known as "consumer generated media", defined as a variety of new sources of online information that are created, initiated, circulated and used by consumers intent on educating each other about products, brands, services, personalities, and issues"
Solis (2010) *Practitioner*	Social media is the democratization of information, transforming people from content readers into publishers. It is the shift from a broadcast mechanism, one-to-many model, rooted in conversation between authors, people and peers
Kaplan & Haenlein (2010) *Academic*	Social media is a group of Internet-based applications that build on the ideological and technological foundations of Web 2.0, and that allow the creation and exchange of user generated content.
Xiang & Gretzel (2010) *Practitioner*	While there is a lack of a formal definition, 'social media' can be generally understood as Internet-based applications that carry consumer-generated content which encompasses "media impressions created by consumers, typically informed by relevant experience, and archived or shared online for easy access by other impressionable consumers"
Oxford Dictionary (2012)	Websites and applications that enable users to create and share content or to participate in social networking

■ Taxonomy of social media websites

Given the multiple definitions above, it is important to understand the functionalities of each of the different platforms in order to classify the options at the researcher's disposal, for which the diagram in Figure 6.3 is useful.

- *Identity* represents the extent to which users reveal their real identities to each other.

- *Sharing* relates to the extent to which users exchange and distribute content.

- *Relationships* can be based on existing structured ones from offline environments or particular interests, or can be unstructured where people with no previous relationships can freely interact.

- *Reputation* is the extent to which the trustworthiness of someone can be assessed in the social media setting.

- *Groups* relates to the possibility of forming communities and sub-communities within a particular platform.

- *Presence* relates to the degree the real presence of the individual behind the screen is disclosed to show that users are available.

- *Conversation* relates to the extent to which users communicate with each other.

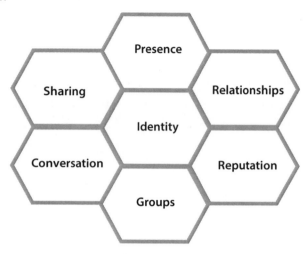

Figure 6.3: Social Media taxonomy (Kietzmann et al., 2011)

Certain social media sites might be more adequate than others to conduct your research enquiry. For instance, if your research looks at reputation and how it affects trust, then you might want to choose as a context a social media website that is reputation-centred as opposed to a site that is built on conversations only. If on the other hand, your research focuses on behaviours in online communities, then sites that allow the formation of these kinds of communities would be the most sensible selection.

Ethical considerations in Internet research

The ethical considerations that are accounted for in this section are based on the harm that participants of research may be exposed to when being part of an academic study. Online research is not likely to be more harmful than offline research, yet it poses other challenges (Kraut et al., 2004). We identify three of the most important ethical considerations when conducting research online: the safeguard of participants, ensuring participants' confidentiality, and gaining participants' consent.

Safeguard of participants

In online research it is harder to assess if a risk of harm to a participant is likely to occur. This is due to the limitations present in computer-mediated interactions where the level of distress of a person as a consequence of being part of a certain study cannot be easily assessed. Exit mechanisms and building good rapport with the participant when running research are strategies that can be useful in order to avoid this from happening (Eynon, Fry, and Schroeder, 2008).

Ensuring confidentiality

Another important element to take into consideration is how the findings in your research are presented, particularly in regard to participant anonymity. In order to ensure confidentiality of the participants, the researcher needs to pay special attention to how the data is presented, the type of information that is disclosed in terms of age, gender or location of the participants, and when quoting from online sources which can be easily found using search engines.

Participants' consent

One of the greatest ethical considerations when conducting online research is the consent of the participant to take part in the study. Depending on the methods and nature of your research, consent will be sought before conducting your study (as in interviews and some types of netnographic studies). It could be the case that you are planning to conduct a covert netnographic study, where you do not tell the subject community who you are and why you are interested in that community. If you decide to do so you will need to make sure to conduct an exhaustive risk assessment of the scope of your research and to take the sufficient preventive measures in order to ensure the confidentiality of it.

■ Summary

This section aims to give an introductory account of using the Internet to conduct research. Although this is not an exhaustive review of the implications of conducting research online, it is intended to serve as a guide to using the Internet in your dissertation.

Overall summary

Both historical sources and the World Wide Web offer a vast amount of data which you can consider collecting in your research. However collecting this material alone does not offer you the opportunity to infer conclusions or answer your research questions. This section should be used in conjunction with the techniques (in Chapter 7), qualitative data analysis (Chapter 8) and ethical implications (Chapter 11) in order to create the best possible project to answer the problems identified in your research using the preceding chapters.

References

Amatori, F. and Jones, G. (2003), Introduction, in *Business History around the World*, ed. F. Amatori and G. Jones, Cambridge: Cambridge University Press, 1-7.

Bolick, C. M. (2006), Digital archives: Democratizing the doing of history, *International Journal of Social Education*, **21**(1), 122-34.

Brundage, A. (2013), *Going to the Archives: A Guide to Historical Research and Writing*, Oxford: Wiley-Blackwell.

Bryce, D., O'Gorman, K.D. and Baxter, I.W.F. (2013), Commerce, empire and faith in Safavid Iran: The *Caravanserai* of Isfahan, *International Journal of Contemporary Hospitality Management*, **25** (2), 204-26.

Bucheli, M., & Wadhwani, R. D. (2014), *Organizations in Time: History, Theory, Methods*, Oxford: Oxford University Press.

Business Insider (2014), "Fears That Teenagers Are Deserting Facebook Are Overblown," http://www.businessinsider.com/teenagers-arent-leaving-facebook-2014-1?IR=T.

Charlton, T. L. (2006). Introduction: Looking for a Vade Mecum. In T. L. Charlton, L. E. Myers & R. Sharpless (Eds.), *Handbook of Oral History* (pp. 1-15). Lanham, MD: AltaMira Press.

Derrida, J. (1998), *Archive Fever: A Freudian Impression*, Chicago: University of Chicago Press.

Eynon, R., Fry, J. and Schroeder, R. (2008). The ethics of Internet research, in *SAGE Internet Research Methods*, P. Hughes (ed), London: Sage, pp 279–304.

6

Eysenbach, G. and Till, J.E. (2001), Ethical issues in qualitative research on Internet communities, *BMJ*, **323** (7321), 1103–05.

Farge, A. (2013), *The Allure of the Archives*, New Haven, CT: Yale University Press.

Foucault, M. (1969), *The Archaeology of Knowledge*, Routledge: London.

Harvey, K. (2009). Introduction. In K. Harvey (Ed.), *History and Material Culture: A Student's Guide to Approaching Alternative Sources* (pp. 1-23). London: Routledge.

Hoffman, DL and TP Novak (2012), Toward a deeper understanding of social media, *Journal of Interactive Marketing*, **26** (2), 69-70.

Hookway, N. (*2008*) "Entering the blogosphere": some strategies for using blogs in social research, *Qualitative Research*, **8**(1) 91-11

Illingworth, N. (2001) The Internet Matters: Exploring the Use of the Internet as a Research Tool, *Sociological Research Online*, **6**(2)

Illingworth, N. (2006) Content, Context, Reflexivity and the Qualitative Research Encounter: Telling Stories in the Virtual Realm, *Sociological Research Online*, **11**(1)

Jones, G., & Zeitlin, J. (2007). Introduction. In G. Jones & J. Zeitlin (Eds.), *The Oxford Handbook of Business History* (pp. 1-6). Oxford: Oxford University Press.

Kaplan, A.M. & Haenlein, M. (2010) Users of the World unite! The challenges and oppportunities of Social Media, *Business Horizons*, **53**, 59-68

Kietzmann, J.H., Hermkens, K., McCarthy, I.P., Silvestre, B.S. (2011). Social Media? Get Serious! Understanding the Functional Building Blocks of Social Media. *Business Horizons* **54**(1), 241-251.

Kozinets, R. V. (1998), On netnography: Initial reflections on consumer research investigations of cyberculture, in *Advances in Consumer Research*, Vol 25, J. Alba and W. Hutchinson (eds), Provo, UT: Association for Consumer Research, 366-371.

Kraut, R., Olson, J., Banaji, M., Bruckman, A., Cohen, J., & Couper, M. (2004). Psychological research online: Report of board of scientific affairs' advisory group on the conduct of research on the Internet. *American Psychologist*, **59**, 105-117.

Maclean, M., Harvey, C., & Clegg, S. (2015). Conceptualizing Historical Organization Studies.*Academy of Management Review*, amr-2014.

Mangold, W. G. and Faulds, D. J.(2009) . Social Media: The New "Hybrid" Element of the Promotion Mix. *Business Horizons,* **52** (4): 357-366

Mann, C. & Stewart, F. (2000). *Internet Communication and Qualitative Research: A Handbook for Researching Online.* London: Sage Publications

Manoff, M. (2004), Theories of the archive from across the disciplines, *Libraries and the Academy,* **4**(1), 9-25.

Maxwell, A. (2010), Digital archives and history research: Feedback from an end-user, *Library Review,* **59**(1), 24-39.

Murray, O. (2001), Herodotus and oral history, in *The Historian's Craft in the Age of Herodotus,* ed. Nino Luraghi, Oxford: Oxford University Press, 16-44.

ONS (2014), Internet Access - Households and Individuals, London: Office for National Statistics.

Perez-Vega, R., Waite, K. and O'Gorman, K.D. (2014) The influence of brand immediacy in consumer engagement behaviours: A revised social impact model, in *Marketing Dimensions: People, Places and Spaces.* Presented at the 47th Academy of Marketing Conference, Bournemouth, UK.

Perks, R., & Thomson, A. (2006). Introduction. In R. Perks & A. Thomson (eds.), *The Oral History Reader* (pp. ix-xiii). London: Routledge.

Portelli, A. (2006). What makes oral history different? In R. Perks & A. Thomson (eds.), *The Oral History Reader* (pp. 63-74). London: Routledge.

Solis, B. (2010), *Engage: The Complete Guide for Business to Build, Cultivate and Measure Success in the New Web,* Hoboken, NJ: John Wiley & Sons.

Sommer, B. W., & Quinlan, M. K. (2009). *The Oral History Manual* (2 ed.). Lanham, MD: AltaMira Press.

Stanton, J.M. (1998). An empirical assessment of data collection using the Internet. *Personal Psychology,* **51**(3), 709–725.

Szabo, A and Frenkl, R. (1996) Considerations of research on Internet: Guidelines and implications for human movement studies, *Clinical Kinesiology,* **50**(3) 58-65

WordPress (2014). A live look at activity across Wordpress.com. Available at http://en.wordpress.com/stats. Accessed 10 August 2014.

Xiang, Z., & Gretzel, U. (2010). Role of social media in online travel information search. *Tourism Management,* **31**(2), 179-188.

7 Qualitative Data Gathering Techniques

Sean Lochrie, Ross Curran and Kevin O'Gorman

As one of our primary methodologies in the Methods Map (see chapter 4), qualitative techniques can yield valuable, revelatory, and rich data. They can be used on their own, or in conjunction with other research tools depending on the nature of the research project. For example, interviews can be used to explain and interpret the results of quantitative research, or conversely, to provide exploratory data that are later developed by quantitative research. MacIntosh & Bonnet (2007, p. 321) note with humour that "[q]ualitative research is sometimes styled as the poor cousin of 'real science'…" This position can represent an added challenge to researchers. This chapter discusses some common approaches to qualitative research methods (see the 'Techniques' section of the Methods Map) and the issues that must be considered with their application in order for them not to be viewed as somehow inferior to 'real science'.

Interviews

A long-established research method, qualitative interviews involve a conversation between the researcher and the subject towards developing understanding of central themes and research questions. Interviewing is now examined in three stages: pre-interview, interview and post-interview, explaining some useful techniques for conducting successful interview research.

◼ Pre-interview considerations: Design and access

You will remember from Chapter 2 that being realistic and ensuring your objectives are achievable is important when formulating your ideas. The same caution must be applied to considering your approach in interviews.

First and foremost, trust your instincts and your 'gut feeling' to guide you. You should not forget that an interview is simply a dialogue between two people. You are familiar with this dynamic and you already possess the basic skills that will ensure a successful outcome.

Table 7.1: Strengths, weaknesses and applications of interview approaches

Strengths	Weaknesses	Applicability
Unstructured		
Provides rich information. Explores previously unknown themes that arise from the interview. Creates relationships which may lead to more information. Uses natural language.	Very time consuming. Resource intensive Lacking in generalizability Can generate lots of often irrelevant data. Susceptible to interviewer bias.	Exploratory research investigating past events when subjective views and experiences are sought in conjunction with other research methods.
Semi-Structured		
Questions prepared in advance to cover critical points, useful when the researcher is inexperienced. Interviewees still retain freedom and flexibility to express their own views. Increased reliability and scope for comparability. Interviewee is able to respond in language natural to them	Time consuming. Resource intensive. Needs good interview skills to keep on topic. Interview questions are open to researcher bias May lack in generalizability.	Multiple interviewers. Only one chance to conduct the interview. Researcher has some knowledge of the topic, In conjunction with other research methods.
Structured		
Can produce consistent generalizable data. Minimal risk of bias. Large sample size. Can be conducted quickly. Sophisticated interviewing skills not required.	Little opportunity for feedback. Question responses are limited and restrictive. Little scope to cater for the unforeseen. Real-time changes to the interviews cannot be made.	Clear focus and a question to be answered. High level of knowledge on a topic to allow for appropriate question formulation. A well-developed literature.

7

Interviews range from unstructured (open-ended) to structured, with semi-structured occupying a middle-ground. Selecting the most appropriate type often determines project success. For example, unstructured interviews in a resource-constrained, narrowly-focused project may prove ineffective, whereas highly focused structured interviews are unlikely to capture the depth of insight required in some exploratory studies. The type of project you are involved in, the nature of your research participants and the time and cost limitations you face must be incorporated into your decision-making. For example, it may be difficult to get the approval to conduct unstructured in-depth interviews with prisoners; it may also not be the best use of the opportunity to ask sterile and prescriptive structured questions if you are lucky enough to interview the CEO of a global company. Table 7.1 illustrates some characteristics of these approaches and suggests suitable applications; however, the boundaries are not fixed between them.

One of the most important considerations will be about what to ask your participants. A common problem is for a researcher to formulate and ask leading questions, either before or during the interview (or in a focus group). Leading questions are designed to direct the interviewee towards a particular conclusion, and therefore may invalidate their responses. The question might contain a judgement or imply a scenario through the order of words used, or through the use of non-neutral language. For example, asking "what sort of problems are caused by gender inequality in your workplace" implies that the interviewees are or should be aware of gender inequality in their workplace (there might be none), and then asks them to think of problems with this, affecting how they think about the subject before they have even begun to respond. A more neutral version of this question could be "what is your experience of gender in the workplace?", although you will be able to think of several other variations. In the same way that you must consider and attempt to account for researcher bias (see Chapter 12), it is vital that you think about how questions might shape responses.

How to conduct the interview is another challenge, with approaches including: video, telephone, or face-to-face interviews. Unstructured interviews elicit more information in a face-to-face format, whereas telephone-based formats may prove suitable for structured interviews when a larger sample is required to strengthen validity, and the practicalities of meeting each respondent face-to-face are diminished. Ultimately, the most efficient way should be selected considering the resources available, appropriateness to the context, and the added value of two-way interaction to the research.

Access to appropriate participants is vital and must be realistic and achievable within any project timeframe. Interviewers must be able to brief gatekeepers and participants on the purpose of the project, as the initial exchanges can affect the rest of the interview. The briefing should include the following elements:

- What the data generated from the study will be used for.
- Reassurances of confidentiality.
- How data will be recorded.
- Length of the proposed interviews.
- How many interviews the participant is committing to undertake.
- Reassurance that the researcher's role is non-judgemental but evaluative.

■ The Interview

The interviewer has to be able to listen, prompt appropriately, and interact with the interviewee effectively. Good interviewers are personable, fostering a trust and rapport with the interviewee. Gaining valuable data from an interviewee who is relaxed and enjoying the process is far easier than one who is on edge and suspicious. Table 7.2 illustrates interview stage techniques that can enhance interview quality

7

Table 7.2: Interview techniques

Activity	Description	Benefits
Pilot study	Ensures the study is designed correctly, but does not contribute towards data. Should resemble the actual study closely.	Improves the robustness of the study. Allows early remediation of project design flaws. Settles the researcher into a routine and process they can execute confidently.
Selecting the setting	Where the interview takes place influences the interview itself.	The interviewee may find hosting the interview more convenient, a neutral setting may elicit more data, some settings may jeopardise interviewee anonymity.
Recording	Discretely, but with permission, record interviews for later transcribing and analysis, improving accuracy.	Can review the interview innumerable times. Records with minimal intrusion.

The interview guide	A pre-prepared set of topics/questions, produced with the aim of providing a form of direction for interviews. Lines of enquiry should correspond to the critical themes underpinning the study.	Aids the researcher, helping to ensure coverage of pertinent themes. Briefs the interviewee (but should not *lead* them).
Non-verbal communications	Interviews include the verbal conversation, and a range of body language. Hand gestures, eye movements and head movements can all add meaning to an interviewee's words. Note taking can record these.	Interviewee body language is an important part of the data, confirming, contradicting or emphasising what the participant is saying.
Funnelling	When the interviewer begins with open, general questions but gradually, as rapport develops, focuses on more specific points.	Builds rapport. Useful when asking more sensitive questions.
Gaining a follow-up	Arranging follow-up interviews is more likely during an interview. The researcher should grasp this opportunity if it arises.	Can verify findings through further discussion with the interviewee.

The application of techniques described in Table 7.2 helps the researcher generate robust and valuable data. At all times, interviewers should be courteous and appreciative of the time being given to them. In addition to interview techniques, Alvesson (200,3 p. 18) emphasises that an interview is indeed "…a complex social situation". Figure 7.1 presents eight issues interviewers should be aware of, according to Alvesson (2003, p. 18).

Interview issues

1   The social problem of coping with an inter-personal relationship and complex interaction in a non-routine situation

2   The cognitive problem of finding out what it is all about (beyond the level of the espoused)

3   The identity problem of adopting a contextually relevant self-position

4   The institutional problem of adapting to normative pressure and cognitive uncertainty through mimicking a standard form of expression

5   The problem (or option) of maintaining and increasing self-esteem that emerges in any situation involving examination and calling for performance

6   The motivation problem of developing an interest or rationale for active participation in the interview

7	The representation / construction problem of how to account for complex phenomena through language
8	The autonomy / determinism problem of powerful macro-discourse(s) operating behind and on the interviewee

Figure 7.1: Interview Issues (Alvesson 2003, p. 18)

■ Post-interview

Post-interview, the researcher will disengage from the field. It may be appropriate to distribute a message of thanks to participants. When agreements have been made to share the results of the research, fulfilment of these is advisable, both from a moral viewpoint but also, should follow-up data be required, access is more likely to be granted by the participant. As soon as is possible, the researcher should transcribe recordings of interviews and organise the gathered data while the interviews remain fresh in their mind.

Focus groups

A focus group can be defined as a group discussion or interview between one researcher and several participants at once. Normally, they consist of small groups of individuals who convene to communicate their opinions concerning a specific area of interest defined by the researcher. Similar to individual interviews, focus groups facilitate the detailed investigation of participants' experiences and observations on a specified theme(s). However, a significant difference is that data is generated from the interaction among those involved, which is managed and guided by a facilitator or moderator (typically the researcher). The key features of a focus group are summarised in Table 7.3.

■ When are focus groups applicable?

In the social sciences, the ability of focus groups to amass rich information on the knowledge and experiences of people renders their applicability broad. Focus groups can be used to explore under-researched issues; to investigate the origins of people's understanding of a subject; to broaden the knowledge of a phenomenon which is unfamiliar to the researcher but familiar to the respondents; and to encourage people to converse on their understanding of an issue and to expand their opinions on it. For example,

7

Alexander, O'Gorman & Wood (2010) used a series of focus groups to explore consumer attitudes towards the potential implementation of compulsory nutritional labelling on commercial restaurant menus in the UK. This approach allowed them to gain comparable results through conducting three focus groups with people with differing attitudes to eating outside the home.

Due to their qualitative nature, focus groups can either be used as an autonomous method or in combination with other approaches. For example, they can be used at the beginning of a research project to obtain data into an under-researched phenomenon. This data can then be used to develop a survey or interview framework for further data collection. Second, focus groups can be undertaken in order to confirm or gain reaction from findings which have been developed through the use of other techniques such as interviews, observations, and surveys.

Table 7.3: Key features of focus groups

Feature	Purpose
Deliberation	Allows for individuals who have had comparable experiences to come together to discuss those experiences.
Flexibility	Individuals have the opportunity to highlight issues that are important to them.
	The researcher can therefore explore ways in which people concur or diverge in relation to particular issues and the reasoning why.
Emotions	Focus groups allow for an extensive understanding of the way people feel.
Moderation	The moderator has less control meaning that themes which may have been undetected in more structured approaches can be identified.
Freedom	Sometimes people are reluctant to discuss things on an individual basis but may feel more supported in discussing them in a group if it becomes apparent that these ideas/sentiments are shared by the other participants. This may generate more valuable data for the study.
Challenge	Individuals' opinions can be queried and challenged by others.
	Through this process people's views can either be confirmed or amended.
Interactive	Interaction between respondents will enhance the prospect of the views expressed being accurate, and therefore, more reliable.
	This is because of the belief that the focus group environment means individuals are compelled to deliberate their accounts and consider their views against the experiences and beliefs of others.
Duration	Focus groups usually last from one to three hours.

■   Focus group process

Before undertaking a focus group there are a number of considerations that must be addressed to ensure its viability and effectiveness. The first two stages occur prior to the actual focus group and include planning and recruiting. Table 7.4 summarises the key elements of the planning and recruiting stages.

Planning and recruiting are fundamental elements of the focus group method. Failure to do these with care can result in the process being ineffective and the data collected being poor and unrewarding.

Table 7.4: Features of the focus group planning and recruiting stages

Aspect	Explanation
Planning	
Define purpose of focus groups	The research objectives must be identified.
	From these the moderator can identify from whom the information needs to be collected, and devise themes that can be used to direct the discussion and highlight key areas which need to be encompassed.
Develop a focus group guide	This is an outline which identifies the issues and themes that are to be explored.
	The guide is constructed in order to enlighten the overall research objectives and to ensure that the focus group discussions correlate with these goals. Similar to an interview guide, this ensures the discussions are useful without being led by the researcher's agenda.
Location	Locations should be somewhere where the participants feel comfortable and preferably that they are familiar with.
	This can improve attendance, and will limit distractions. It must be accessible and where people can easily see and hear each other.
Transcription	The researcher must plan how they will record the focus group.
	A recording device can be used to capture spoken words. There are instances when the interaction is recorded by video camera.
	Regardless of approach, prior consent must be obtained.
Recruiting	
How many groups to run?	This will depend on the nature of the research, the variation of people that need to be in involved, time restraints, and cost limitations.
Sampling method	Focus groups follow a purposive sampling strategy. As the aim is to obtain an in-depth understanding of a specific population, random sampling is unsuitable.

7

Selection criteria	Selection criteria must be well defined. This may relate to: age, organisational department, demographics, gender, or particular experiences.
Dynamics of the group	Groups need to be balanced so that members have a level of commonality, so that the interactions will be meaningful, but amply dissimilar so they don't have exactly similar beliefs.
	However, difficulties may occur if groups contain people from differing levels of an organisation. This can lead to views being inhibited and habitual roles emerging.
Size of groups	Groups usually consist of between six and ten people.
	More than ten can lead to difficulties in controlling the conversation, lack of substance, and individuals not contributing.
Accessing participants	Obtaining participants can be accomplished through: sampling through existing lists, advertising, snowball sampling, and gaining access and aid through organisational gatekeepers.
Inviting participants	Possible members should be contacted and informed of the purpose of the research, the time and location of the meeting, the technique that will be used to record the discussion, and the topic of the debate.

Conducting the focus group

Conducting a focus group can be broken down into a series of stages: introduction, ice-breaker, initial questions, important questions, closing questions – Table 7.5 highlights these. It is essential that the discussion is driven by the focus group guide. While this guide will allow for the collection of information relevant to the study's objectives, it should not unduly constrain participants. This can uncover issues which could enlighten the research through the moderator encouraging participants to raise subjects of their experiences, providing lucidity and intensity into the discussion.

The role of the moderator is of vital importance within the process. They have the responsibility to ask questions that will encourage discussion within the group. They will also try to ensure that the discussion is significant and within the parameters of the research, but without constraining the views of the participants. They will use discussion aids and probes to help gain a deep understating of the issues to be discussed or need further debate; attempt to involve all group members; and when relevant, investigate beyond facts to the feelings of participants. Moderators will also bring discussion points to a close when the dialogue is going off course. Such facilitation is essential to ensure that the discussion focuses on both the research interests and the relevant aspects that participants regard as important.

Table 7.5: Phases in conducting the focus group

Introduction

In this stage it is important to create an environment which allows people to feel comfortable to talk in.

The researcher should introduce themselves, summarise the research project; what will be done with the collected data, and confirm confidentiality.

Ground rules may also be discussed, for example: everyone should have the opportunity to speak; and all remarks should be directed to the collective.

Ice-breaker

Participants should be given the opportunity to introduce themselves.

When possible, allocate name badges to the group, this will allow the moderator to follow the discussion and ensure that, when needed, participants can be asked questions if they are struggling to interact.

Initial questions

The research topic should be introduced in more depth.

The group should be asked to deliberate the subject in order to clarify any difficulties and any differences in the understating of key issues.

Important questions

This is where the main debate will commence. Participants will discuss the important themes that are central to the research.

Commonly, the moderator will use probes to develop specific areas of interaction to gain a more in-depth understanding of issues raised or use discussion aids to instigate debate.

It may also be valuable to record physical behaviours throughout the focus group.

There should be a limited number of questions/themes to be addressed – usually, between two and six. More than this and the ability to gain an extensive insight may be diminished.

Closing questions

This relates to how the focus group is brought to an end.

The closing question should give the participants the opportunity to have a final remark – this could entail them either stating something they feel has not been fully covered or stating a concluding opinion.

The moderator can also use the closing stage to reconfirm areas of uncertainty or ask for clarification from members as to the accuracy of their interpretation on a specific matter.

7

Dealing with challenges

When conducting focus groups a number of challenges are often encountered. Table 7.6 highlights these and offers possible solutions.

Table 7.6: Focus group challenges and solutions

Challenge	Solution
A small number of people are dominating the discussion	The moderator can intervene by confronting the dominant individuals. This should be done in a friendly and constructive manner to ensure that their involvement is not lost. Recognise their opinions and then ask others for their views.
The discussion is at an impasse	Intervention by the moderator can be used to either summarise the key points of the issue discussed, giving participants the opportunity to readdress specific points; or there is an agreement to focus on the next question/theme. By giving participants a choice so they feel involved.
Inactive participants	The moderator can ask the individual for their views; or they can remind the group of his/her gratitude that several and contrasting views are being projected. By stating this to the group the moderator is not isolating anyone and is fostering a comfortable environment for all the participants. Through this the participant can decide themselves if they are comfortable to speak.
Multiple conversations at once	Intervention by the moderator can be used to allow a more manageable approach to resume. For example, remarking on everyone's enthusiasm on the issue but recommending that a more systematic way of expressing the views in turn would be beneficial.
Quiet groups	Participants may be asked to divide into smaller groups to discuss specific issues then asked to report back.

Limitations of focus groups

While focus groups offer a useful methodological approach, they do have a number of limitations.

- They are difficult to organise – acquiring participants is a lengthy process and, at times, requires persuasion through inducement/incentive.

- Transcription difficulties – as focus groups involve multiple viewpoints interacting simultaneously the recordings will be complex to transcribe and the process lengthy.

- Information overload – focus groups tend to accumulate large amounts of data which can be difficult to dissect and manage.

- Limitations on control – unlike an interview, there is less control in a focus group. Therefore, it is easy for the discussion to diverge into areas which are not relevant. Constant interventions when this occurs may harm the quality of the information gathered.

- Group effects – some people are negatively influenced by the dynamics of the group. For example, a focus group of various members of an organisation may be influenced by position, gender or social standing. This can lead to the collection of inaccurate information.

Despite these limitations, the application of focus groups within research offers a rewarding avenue from which to collect rich multiple-perspective data which has the ability to illuminate any research project.

Ethnography and observations

As researchers entering the field, we face the challenge of grappling with things which are at once "strange, irregular and inexplicit" (Geertz, 1973, p. 10). Ethnographic studies may begin with very simple questions (e.g.: "why are the nurses crying"; Weinberg, 2003) and move forward from there. The challenges ethnographers face in generating rich data that illuminates understanding of human, social and cultural interactions within a specific setting are significant. This section introduces ethnographic research, before exploring fieldwork considerations, and applicability.

Traditionally associated with anthropological studies, particularly the study of indigenous peoples, ethnographic research has now been applied in various contexts. An ethnography is an in-depth research approach, developing intimate understandings of human interaction and behaviour first hand. Embedded and immersed over a prolonged time period, the ethnographer conducts fieldwork from within a societal subgroup: observing, listening, and interacting with other members to gain an 'insider' understanding of social phenomena. The principal aims of this approach include:

- Exploring relationships affecting interactions within specific situations.

- Investigating spaces where people make decisions within a relational, not individual process.

- Challenging assumed processes and suggesting new questions regarding social phenomena.

Ethnographic research projects are essentially unique, and therefore the technique cannot be easily mastered in advance. A good ethnographer requires patience, a clear vision, people skills, and a willingness to commit to long term research. Table 7.7 highlights the strengths and weaknesses of ethnography and observation as a methodological approach.

Table 7.7: Strengths and weaknesses of ethnographic and observational research

Strengths	Weaknesses
Rich data can be gathered.	Observer bias can be a problem Notes will be subjective and selective
They take place in natural settings rather than in created research settings.	There is the prospect that the researcher may misinterpret what they witness.
Can be used as a starting point to create themes to inform a more structured data collection process. Helpful when the information about a specific topic or context is minimal.	Difficulties in documenting what information is important. Particularly relevant for non-participant observation where there is the possibility of information overload.
Behaviours can be identified which the subjects were not aware of or did not wish to reveal.	The observer effect. The subjects may alter their behaviours if they know they are being watched.
Behaviours can be identified which may not have been unearthed through other techniques.	Can be time-consuming as long periods of engagement and commitment are required.
Can be used to validate evidence gathered from other techniques. For example, as part of a case study.	Cognitive data cannot be observed. For example: motivations; attitudes; and perceptions.

Observations can be a fruitful approach for gathering rich information to enlighten research, as well as complementing and informing other qualitative techniques. To be successful, researchers must carefully select the appropriate observational approach and this will be dependent on the objectives of the study. Attention must also be given to the key elements of the process to ensure the validity of the approach. While observations can be intensive and sometimes complex, the approach is an important technique in the qualitative researcher's toolkit.

Observation involves the monitoring and recording of naturally occurring activities and/or events. By observing situations as they occur for a short period of time, the researcher has the prospect of understanding the intricacy of what is being investigated. This could include: how people interact or work together; how processes function; and how relationships are formed. Observational research can take the form of either participant or non-participant. Typically observations are used in conjunction with other data gathering techniques as a means to inform and consolidate evidence gathered from other avenues, and are extremely popular in case studies.

Table 7.8: Categories of observer's roles

Role	Description
Complete participant	The researcher is a full participant in the situation which is being studied The purpose of the research is not disclosed. Raises ethical questions – not appropriate where there is potential to create detriment to those being studied.
Participant-as-observer	The researcher is a full participant in the situation which is being studied. The members of the group are aware of the researcher and the purpose of the study. Requires attaining the support and trust of those involved.
Observer-as-participant	Observing is the primary purpose. The members of the group are aware of the researcher and the purpose of the study. Some interaction with members is required when necessary. The researcher gains less emotional involvement in group experience than they would if they were 'participant-as-observer'.
Complete observer	The researcher does not take part in the situation or activities of the setting. The purpose of the research is not disclosed. Information is gathered by the researcher in an inconspicuous manner.

In non-participant observation, the researcher examines the phenomenon as an outside observer via direct or indirect observations. Direct observation occurs when the researcher directly perceives the experience or the environment and documents it, for example, during a meeting to investigate how leaders attain strategic change in organisations where leadership roles are shared. Conversely, indirect observations occur when the researcher observes the behaviour after its occurrence, for example, through video technology. Participant observation requires the researcher to engage with the phenomenon being investigated. In doing so the researcher actively participates and engages with the subjects and/or the activities of the research context. For example, McMillan, O'Gorman & MacLaren (2011) undertook participant observations for a three month period in Nepal, allowing them to illustrate how commercial hospitality has catalysed sustainable social change through empowering women. Through participation the researcher becomes a significant component of the study's design. This requires the researcher to balance their function as both a participant and as an external entity, meaning their role is both involved and disconnected. This also requires the investigator to preserve their role and veracity as an explorer and their capacity to critically deliberate what they are observing.

■ The observational process

Regardless of approach, before entering the field a number of issues must be addressed to ensure the effectiveness and legitimacy of the proposed research. Once in the field the researcher must consider a number of essential factors. Table 7.9 highlights the main issues in each of three stages.

Table 7.9: Issues in the observation process

Issue	Description
Preparing	
Access	Must be negotiated and the extent to which the researcher's role as either overt or covert must be distinguished.
Knowledge	Ensures familiarity with the context that is going to be observed. Allows for appropriate data to be collected. Ensures awareness of behaviours which must be respected.
Ethics	Informed consent obtained from the participants. Ethical approval from the relevant organisations.
Data collection aims and objectives	Allows for a more structured approach when documenting observations. Ensures that the relevant data are gathered.
Observation guide	To remind or aid the researcher in gathering information in relation to specific themes. Should not excessively constrain the researcher by confining them to specific areas of interest. Be aware of other observations beyond the guide.

In the field	
Conduct	For participant observations, build affiliations with members. Creates trust and co-operation.
	The researcher must maintain a positive and non-intimidating self-image. This can be achieved through concise and honest self-introductions.
	Preparation by the researcher may be required to familiarise themselves with the norms of the context in order to understand specific conventions.
Recording data	Can be difficult due to the persistent flows of information that could be recorded.
	Note taking should follow pure observations.
	The observation guide will help in determining what to record.
	Unstructured observations must be carefully managed.
Handling problems	Common challenges include: difficult individuals or groups; personal disputes; and discovering dishonesties.
	Tensions or unnecessary unease should not be created by the observation. Respond similarly to the expectations of the environment.
Data analysis	Typically occurs throughout the process and is rarely left to the final stages.
Departing	
When to leave	Practical necessities: time restraints require the researcher to leave the field or funds have run out.
	Theoretical saturation has been realised. No new insights are being gained.

7

Ethnographic fieldwork

Ethnographic fieldwork, is a long term commitment, for example, Kozinets (2001) spent 20 months conducting fieldwork investigating social interactions and consumption within the Star Trek Fandom subculture. Understanding the six research stages of ethnographic research can assist in planning and conducting a study. These are described in Table 7.10.

In the field, the ethnographer can utilise a range of data sources, most often, open-ended interviews and participant observation (see page 132), as well as appropriate artefacts, official documents, and news and magazine publications. Additional academic sources can be useful in framing and justifying the study. An ethnographer should consider the issues described in Table 7.11 when initialising research.

Table 7.10: Stages of ethnography

Stages of ethnography	Description
Problem identification	Consult previous research and consider pilot studies to determine the feasibility of the project.
Entering the setting	Researcher becomes immersed in the group under study. Ethical considerations are needed. First impressions count, the ethnographer should prepare a simple lay explanation of the project and present it when necessary.
Data collection	Data is gathered primarily through participant-observation and informal interviews, supplemented by artefacts and literary sources. Detailed field notes are critical.
Interpretation	Themes are identified within the data, informing further data collection.
Verification	Data is verified, through follow up interviews or triangulation techniques.
Dissemination	Data is written up from field notes into a report or research paper.

Table7.11: Ethnographic research considerations

Consideration	Description
Time	Generally, several months to a year is required to gather enough data.
Ethnographer as research instrument	Efficiently filter irrelevant data at an early stage. The ethnographer has a strong influence over the project's results.
Naturalistic observation	The research setting is natural and real, therefore the ethnographer has little control over it. Ethical and safety issues should be considered carefully.
Interactive-reactive nature	Throughout the ethnography the research focus and techniques can be altered.

■ Covert or overt

Data collection can either be defined as overt or covert. In the overt approach the researcher acknowledges to participants that they are being observed for a particular purpose. The approach may result in those being observed altering their behaviours and responses, due to their consciousness of being watched. Conversely, covert observation is conducted without the knowledge of those being viewed. Therefore, those being observed should not be influenced by the process. However, a limitation of this approach is that those being observed may become distressed or angry if/when they discover they have been part of a study, even if the organisation has agreed to the researcher's access. Therefore, building rapport with the participants and gaining group acceptance and trust is essential for a covert study. Table 7.12 highlights how covert and overt approaches relate to participant and non-participant observations.

Table 7.12: The role of the researcher

	Covert	Overt
Participant	Complete participant	Participant-as-observer/ observer-as-participant
Non-participant	Complete observer	Non-partaker

Observations can also be structured or unstructured. An unstructured observation infers that the observers are unrestricted and are free to view and document anything they feel is meaningful or important. On the other hand, structured observation necessitates less inclusive data collection as the observer only documents occurrences that are of specific relevance to the subject being explored. However, the structure must be derived from somewhere. Typically, this may be created through engagement with the literature concerning a specific topic or theoretical lens, and/or from previous frameworks used by past researchers. Therefore, the observations are guided towards specific issues or pre-existing hypotheses. In situations where there is a lack of information to create an effective structure, a pilot study using unstructured observations may help generate themes or issues which could be used to devise a framework for a future structured study.

■ Notes

Ethnographies are often conducted over a long period of time and produce a vast amount of data, so the ethnographer's ability to record data through research notes is vital. Without effective field notes, pertinent data is forgotten or open to misinterpretation at a later date. Field notes should be organised, detailed and complete, to allow for effective analysis, and include:

■ Shorthand notes written as an event unfolds, filled out fully shortly after.

■ Full descriptions of everything that occurs – seemingly unimportant information may become useful later.

■ Relevance to the guiding research question, allowing identification and refinement of the project around emerging themes.

■ Reflection from the ethnographer's perspective, which can offer useful insights.

Ultimately, field note taking is a personal process that can be developed and honed as the ethnographer becomes more experienced.

■ Applications

Selecting the best fit approach to a research project influences its success. Time, funding, the researcher's experience and even their personality can influence selection of a research approach. Table 7.13 shows some notable advantages and disadvantages of ethnographies.

Table 7.13: Advantages and disadvantages of ethnographic research

Advantages	Disadvantages
Phenomena are observed in a natural state, uncontrived.	Time-consuming, can be expensive.
Peoples' actual behaviour is revealed.	Too much data can distract the researcher and lead to vital points being overlooked.
Deeper insights than short-term research.	Generalization can be limited as the researcher only studies one sample.
Emergent themes offer the opportunity to research unconsidered phenomena.	Vulnerable to researcher bias.

Executed correctly, within an appropriate project, ethnographic research can generate deep and rich insights into a social phenomenon, however, the required investment of time and close interactions with the subjects requires a high level of researcher commitment and the appropriate people skills.

Diaries

Within the realms of management research, diary use is becoming increasingly popular. Diaries can be split into two distinct groups; **generated**, (where the researcher asks participants to complete them with observations), and **existing** (pre-existing diaries). The merits of each are discussed below.

■ Generated

Generated diary studies can be useful in investigating phenomena from the participant's perspective. Diary-keeping allows for recording of participants' more intimate, personally held views, as they occur in their natural settings.

Diaries record participants' views of events far quicker than other techniques (e.g. interviews), and can be in audio, or audio-visual form (Murthy, 2008), allowing recordings to be made throughout the day, in close to real-time. Hence, diary studies can generate rich, highly accurate data. Table 7.14 describes some of the principle issues affecting empirical diary research.

Table 7.14: Diary research issues

	Description
Multiple perspectives	A diary approach can allow various perspectives of a given issue to be analysed, sometimes across organisational boundaries, which can enhance the generalizability of the research. However, this can significantly increase the complexity of subsequent analysis, so careful consideration is required.
Limits researcher bias	Unlike interviews, diaries untangle the researcher from the data collection process, thus limiting researcher bias. However, interviews can offer valuable interaction between researcher and subjects.
Promotes multi-tasking	Diary-based research can be significantly more efficient than other approaches, as the researcher is free to collect data through different techniques while a diary program is ongoing. Researchers must be conscious of subsequent added complexity in analyses and philosophical implications if they combine various data-collection techniques.
Time efficient	Although from initiation to completion diary projects can last a long time, they can be a surprisingly efficient as they can produce significant amounts of data. Researchers can face difficulties in finding diary research participants, and crucially, ensuring they sustain diary recording activities for the duration of a research project.

Table 7.14 highlights the complexities of diary research. An inexperienced researcher should proceed with caution. Particularly within a time-constrained project, motivating participants to maintain a complete and detailed diary can be challenging, if not fatal.

■ Existing

Within qualitative research, dairies can be used as the main source of information for a study or in conjunction with other techniques, such as observations or interviews. Diaries are ideal for providing documentary evidence in the form of raw biographical and historical material because they are intimate, personal and offer an insight into the lives of particular individuals. Due to their often historical nature, diaries are also able to convey thick descriptions of everyday life experiences which are inaccessible to researchers through other forms of data collection (Bryce, MacLaren and O'Gorman, 2012). Therefore, diaries reflect people's behaviour, conveying opinions, reporting events, or recounting what individuals decided and did. As a result, through diaries, researchers can explore behaviours without having to stimulate it themselves. While being kept typically for purposes other than research, diaries are becoming more popular within management studies. For example, Coulson, MacLaren, McKenzie and O'Gorman (2014) use diary inserts from soldiers serving in Afghanistan to explore Pashtunwali and tourism in the country. The use of diaries in this study was supported by other techniques such as oral history interviews and netnography.

Despite their benefits, diaries are associated with a number of challenges. Due to their subjective nature, diaries are seen to carry a form of personal bias. Therefore, questions are raised over the honesty and accuracy of diaries where entries may be distorted by the writer's feelings and intensions. Furthermore, as with other forms of data collection, gaining access to diaries can be challenging. This is especially pertinent if the desired record is held by a particular business, library or institute. Nevertheless, the value of the information which can be found within diaries should be a motivator to the ardent researcher who wishes to contribute to their investigation through an often overlooked, but invaluable, form of data collection.

Conclusions

This chapter has introduced some of the common approaches to qualitative research methods, as illustrated in the Methods Map. Qualitative research regularly focuses on investigating occurrences in the environments in which they naturally transpire and uses social actors' meanings to comprehend the phenomena. The approaches identified in this chapter, whether it be interviews, focus groups, observation or diaries, demonstrate essential avenues from which the researcher can understand the environment in which their study in embedded. However, researchers employing qualitative approaches must be cautioned that none is a straightforward process and that careful planning and consideration must be placed on the possible limitations of a given method. Despite this, qualitative methods, if employed wisely, can gather and expose enlightening information which can render any study fruitful and worthwhile.

References

Alexander, M., O'Gorman, K. D., & Wood, K. (2010). Nutritional labelling in restaurants: Whose responsibility is it anyway? *International Journal of Contemporary Hospitality Management,* **22**(4), 572-579.

Alvesson, M. (2003). Beyond neopositivists, romantics, and localists: A reflexive approach to interviews in organizational research. *Academy of management review,* **28**(1), 13-33.

Bryce, D., MacLaren, A. C., & O'Gorman, K. D. (2013). Historicising consumption: Orientalist expectations of the Middle East. *Consumption Markets & Culture,* **16**(1), 45-64.

Coulson, A. B., MacLaren, A. C., McKenzie, S., & O'Gorman, K. D. (2014). Hospitality codes and social exchange theory: The Pashtunwali and tourism in Afghanistan. *Tourism Management,* **45**, 134-141.

Geertz, C. (1973) *The Interpretation of Cultures,* New York: Basic Books.

Kozinets, R. V. (2001). Utopian enterprise: Articulating the meanings of Star Trek's culture of consumption. *Journal of consumer research,* **28**(1), 67-88.

MacIntosh, R., & Bonnet, M. (2007). International perspectives on validity in action research: introduction to the special issue. *Management Research News,* **30**(5), 321-323.

McMillan, C. L., O'Gorman, K. D., & MacLaren, A. C. (2011). Commercial hospitality: A vehicle for the sustainable empowerment of Nepali women. *International Journal of Contemporary Hospitality Management,* **23**(2), 189-208.

Murthy, D. (2008). Digital ethnography an examination of the use of new technologies for social research. *Sociology,* **42**(5), 837-855.

Weinberg, D. B. (2003). *Code Green: Money-driven hospitals and the dismantling of nursing.* Ithaca; Cornell University press.

7

8 Qualitative Data Analysis Approaches

Katherine J C Sang and Rafał Sitko

Analysing the vast amounts of data generated by qualitative research can be daunting. The purpose of this chapter is to provide suggestions on how to move beyond describing what participants have said, to analysing the data. In this chapter researchers will learn more about the most common approaches to analysing qualitative data, namely, Grounded Theory, thematic and template analysis, discourse analysis and hermeneutics. On the Methods Map (see Chapter 4), these can be found in the 'Inductive' section of the Data Analysis area. Situations where each approach may be more suitable are suggested. By the end of the chapter readers should be able to identify which approach is appropriate to their data set.

Coding

Whether working with transcripts of interviews or focus groups, field notes, or any other form of text, researchers will find themselves with large amounts of data, which they need to make sense of. Reducing qualitative data into more manageable 'chunks' underpins most forms of qualitative data analysis. This is, crudely, the process of 'coding' data. These codes can be developed *a priori* (before) or *a posteriori* (after) data collection. With the former, codes will often be drawn from the literature and underlying theoretical framework. The latter refers to codes that emerge from the data itself, often associated with Grounded Theory. In contrast, template analysis (discussed later) allows for both *a priori* and *posteriori* codes. The remainder of this chapter details various approaches to coding data. What all approaches share is a careful reading of the text, for example, interview transcripts, the identification of themes and tensions within the data. There are a number of types of codes which researchers may use. The most familiar of which are open, selective and axial which are outlined in Table 8.1.

Table 8.1: Examples of types of codes (adapted from Gilbert, 2008).

Type of code	Description
Open	The breaking up of data into chunks or parts. May require the coding of each line of data (for Grounded Theory) Identification and refinement of concepts
Selective	The identification of relationships between codes, for example, a central category (or higher level code) and the codes related to that.
Axial	The rebuilding of data through the identification of links and cross links between the codes or chunks of data

Table 8.2 shows an example of the coding of a transcript from a focus group. This sample of data is from a focus group exploring the well-being of staff within universities in the UK. The section of data outlines one participant's reflections on their working life as a research only member of staff. Codes, such as 'job insecurity' have been attached to sections of text where participants describe the precarious nature of their work.

Table 8.2: Sample of focus group data with example codes.

Text	Example codes
From recent experience, when you are a Research Assistant, or Associate Fellow, you are not really involved in the teaching side of it, so you might do one odd lecture here and there. The majority of your time is as a researcher, so you have to constantly be getting in research funding. It can be a horrible way of surviving. You never know if you are going to have a job in ten months' time. You know when that funding will end.	Researchers have little opportunity for teaching Job insecurity
For the E.U one, someone else in the school managed to get funding, but it took him four to five solid months of working on a proposal. You can't spend five months on a proposal, if you are doing research for previous research funding. Horrible way of living.	Time commitment of applications Job insecurity
I don't know if it is different for the teaching side of it, if you have actual contracts that stipulate actual numbers of years, but when you get ten months' funding here, six months' funding there, it is horrible. It is also more work for the admin staff, who have to constantly be working on the research proposals.	Lack of understanding of other staff members' contracts Impact on non-research staff

8

Once a series of codes has been developed, these are then organised into a hierarchy of codes. For example from the table above, a high level code might be 'sources of stress' with lower level codes being 'job insecurity', 'time commitment of applications'. This ordering of codes moves coding beyond describing the data, towards analysis. However, this process can be subjective and it is important to consider whether another researcher would identify similar patterns within the data.

The extent to which qualitative researchers wish to ensure reliability and validity of their research is debatable (Golafshani, 2003). Kreiner et al (2009) provide a detailed account of coding of interview data within a research team. This provides an opportunity to explore avenues for ensuring reliability within data analysis. In their study of how individuals navigate the borders between their working and non-working lives, Kreiner et al (2009, p. 709) set out the following two-step coding system in their data analysis (see Table 8.3).

Table 8.3: Stages in posterior coding of interview data adapted from Kreiner et al (2009)

Stage	Action
Developing posteriori codes	Each interview transcript read in detail by two of the three research team with codes developed inductively from the data. Codes could apply to words, sentences, paragraphs or passages of text. Each researcher coded each interview transcript independently Each new code placed into a database with associated meanings and parameters clearly stated.

Joint analysis of texts	The transcripts were analysed in a joint coding meeting where the coding was compared.
	
	Final codes to be used were finalised.
	
	There were three scenarios
	
	    Both coders applied the same code to the same section of text (code finalised)
	
	    One coder applied a code to a section of text (second researcher reread the section and reconsidered if the code should be applied – if yes, code finalised)
	
	    No codes placed on the text

The advice set out in the table is appropriate to a research team of at least two people. Student researchers may be working alone, and as such alternative methods of quality assurance of the coding and analysis need to be considered. King (n.d and 2007) suggests that when analysing qualitative data it is important that the researcher is aware of their own effects on the data collection and analysis. This can be achieved through 'reflexivity' and keeping detailed research diaries which allow the researcher to write down their thoughts and reflections throughout the research process.

The following sections of the chapter move to detailed presentation of particular approaches to the analysis of qualitative data, beginning with 'Grounded Theory'.

Grounded Theory

Grounded Theory is an approach to analysing qualitative data that was developed by Glaser and Strauss in 1967 to assist researchers in building theory from data, rather than using data to test existing theory. The approach has had considerable influence in the field of management research, despite frequent misuse, with studies citing a Grounded Theory approach frequently not doing so (Goulding, 2005). Suddaby (2006) provides a helpful guide to what grounded theory is not, and provides several examples of the robust use of the approach. However, researchers often successfully *draw* on Grounded Theory to explore aspects of working life by applying the rigorous data analysis techniques to collected data, rather than to the entire research process. An example of this is Richards (2008) who drew on Grounded Theory approaches to analysing data to explore the role of blogs in employee resistance. For those intending to adopt a Grounded Theory approach, consulting Glaser and Strauss (1967) for detailed guidance is recommended. Silverman (2006, p.235) provides a simplified series of stages to a Grounded Theory approach to data analysis:

1 An initial attempt to develop categories which illuminate the data

2 An attempt to 'saturate' these categories with many appropriate cases in order to demonstrate their relevance

3 The development of these categories into more general analytic frameworks with the relevance outside the setting.

It is evident that the emphasis is on developing categories (or codes) from the data, with the relevance of a category in part determined by the number of cases (examples, or participants) attached to it. This quantification may not always be appropriate, and as Silverman (2006) cautions, it may not be possible to collect or analyse qualitative data without being informed in some way by existing knowledge or theories.

> *Exemplar paper*: Black, I., & Tagg, S. (2007). A Grounded Theory of doctors' information search behaviour. Implications for information provision, pharmaceutical market entry and development. *Journal of Marketing Management*, **23**(3-4), 347-366.

This study of physicians' information use adopted an orthodox Grounded Theory approach, as theory was generated from the data to avoid the imposition of prior theoretical assumptions on the data. The authors began their analysis with open coding where sections of text are examined and conceptualised line by line. Once key 'open' codes had been identified, the researchers then moved to selective coding whereby the relationships between codes are formalised and theory development begins, through axial coding. This process was conducted until data saturation had been reached, whereby no new codes or concepts were emerging from the data. It was at this stage the researchers were able to relate their data back to the literature for theory development. It is clear from the exemplar paper that Grounded Theory is a time-consuming and technical process which requires a cyclical process of data collection and analysis. This may not be suitable for all qualitative research projects, particularly those with large data sets.

The chapter now moves to alternative approaches to analysing text.

Thematic analysis

Despite its popularity among social scientists this approach is poorly demarcated as it does not have an identifiable heritage and there are few clear guidelines for using it (exceptions include e.g. Ryan and Bernard, 2003; Braun and Clarke, 2006). What can be even more confusing is that identifying themes and codes is an activity also used in other methods of qualitative data analysis. However, compared to other approaches thematic analysis does not build a new theory (Grounded Theory), does not use a set of codes generated before and after data collection (template analysis), does not highlight the use or role of the language (discourse analysis) and does not focus on unearthing the symbolic meaning of communication (hermeneutics). Simply, it is a "method for identifying, analysing, and reporting patterns (themes) within data" (Braun and Clarke, 2006, p. 79). Although, this process may seem uncomplicated it is important to follow a few rules to allow the research to be compared or synthesised with similar studies. Table 8.4 outlines the key steps of thematic analysis identified by Braun and Clarke (2006).

Table 8.4: Phases of thematic analysis. Adapted from Braun and Clarke (2006).

Phase	Description of the process
1. Familiarisation with the data	Data transcription (if necessary). 'Active' reading and writing down initial ideas.
2. Generating initial codes	Coding data (posteriori) in a systematic fashion across the entire data set.
3. Searching for themes	Re-focusing the analysis at the broader level. Forming codes into potential themes.
4. Reviewing themes	Checking themes against the coded extracts and in relation with each other. Forming a thematic 'map' of the analysis.
5. Defining and naming themes	Further refinement of identified themes. Locating the overall story of the analysis.
6. Producing the report	Writing-up the analysis results with vivid extract examples and comprehensive commentary.

According to the presented framework the analysis should start by becoming familiar with the data. This is especially true in cases when transcription has been prepared by a third party. The whole content should be read at least once, up to several times depending on the size of the data set. Although, this first step may be time consuming it is important to create a list of initial ideas emerging from the data. The second step involves organising notes from across the entire data set into codes (see Tables 8.2 and 8.3). While some extracts may not provide any codes, others could be marked with numerous. Generally, it may prove beneficial for the next stages of analysis to generate as many relevant codes as possible. It is likely that some codes will be contradictory or seemingly unfitting but these also should be noted. In the third stage codes are combined into broader patterns, i.e. potential themes. Some clusters may pile up as main themes when others, more specific, will form subthemes. Step four concerns revising themes. At this stage themes should be checked against the coded extracts and in relation to each other. Extracts may not fit into initially proposed patterns. Themes might not have enough evidence to support them or the underlying data may be too diverse to form a single coherent category. Furthermore, two seemingly separate patterns may concern the same topic and collapse

8

into each other. In another case, themes may be too different and not match meaningfully. With thoroughly revised themes it should be possible to form a 'map' similar to Figure 8.1. Table 8.2 showed an example of coding of a focus group transcript with staff in a university in the UK. The figure below shows how the codes identified; job insecurity, bureaucracy and time commitment can be arranged hierarchy under the theme of 'well-being of staff'

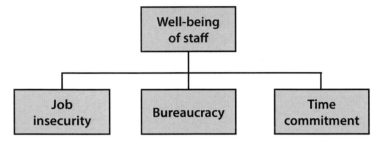

Figure 8.1: Showing the relationships between codes/themes.

The fifth step is further refinement of the themes. At this point it should be considered how identified themes fit into an overall argument. The aim is not to summarise the transcript but to analyse the data and reveal its hidden relationships. Themes have potential to expose paradoxes, differences between seemingly similar elements and common points among very different aspects. Their role is to expose what is interesting about the data. The message the themes send should be interesting but also clear, thus their names have to be concise and catchy. The final step involves writing up the analysis. On the basis of identified themes the report should tell the reader the story of the data. It is important to support the argument with examples of data extracts. However, these have to be a well embedded part of the analysis rather than an end in itself.

Template analysis

If a qualitative data set is large, then Grounded Theory may not be an appropriate way to manage and analyse the large amount of data generated. One alternative is Template Analysis, which is widely used in management research (Daniels et al., 2004). Template analysis allows for textual data to be thematically organized and analysed according to a set of codes developed a priori (King, 2004). It is considered ideal for those who consider Grounded Theory as too prescriptive in terms of its method and for those researchers using data sets of over 20 (King, 2004). King (2004) provides a systematic procedure for conducting template analysis, and like Grounded Theory it makes use of codes to order textual data. A code is a label attached to a portion of text, and can be descriptive or analytical in nature. King (n.d.) sets out seven steps for undertaking template analysis. They are outlined in Table 8.5.

Table 8.5: The seven stages of template analysis. Adapted from King (n.d.).

Step	Action
Themes and codes	The identification of a priori codes. Likely to be developed from the literature and interview/focus group template.
Transcription	Careful transcription of the data. Detailed reading of the transcriptions to ensure familiarity with the data.
Themes and codes	A first round of coding the data. Identify those sections of the data which are relevant to the research questions. Now a priori codes can be attached to sections of the data. At this stage researchers can begin to identify codes emerging from the data and may need to develop new codes.
Producing the initial template	The researcher can either choose to develop this following initial coding of all transcripts, or after coding a sub set. It will be necessary to provide a number of levels of codes, but not so many that the analysis becomes confusing. It is likely that during analysis researchers will also likely want to produce a hierarchy of codes.
Developing your template	At this stage the template can be applied to the entire data set. However, it is still possible to adapt and add to the template as analysis progresses.
Interpreting and writing up	At this stage the data is interpreted and the findings written up.
Quality checks and reflexivity	To check the quality of analysis, researchers may want to have the coding independently checked by another researcher. Alternatively the analysis can be examined by respondents. It is important to keep a clear diary of the steps taken during analysis and to engage in reflexivity. This means to be aware of the researcher's influence over the data collection and analysis.

8

Exercise: template analysis

Read through the sample interview transcript. The aim of the study was to understand some of the causes of stress for architects, how university relates to working life and how this might be different for men and women.

1   What are the a priori themes of the interview?

2   Do any new themes emerge from the interview and if so what are they?

3   What are the relationships between the themes?

With another person in your class, discuss your analysis of the interview transcript. Did you identify the same themes and relationships or were they different?

Interviewer(I): How much did you know about being an architect before you went to university?

Brian(B): [laughs] Nothing! It was really stupid actually. I thought it was going to be all creative and I'd be doing exciting stuff. I mean, that's what it was like at university, but you know, when I got into practice it was nothing like that.

I: In what way?

B: Well, I never got to be creative, I was doing boring project management things, like admin, dealing with builders and clients. It was nothing like Uni.

I: How well did University prepare you for working life?

B: Not at all! It's criminal really. Uni was all creative projects, designing new museums and stuff. I get into practice and I am designing the door frames for toilets in a school. So I don't get to be creative at all, and I thought I would be. It's really stressful for me actually. I am so bored a lot of the time, but I am working really long hours.

I: What sort of hours did you work as a student?

B: Well, you're right you know, University was really long hours. It was so stupid – we would spend hours in the studio – pulling all nighters, but you know, it was fun, I was young and we all did it together. We ate bad food, drank beer and had a laugh. That's easy to do at 19, not so easy at 35. We started off badly and it hasn't changed. Really the lecturers should have stopped it, but they always said that they did it as a student and if you aren't willing to work all hours then you aren't an architect. We were told 'architecture is a lifestyle not a career'. Thinking back it makes me angry – it left us vulnerable to being exploited by employers who wanted us to work 80 hour weeks for barely any money in return.

I: 80 hours a week? How can you balance that with your home life?

B: You can't! You can't! You can only do it if you're young and have no kids. I do have kids, but my wife gave up work. She was an architect too, but you just can't do the two. I mean, some architects who work in local councils get maternity leave, they get part time work, they get paternity leave. You work in a small practice you get nothing. I see lots of women dropping out [of architecture]. They're really good at their job, but they can't do that and have kids. Not small kids anyway.

I: So there are no women in architecture who have kids?

B: Oh, there's some, but they give up work or they set up their own practice and work part time. They can set their own hours, work at night, that sort of thing. Even when they do work part time, they work 40 hours a week – so it's not part time really. Not when I think of people I went to Uni with who do a different job. They earn a lot more money and don't work so many hours.

Discourse analysis

As Potter (1997) identifies, 'discourse analysis' (DA) covers many approaches to analysing social life and the role of language. This can range from detailed analyses of sentence structure and ordering of speakers, to poststructuralist accounts of how power is communicated through discourse. The perspective adopted for discourse analysis will depend on the underpinning ontological and epistemological perspectives of your study. While the previous approaches to analysis have provided frameworks for identifying themes in the data, discourse analysis adopts a more fine grained analysis of the language used in particular contexts (Dick, 2004). As such, discourse analysis requires a particular approach to the transcription of the recordings, regardless of the type of interview or focus group conducted. However, DA can also be applied to textual analysis of other documents, such as reports. Ness (2012) details the Critical Discourse Analysis approach adopted in a study of documents relating to women's exclusion from the construction industry. Critical Discourse Analysis (CDA) is an approach to understanding how discourse can reveal social and political inequalities (Wooffitt, 2008). As such this approach is concerned with emancipatory approaches to research and is appropriate to studies of marginalised groups within society, including the workplace. As Ness (2012) argues, any analysis of a text must consider its context, and this underpins the detailed context and reading of the text which is presented in this key paper. As with other examples of DA and CDA (see for example, Rodriguez, 2013), Ness identified recurring themes and contradictions within the text:

> *"The intertextual context [the construction industry and gendered assumptions] has apparently been evoked in two ways – to challenge it ('women can work in construction') and yet to reproduce it ('there are some jobs in construction which women cannot do'). This seems rather extraordinary, but the double think can perhaps be explained by looking at this discourse as part of a social process, seeking to explain the relations of power and domination underlying it, and to explore the relationship of discourses to processes of struggle and change" (Ness, 2012, p. 661)*

This excerpt reveals a number of key aspects to CDA (which would also apply to DA). Firstly it is clear that Ness has read the report in question (*Respect for People*) in great detail and identified an emerging theme; that of women's suitability for construction jobs. Secondly through this detailed reading, a tension has been identified. Namely the opposing statements above. Thirdly, DA here is concerned with analysing these statements in the context of the construction industry and broader societal gender power relations. Finally, it is evident that the DA here is employed to analyse the relationship between the discourse (the report) and its context (society).

Hermeneutics

The Greek word *hermēneia*, meaning interpretation or understanding, encapsulated a wide range of interpretation and clarification, which covered speech, translation, and commentary. Hermeneutics has now become the theory of textual interpretation. Originally concerned with interpreting sacred texts; it has developed over time into a data analysis technique (O'Gorman, 2010). The method is dependent on the inferences made by the researcher and the meanings the researcher then attributes to elements of the text. Increasingly, hermeneutics is being adopted as a data analysis technique across business research and is seen regularly in the core business literature as an accepted and effective means of data analysis. O'Gorman (2008) adapted and developed both the epistemological practices (Table 8.6) and the methodological principles (Table 8.7) in hermeneutical research. The first column gives the name of the epistemological practices or methodological principles whereas the second column gives a generic description of how these could be applied to any research project. When discussing a research project a third column could be added to illustrate how these practices and principles are applied to the project and what the particular results are.

Table 8.6: Epistemological practices. Adapted from O'Gorman and Gillespie (2010).

Practice	Generic description of practice
Bracketing of previous experience and turning toward lived experience	Presuppositions, biases, and any knowledge of the phenomenon obtained from personal and scholarly sources must be set aside. After data collection the researcher then enters into a dialogue with the text using the understanding gathered and drawing on their pre-understanding to interpret the phenomena.
Investigating the phenomenon	It is important to clearly define the phenomenon under investigation in order for the data collection to remain focused.
Reflecting on essential themes	Moving from data collection to data interpretation involves a process of phenomenological reflection. The first step is to conduct thematic analysis, which helps give a degree of order and control to the task.
Writing and rewriting	During the analysis, the procedure of asking questions of the text, and listening to it, in a dialogic form, is central in the writing and rewriting phase. Reflection and writing can be false dichotomies as they tend to be symbiotic tasks.

Table 8.7: Methodological principles. Adapted from O'Gorman and Gillespie (2010).

Principle	Generic description of principle
Maintain a strong & oriented relation	Writing and interpretations must remain oriented to the phenomenon under investigation, thus superficialities and falsities will be avoided
Considering parts and whole	The overall interpretation is consistent with the various parts of the analysis. Step back and look at the whole, and how each of the parts needs to contribute towards it.

8

When the methodological principles and practices are combined they form a hermeneutic circle of interpretation, used to reflect upon, discuss and analyse data. This is normally done by making three consciously distinct revolutions of the hermeneutical circle; this process is shown in Table 8.8, taken from O'Gorman and Gillespie (2010) and used here as an example. The first column shows the level of analysis, the second column describes how that analysis took place, and finally the third column shows a summary of the results obtained from each stage of analysis.

Table 8.8: Review of the hermeneutical process. Adapted from O'Gorman and Gillespie (2010).

Description of the analysis	Summary of the results obtained from the analyses
Thematic level	
To look for common themes used by the 20 leaders interviewed, to create corporate culture within their organisation	Variety of devices developing and sharing a core values statement signs, symbols, rights, ceremonies. All leaders seemed to place emphasis on the importance and centrality of telling stories.
1st Reflective level	
Showed that storytelling is used by all the leaders – the interviews were re-read and reflected upon for aspects of storytelling	From reflecting on the interviews it became clear that six principle categories of storytelling were identified; verified by working with other investigators to ensure that the emergent presentation of results reflected the data. There was a considerable amount of writing and rewriting at this stage, the majority of which did not end up in the final draft.
2nd Reflective level	
Interviews were analysed in order to explore for sub-categories showing storytelling usage.	Taxonomy of the uses of storytelling by leaders in the hospitality industry was developed. However, at this stage, the warnings and concerns that the leaders expressed about storytelling were also recorded to give a holistic picture.

The process began with an initial thematic analysis to explore the common devices used by the leaders; this identified that the leaders all told stories. Then a first reflective analysis identified how the leaders used storytelling and finally a second reflective analysis allowed for the collation of examples of storytelling. These three revolutions of the circle can also form the structure for the discussion and findings section, helping to bring into focus a sometimes-unclear picture.

Computer aided qualitative data analysis (CAQDAS): a short note

The previous sections of this chapter have set out some of the common approaches to analysing qualitative data. Ho wever, the question remains of how to manage a large data set. The option remains to do manage the data manually, with pieces of paper, sticky notes and highlighters. This is what many researchers do and is a perfectly valid, if not space saving, approach.

However, for large data sets, researchers may wish to make use of one of the many software packages which have been designed to assist qualitative researchers. Unlike those for quantitative data, the software will not analyse the data, but can be used to manage the many hundreds of pages which can result from transcription, and through coding, allow for easy retrieval of quotes. Further, if researchers wish to combine different sources of data, including visual or audio material, many of the software packages can do this as well. This can be particularly useful if researchers are working as part of a team (Silverman, 2006). However, it is important to remember that CAQDAS is primarily a data management and presentation tool, it is no substitute for careful reading of the text or theory development.

Further reading and References

Black, I., & Tagg, S. (2007). A Grounded Theory of doctors' information search behaviour. Implications for information provision, pharmaceutical market entry and development. *Journal of Marketing Management*, **23**(3-4), 347-366.

Braun, V., & Clarke, V. (2006). Using thematic analysis in psychology. *Qualitative Research in Psychology*, **3**(2), 77-101.

Daniels, K., Harris, C. and Briner, R. B. (2004). Linking work conditions to unpleasant affect: cognition, catergorization and goals. *Journal of Occupational and Organizational Psychology*, **77**, 343-63.

Dick, P. (2004). Discourse Analysis. In Cassell, C., & Symon, G. (Eds.), *Essential guide to qualitative methods in organizational research*. Sage Publications, London, 203-213.

Gilbert, N. (Eds.). (2008). *Researching Social Life*. Sage Publications, London.

Glaser, B. G., & Strauss, A. L. (1967). *The Discovery of Grounded Theory: Strategies for Qualitative Research*. Transaction Publishers.

Golafshani, N. (2003). Understanding reliability and validity in qualitative research. *The Qualitative Report*, **8**(4), 597-607.

Goulding, C. (2005). Grounded Theory, ethnography and phenomenology: A comparative analysis of three qualitative strategies for marketing research. *European journal of Marketing*, **39**(3/4), 294-308.

King, N. (2004). Using templates in the thematic analysis of text. In Cassell, C. and Symon, G. (Eds.), *Essential Guide to Qualitative Methods in Organizational Research*, Sage Publications, London, 256-70.

8

King, N. (n.d.). *Template Analysis* http://hhs.hud.ac.uk/w2/research/template_analysis/ last accessed 19th February 2014.

Kreiner, G. E., Hollensbe, E. C., & Sheep, M. L. (2009). Balancing borders and bridges: Negotiating the work-home interface via boundary work tactics. *Academy of Management Journal,* **52**(4), 704-730.

Ness, K. (2012). Constructing masculinity in the building trades: "most jobs in the construction industry can be done by women". *Gender, Work & Organization,* **19**(6), 654-676.

Oehlert, Gary W. (2000). *Design and Analysis of Experiments: Response surface design.* New York: W.H. Freeman and Company

O'Gorman, K. D. (2008). *The Essence of Hospitality from the Texts of Classical Antiquity: The Development of a Hermeneutical Helix to Identify the Philosophy of the Phenomenon of Hospitality,* University of Strathclyde, Glasgow.

O'Gorman, K. D. (2010). *The Origins of Hospitality and Tourism.* Goodfellow, Oxford.

O'Gorman, K. D. and Gillespie, C. H. (2010). The mythological power of hospitality leaders? A hermeneutical investigation of their reliance on storytelling. *International Journal of Contemporary Hospitality Management.* **22**(5), 659-680.

Potter, J. (1997). Discourse analysis as a way of analysing naturally occurring talk. In D. Silverman (ed.) *Qualitative Research: Theory, Method and Practice,* Sage, London, p. 144-160.

Richards, J. (2008). 'Because I need somewhere to vent': The expression of conflict through work blogs. *New Technology, Work and Employment,* **23**(1-2), 95-110.

Rodriguez, J. K. (2013). Joining the Dark Side: Women in Management in the Dominican Republic. *Gender, Work & Organization,* **20**(1), 1-19.

Ryan, G. W., & Bernard, H. R. (2003). Techniques to identify themes. *Field Methods,* **15**(1), 85-109.

Silverman, D. (2006). *Doing Qualitative Research: A Practical Handbook.* Sage Publications, London.

Suddaby, R. (2006). From the editors: What grounded theory is not. *Academy of Management Journal,* **49**(4), 633-642.

Wooffitt, R. (2008) Conversation analysis and discourse analysis in Gilbert, N. (Eds.). . *Researching Social Life.* Sage Publications, London, 441-461.

9 Quantitative Data Gathering Techniques

Babak Taheri, Catherine Porter, Nikolaos Valantasis-Kanellos and Christian König

The role of managers and researchers is concerned with analysing and solving problems. These problems come in many forms with common features and normally include some numerical information. Both managers and researchers need to understand a range of quantitative methods. In order to perform quantitative analyses, we need data. This chapter focuses on how to collect quantitative data: sampling and measurement issues, surveys and experimental research.

The nature of quantitative research

Following the path of our Methods Map (see Chapter 4), quantitative methods are part of an **objective** ontology; and a **positivist** epistemology. Social science research has tended to be influenced by the hypothetico-deductive paradigm (a research approach that starts with a theory about how things work and derives testable hypotheses from it). Quantitative studies are defined as: quantifying the problem or research question and establishing the mechanisms through which one or more (quantitative) variable(s) may affect another variable. The following phrases are linked with a quantitative methodology and are used interchangeably: a deductive approach, an etic view, objective epistemology, a structured approach, systematic approach, numerically-based data collection, statistical analyses, and replicable research design. In other words, quantitative studies have four main characteristics: systematic/reconstructed logic and linear path (step-by-step straight line); hard data in nature (e.g. numbers); they rely on positivist principles, they have an emphasis on measuring variables and testing hypotheses; finally, they usually verify or falsify a relationship or hypothesis we already have in mind. Advantages of using quantitative data relative to quantitative data include broad comparability of answers, speed of data collection, and the 'power of numbers'. Qualitative questions can be asked in a quantitative survey, but responses (and ensuing data) are much more structured (and some may say, restrictive).

The data that you need to collect will very much be driven by what research question you are trying to answer. This needs to be very specific, and will drive both your data collection *method*, and *sampling*. We discuss these below.

Box 9.1: Examples of research questions suited for quantitative analysis

In its simplest form a quantitative research question will try to quantify the variables you wish to examine.

> *e.g. What is the daily consumption of soft drinks of students at a particular Scottish University?*

> *What is percentage of students in a particular Scottish University students consume soft drinks daily?*

Another researcher might wish to identify the differences between two or more groups on a single or multiple variables.

> *e.g. What is the difference in the daily consumption of soft drinks between male and female students at a particular Scottish University?*

Finally, a researcher might wish to explore the relationship between one or more variables on one or more groups. This type of research is mostly associated with experiments and the identification of causal relationships as will be discussed later in the chapter.

> *e.g. What is the relationship between weather and soft drink consumption for a particular Scottish University's students (or male and female students)?*

Defining dependent and independent variables

Data analysis and design involves measuring variables which can be dependent or independent. We define dependent and independent variables as follows: dependent variable is what you as a researcher think will be affected by another variable (or by an experiment), while the independent variable(s) is what you think will affect the dependent variable. These will be identified directly from your research question. For example, if you are studying the effects of a new marketing program on customer satisfaction, the program is the independent variable and what aspect(s) of satisfaction are influenced or changed by the programme are the dependent variables. Other independent variables may include the age and gender of customers, the amount spent prior to the new marketing program, and other questions about their characteristics.

For all quantitative studies, a crucial component of design is selection and measurement of the dependent variable. It is crucial because the usefulness of the research depends upon the relevance of the dependent variable and its representation on the outcome of interest. Researchers must be cautious, as dependent variable selection reflects the problem definition process, and can thus influence the decision making. The above example suggests careful selection of which aspect of satisfaction to measure. Another example is if we were studying stress levels among office workers, and chose the dependent variable to be 'frequency of employee-to-employee disputes,' then the researcher would have to justify why such disputes are considered to be an appropriate indicator of stress rather than, for example, average number of absences throughout the group.

We briefly discuss experimental design here, as experiments can be seen as the 'purest' way to establish an association between two variables, and therefore score well on the concept of internal validity. We then extend the concepts to non-experimental (or survey-based) data.

■ Experiments

Experiments have wide applications in social science. Experiments are considered as very reliable, and an efficient means of data collection and verification or refuting theories. The study of causal links is the main purpose of experiments. In particular, researchers aim to identify if one change in an independent variable, caused by manipulation (of data), will affect a dependent variable. The main difference between experiments and surveys is that researchers have increased control over the conditions and events of the experiment, as in many cases experiments are conducted in laboratories. Moreover, according to Oehlert (2000) experiments enable direct comparison between items of interest and can offer minimised comparison bias and error. The sampling unit of the experiment which provides measures based on experimental manipulation is referred to as the subject of the experiment.

■ Experimental design process

Experimental design involves *four main design elements* (Zikmund, Babin, Carr, & Griffin, 2010). The first is *manipulation of the independent (experimental) variable*. Moreover, the way an independent variable is manipulated is defined as *experimental treatment*. This fact creates two groups. The *Experimental group* is the first and is represented by participants exposed to planned treatments. The second is called the *control group* and is represented by participants on which none of the planned treatments are made. It should be stated that the *control group* is therefore used to highlight the outcomes that occur among the *experimental group*. For example, if we were studying the stress levels among office workers in an environment where there is reduced daylight through blackened windows, then we would first need to run the study in an environment where there is a *normal* amount of daylight (a *control group*), so that it could be demonstrated that it was indeed the change in exposure to daylight that was the cause of increased disputes among workers in the *experimental group*, when the daylight exposure was reduced. The second step is selection and measurement of the dependent variable (discussed above, employee-to-employee disputes). The third step is selection and assignment of experimental subjects or test units while the fourth is control over extraneous variables (environmental variables affecting the dependent variable). Box 9.2 shows an example of a research that used experiments in order to address the research aim.

Box 9.2: Experiment design example - Priority queues

Alexander et al. (2012) followed a sequential exploratory design mixed methods approach in order to identify how priority queuing affects priority pass holders and ordinary customers of theme parks. Initially they formulated hypotheses based on qualitative data collected during site visits. These hypotheses aimed to assess the negative effect of longer waiting times experienced by main queue customers, the effect of priority queue on customers in the main queue and the influence of main queue waiting time on the value anticipated by priority pass holders. The hypotheses were then tested by two factorial between subjects experiments, following the hypothetico-deductive paradigm used widely in social science research, as argued earlier in this chapter. The focus here is to show how experiments were used to address the research aim.

The viability of the manipulations (waiting time, presence of a priority queue (experiment 1) and cost of priority passes (experiment 2)) was assessed with three pre-tests on a different sample of 30 students from a relevant course.

The design of the two 2x2 between subjects factorial experiments was as follows. Two levels of waiting times acted as the first factor for both experiments. The existence or not of priority queue and two levels of priority pass costs acted as the second factor for each of the experiments respectively. From these factors 8 scenarios in total were constructed. 240 students from a relevant course were the experiments' sample. Each student was randomly handed one short scenario. Once students read the scenario they completed a small questionnaire addressing the issues of word of mouth, repurchase intention (dependent variables), and satisfaction (intervening variable).

Experiment 1 showed that increasing queue lengths negatively affect both customer satisfaction and loyalty outcomes. On the contrary experiment 2 showed that customer satisfaction and the depended variables of word of mouth and purchase intention of priority pass holders were positively affected by increasing queue lengths. For a detailed discussion of these experiments and the tests used to check manipulations and consistency among variables, as well as the approach used to achieve mediation please consult Alexander et al. (2012).

Alexander, M., MacLaren, A., O'Gorman, K. and White, C. (2012) 'Priority queues: Where social justice and equity collide', *Tourism Management*, **33**(4), 875-884.

9

Sampling and measurement

■   Population, sample size and type of sampling

Considerable efforts should be made to ensure that the sample obtained is representative of the population under investigation (i.e. 'the generalizability issue'). A population is normally a collection of all the concerned units that researchers would like to study within a particular problem space. It is vital to clearly define a research population (and your unit of analysis) before beginning to collect your sample. This could be as broad as 'all firms in the UK' to 'small-scale entrepreneurs in the music industry in Glasgow.' Normally, it is impossible (and unnecessary) to investigate all members of a given group. Therefore, researchers use two broad types of sampling techniques: probability/random and non-probability/non-random. Probability sampling is a way of achieving samples that are representative of the whole population of interest and involve random selection. Non-probability sampling involves a specifically chosen sample based on particular characteristics or similar differentiating features relevant to the study; therefore it cannot be determined whether the results of the study are representative of the entire population. There are two main requirements for probability sampling. First, an adequate sample frame – a comprehensive list of all members of our population of interest; second, an ability to randomly select based on features present in the sample frame. See (Walter, 2013) for more details. Table 9.1 shows a summary of probability and non-probability sampling.

No small sample is likely to produce results that accurately represent the entire population. Debatably, it is always possible to pick, strictly by chance, a group whose members happen to be different in some attributes from the population as a whole (this is referred to as the sampling error). This brings attention to the systematic bias (i.e. extraneous sampling factors) which affects survey results and reduces data validity, including frame bias (a wrongly chosen population), selection bias (under-representing certain types of population members), non-response bias (data skewed based on who from the chosen sample actually engaged with the study), interviewer bias, questionnaire bias, respondent bias and processing bias (interviewer writes down the wrong answers); see De Vaus (2007) for more information.

Table 9.1: Types of sampling

Probability sampling
Simple random: Every unit has an equal chance of being selected; it requires a good sampling frame; the population is geographically concentrated.   e.g. In 2013 HWU had 6,494 registered undergraduate students at all three Scottish campuses. A simple random sample would imply that all 6,494 students would have the same opportunity to be selected for the purposes of a specific study, as the researcher would randomly pick names from the university's registry to match the number wanted in the study.
Systematic: Similar to simple random sampling except that it is simpler; constructed from the periodicity of sampling frame; the selection of a unit is dependent on the previous unit.   e.g. after choosing the first student from the 2013 HWU undergraduate students' registry, instead of selecting random names, the researcher would use a particular pattern, such as selecting every 6th student for inclusion in the sample of the study.
Stratified random: The population is divided into strata, and these strata make up the final sample in the study; mainly based on homogeneous subgroups, e.g. gender and age,   e.g. the researcher would divide HWU undergraduate students into male and female, then select a specific proportion of the sample from each of these groups. If the proportion of students selected from each stratum is the same, this is *proportional stratified random sampling*. If the strata are not equal, proportional stratified random sampling would result In the smaller groups being under-represented in the final sample. If, for example, the researcher had divided students in strata according to their ethnic background, then some of the strata would be considerably smaller than others. To avoid under-representation of the smaller strata, the researcher should select larger proportions of students from these and smaller proportions from the larger strata. This is *non-proportional stratified random sampling*.
Multistage cluster: It involves several different samples; researcher mainly wants to study clusters in geographical areas.   e.g. the researcher wants to study the effectiveness of case studies as a teaching method in UK universities. It would be inefficient to randomly select students from a registry list of all UK universities. A more sensible approach would be to divide the country into regions and pick some of them for further exploration. The researcher would then create a list of the universities in the selected regions and maybe try to focus even more by selecting some departments and then a sample of those. Each of the decisions about a selection at every step of this process is randomly made. Thus this multistage sampling technique aims to break the entire population into multiple clusters to make the study more effective from a cost and time perspective.

9

Non-probability sampling
Convenience: Accidental, haphazard, chunk and grab sampling; selection of participants for a study is based on their proximity to the scholar.   e.g. using the earlier example, if the researcher would like to examine the consumption of soft drinks by undergraduate students of HWU, instead of using the all-campus registry, the researcher could aim to include students from his/her own campus and more specifically his/her department instead of all schools and departments of the university.
Purposive: Researcher decides who/what study units will be involved in the research.   e.g. the researcher who wants to examine the consumption pattern of a particular soft drink among a specific group of people, might aim to include in the sample people11 who have been seen to consume this particular drink rather than any other and who belong to the specific group of the study. Students who consume a different brand of soft drink or do not belong to the specific group will inevitably not be considered as part of the sample.
Snowball: Researcher does not know about formal/informal network connections at the start of study, but when he/she begins the research process by identifying someone who meets the criteria for involvement in the study, this person acts as the link to the next participant through their own network, hence the sample 'snowballs'.   e.g. a researcher is trying to identify the consumption pattern of a soft drinks in bridge clubs in Edinburgh, but does not have access to the list of people registered in these clubs. He/she is thus not aware of which people might be members, and cannot find them in any publicly available lists. In this case the researcher needs to identify one person who is member of such a club and is willing to participate in the study. This person can then refer the researcher to other members of the club, who could then repeat the process until the researcher would reach the required sample size.
Expert: The researcher identifies some people as expert with demonstrable experience in some particular area.   e.g., the researcher wants to study how the latest version of Excel is perceived amongst its advanced users. The researcher could aim to include only those individuals that possess a Microsoft Office Specialist Master. As experts, their opinion would be considered more valuable than that of others who hold a lower certification. The same would also apply with years of experience in a particular role, in the case that the researcher would like to include in the sample professionals from a particular industry.
Quota: The researcher specifies the minimum number of sampled units wanted in each category; sets organised quotas, in terms of characteristics, in order to find out the distribution of the variable in the population.   e.g. the researcher wants to identify the consumption pattern of soft drinks among male and female students of UK, German, French, and Greek origin. The use of quota sampling enables the researcher to include in the sample a specific proportion of male and female students of those ethnicities, and to provide a comparison amongst them.

There is considerable debate over what constitutes an acceptable sample size for the results to be statistically valid. However, there is no golden rule that determines a suitable sample size, and it will often depend on your budget. It is generally acceptable that the bigger the sample is, the more generalizable are the results of the study. Different authors recommend diverse sample sizes as appropriate for quantitative research, including an absolute sample ranging from 200 to 300 participants (De Vaus, 2007; Hair, Black, Babin, & Anderson, 2010).

Previous studies suggest a general guideline for using confidence intervals (an estimated range of values which include an unknown population parameter with certain probability) to configure sample size. For example, for a sample of 500, confidence levels range from 1.9 percent for homogeneous populations to 4.4 percent where there is a 50/50 split on variables. There are three factors that determine the ideal sample size, namely: confidence level (corresponds to a Z-score), population size, and the margin of error, which is beyond the scope of this chapter (see De Vaus (2007) for more information). Finally, in the real world, some respondents may decide not to participate in the survey at all. This may become an issue when non-respondents differ from respondents in a non-random manner, which consequently introduces sampling bias (Walter, 2013). For example, the responding members of any sample may be more educated and older than the actual education and age distribution represented in the population from which the sample is drawn. Researchers generally use a formula to calculate response rate:

Main measurement types

Measurement is the process of putting participants into the categories or values of a variable; and researchers are not able to identify variation unless it can be measured. Hair et al. (2010) also describe two further classifications of measuring quantitative data.

- *Nonmetric measurement scales* describe differences by indicating the presence/absence of a characteristic (i.e., nominal and ordinal scales).

- *Metric measurement scales* are used when subjects differ in degree on a particular attribute (i.e., interval and ratio scales).

Table 9.2 shows the main measurement types. In quantitative research, question reliability occurs when a question is answered in the same way on different occasions if given to the same individual. Content validity is about ensuring that a measurement technique measures the concept it is designed to measure. The reliability of scales can be measured using a number of statistical techniques and falls into two different parts, namely: single item scales and multiple attribute scales. Four types of validity commonly used are: face, criterion-related, content, and construct validity (Please see De Vaus, 2007 for more information).

Table 9.2: The measurement types

Measure	Description
Nonmetric measurement scales	
Nominal	The numerical values only 'name' the attribute uniquely. It normally presents categories or classes including demographic attributes (e.g. sex, gender, religion), forms of behaviour (e.g. purchase activity), or action that is discrete (e.g. loves or not, happens or not). For example, in the study of a basketball team players are identified by the number on their shirts – this number identifies the individual player. However, a player with number 20 is not considered to be twice as good as the player who wears number 10 on their shirt. The number is a nonmetric representation.
Ordinal	The attributes can be rank-ordered. The distances between attributes do not have any meaning. For example, on a survey you might code Educational Qualification as 1=basic education; 2=Higher diploma; 3= A level and college; 4= University education. In this measure, higher numbers mean more education but, for example, a Higher diploma is not considered to be twice as good as basic education.
Metric measurement scales	
Interval	The distance between attributes does have meaning. The interval between values is interpretable. The steps between the values/scores are equal in size. The values can be added, or calculated, computed to gain an average and so on. For example, we could measure consumer satisfaction toward a particular service along a 5-point scale (1 not at all satisfied and 5 highly satisfied) and confidently calculate an average satisfaction rating.
Ratio	There is always an absolute zero that is meaningful. This means that you can construct a meaningful fraction with a ratio variable. In social research most 'count' variables are ratios, for example, the number of consumers who paid to get access to our theme park in the past six months. Why? Because it is possible to have zero consumers and because it is meaningful to be able to say, "we had twice as many paying customers visit the theme park in the past six months as we did in the same six month period last year."

Surveys

■ Why surveys?

A survey is a structured method of asking the same questions in the same order, to different respondents, and creating a database of answers for analysis. Whilst the experimental method manipulates an independent variable in order to assess the outcome of a dependent variable, surveys allow us to exploit natural variation in these variables, and look for associations; for example, sampling and collecting data from workers in high light environments versus low-light environments.

The terms 'questionnaires' and 'surveys' are often used interchangeably. However, Sarantakos (1988, p. 223) emphasises that, "in general, surveys are methods of data collection in which information is gathered through oral or written questioning. Oral questioning is known as interviewing, written questioning is accomplished through questionnaires". A questionnaire or 'interview schedule' can be a printed or an on-line list of questions. A survey is the entire process of conducting an investigation which involves a number of subjects. A questionnaire survey is a survey involving the use of a questionnaire.

The main merits of questionnaire surveys are as follows: an ideal method of providing policy-related data; quantification easily communicated/ understood; repeat surveys can study change over time, surveys can cover a wide range of activities and can study attitudes, meanings and perceptions of a population as a whole. However, this self-reported data collection instrument has its limitations such as exaggeration/under-reporting, accuracy of recall and sensitivity of some questions.

■ Survey design

Survey design has six main process stages:

1 Research questions/conceptual framework;
2 List of information requirements;
3 Questionnaire survey or other methods? (i.e., research strategy);
4 Draft design;
5 Pilot study; and
6 Final design.

9

Oppenheim (2000) explains two main types of survey design, *analytical* or *explanatory* and *descriptive*. The descriptive survey is designed to establish the proportion of any given population who share particular characteristics. Therefore, descriptive surveys enable us to describe the 'who' (demographic characteristics of individuals), 'what' (activities) and 'how' (social and economic status) of the population. On the other hand, an analytical survey is intended to examine relationships and differences between sample groups, i.e. the 'why'. The descriptive research is undertaken to use attitudes and behaviours of respondents in order to explain the variability in different phenomena. Conversely, the analytical survey describes cause-and-effect relationships and is mainly used for testing hypotheses.

In gathering survey data, questionnaires can be administered in two ways: *researcher-administered* or *self-administered.* When a questionnaire is researcher-administered it may be conducted face-to-face, in-home/door-step, executive (business-to-business version of in-home interviews may be conducted at an office), telephone and even via media such as Skype, in the contemporary world. *Self-administered* is where the respondent may complete the questionnaire on his/her own, e.g. postal, hand delivery, fax and online delivery (e-mail or web surveys).

Self-administered questionnaires are normally the least resource-heavy data collection method both in time and money, and also the respondent is not subjected to the problem of a researcher's influence or bias; it can include all main question types and is less immediate for respondents. However, this method has some downsides such as: low response rates, normally more missing data, and possibly misinterpretation of questions. Self-administered questionnaires are usually used for random sampling.

On the other hand, researcher-administered questionnaires have some advantages, such as more flexible questions, and they offer immediate access to potential respondents and allow the researcher to address respondents' concerns directly. However, there are several factors that limit the reliability of questionnaire methods. The researcher might potentially influence the respondents' answer by his or her presence and behaviour, and this may decrease the respondents' honesty as their reply is based on what they interpret to be the 'right' or think the researcher expects to hear. Researcher-administered questionnaires are usually used for non-random sampling.

There are two different ways of operating on-site interviews: First, the interviewer can be stationary and interviewees mobile, for example when the interviewer is located near the main exit or entrance gate of a theme park and visitors are interviewed as they leave or enter. Second, the interviewees can be stationary and the interviewer mobile, for example when interviewing users of a place where the visitors are sitting, e.g. users of a picnic area.

■ What questions should I ask?

A questionnaire allows researchers to work with large samples and to establish numerical comparisons. The main limitation of questionnaires is that the answers may be perfunctory in some cases. Finally, researchers should consider the feasibility of the questionnaire method for their study such as costs, facilities, time and sensitivity. This point should not be taken lightly. We often are drawn toward questionnaires as a method of choice as they seem more manageable, straightforward and achievable, particularly when there are time constraints and limited resources available for the research. However, poorly designed questionnaires can yield a distinct lack of useful data, and information gathered from questionnaires is only useful if the sampling is done appropriately (i.e. non-random) and an adequate number of responses is achieved. Thus designing your questionnaire well, whatever form it takes, is essential.

We focus now on the format of the questionnaire, whether it be administered orally or written. The questionnaire format depends on the aim of the research, nature of questions, sample characteristics and resource limitations. Bear in mind that the questions you ask should be directly relevant to your research. Each question should provide information that will be useful in your subsequent analysis. In terms of style, short structured questions are mostly simple to pose and not overly time-consuming to answer, which might be an advantage when attempting to question individuals who may not be willing to take time out. This can increase sample size. Nevertheless, structured questions can enforce a specific answer upon the respondents, since there may be a limited choice of possible pre-selected answers.

■ Constructing a questionnaire

Constructing a survey *instrument*, or questionnaire, is an art in itself. The most important issue in developing one is the sequential formation, clarity and readability of the questions. The main purpose of a questionnaire is to translate the research objectives (aim and research questions) into a specific formulated/structured way to provide a platform where theory or constructs can be tested (in the form of hypotheses) using quantitative data. Researchers should try to motivate respondents and grab their attention by using a well-formatted questionnaire and a correct sequence of questions. De Vaus (2007, p.97) introduces a 16 question wording-checklist (Figure 9.2).

Figure 9.2: Checklist to assist in the wording of questions

Is the language simple? It should be.

Can the question be shortened? It should be as short as possible.

Is the question double-barrelled? There should be one 'clause' in your question.

Is the question leading? It should not direct the respondent toward a specific answer

Is the question negative? It should be as neutral as possible.

Is the respondent likely to have the necessary knowledge? It should be based on accurate assumptions about the respondent's ability to answer it.

Will the words have the same meaning for everyone? Some phrases/words can have loaded meanings for certain groups – beware of this.

Is there a prestige bias? It could be embarrassing for respondents to answer honestly or they could attempt to project a sense of status through their answers.

Is the question ambiguous? e.g. "How often do you wear Chanel?" The respondent may wear Chanel clothing once a month but Chanel perfume every day, thus they may not be sure how to answer.

Is the question too precise? You could be asking something so specific that you may be excluding the individual from effectively participating.

Is the frame of reference for the question sufficiently clear? e.g. "How long do you spend commuting?" This could mean: from your house to your place of work; the actual travel time spent in a car/plane/bus; the total time spent commuting in a whole working day (to and from work); and many other variations.

Does the question artificially create options?

Is personal or impersonal wording preferable?

Is the question wording unnecessarily detailed or objectionable? See points 1 and 2

Does the question contain gratuitous qualifiers? e.g. "When you are driving your kids to school in the morning do you play music?"

Is the question a 'dead giveaway'? Does it betray your research agenda and objectives thus potentially skewing the respondent's entire set of responses?

Questions can be divided into two extensive types: *structured* and *unstructured*. From an instrument design perspective, the structured questions create greater difficulties. From a content point of view, it may in fact be more difficult to write good unstructured questions. There are two main question formats you may consider for your questions: *open-ended/ unstructured* questions (i.e., respondents can reply in their own words) and *closed-ended* questions (i.e., respondents have a limited set of options from which to choose an answer). Open-ended questions are much more difficult to answer using quantitative methods, without further categorization. There are a variety of closed-ended questions available including numerical rating scales, ranking, binary choice formats and multiple choice formats. Figure 9.3 shows examples of closed questions.

Figure 9.3: Closed-ended questions

Type of closed-choice question	Example
Dichotomies questions	Do you smoke cigarettes? ☐ Yes ☐ No Sex: Male Female
Multiple choice formats	How often do you visit museums and art galleries? ☐ At least weekly ☐ Two or three times a month ☐ About once a month ☐ Once every three months ☐ Never Age: ☐ 18-25 ☐ 26-35 ☐ 36-45 ☐ 46-55 ☐ 56-64 ☐ 65 and older
Semantic differential	Please rate your emotions according to the way the experience made you feel <table><tr><td></td><td>1</td><td>2</td><td>3</td><td>4</td><td>5</td><td>6</td><td>7</td><td></td></tr><tr><td>Unhappy</td><td></td><td></td><td></td><td></td><td></td><td></td><td></td><td>Happy</td></tr><tr><td>Annoyed</td><td></td><td></td><td></td><td></td><td></td><td></td><td></td><td>Pleased</td></tr><tr><td>Unsatisfied</td><td></td><td></td><td></td><td></td><td></td><td></td><td></td><td>Satisfied</td></tr></table>

9

Likert scales Note: The use of longer scales (a ten-point) allows for the detection of finer differences between respondents that would not be possible with a five-point scale	Please indicate your level of agreement with following statements: Visiting this museum is an enriching experience for me ☐ Very strongly disagree ☐ Strongly disagree ☐ Disagree ☐ Neither agree nor disagree ☐ Agree ☐ Strongly agree ☐ Very strongly agree Visiting this museum helps me to express who I am ☐ Very strongly disagree ☐ Strongly disagree ☐ Disagree ☐ Neither agree nor disagree ☐ Agree ☐ Strongly agree ☐ Very strongly agree
Ranking format	Please identify the top three aspects you most enjoyed at this visit (Use each of the numbers only once. 1 indicates the most-enjoyed aspect and 3 indicates the third most-enjoyed aspect) People ………………..( ) Climate ………………..( ) Open space……………( ) Heritage………………..( ) Beaches………………..( ) Lifestyle and culture…..( ) Safe to travel ………….( ) Wildlife………………...( )
Filter or contingency questions	Have you ever booked a holiday? ☐ Yes ☐ No If yes, about how many times have you booked a holiday? ☐ Once ☐ 2 or 5 times ☐ 6 to 10 times ☐ More than 10 times

Internal and external validity of quantitative results

The concepts of validity and reliability have a substantial impact upon how researchers think about their work. Reliability focuses on being able to repeat the study (by an independent researcher) and expect the same results. The validity concept can be seen in quantitative-based studies as both internal and external. Internal validity poses the question: can researchers be reasonably sure that the change/lack of change or association was caused by the treatment or independent variable? External validity is the extent to which the results are generalizable and can be applied to other samples. This is less clear for experiments, but more likely, for example, in the case of research using a randomly chosen survey sample.

For surveys, a well-sampled and executed quantitative survey can still have high internal validity (though one needs to be more careful about asserting causality, rather than associations), and external validity if it has findings that can be generalized from the immediate sample. Internal validity also can be achieved through a pilot study which can be carried out in the stage of data collection to assure that the questions and the measurements are appropriate. Pilot surveys can help us in various ways, including testing questionnaire wording and layout and question sequencing, gaining familiarity with respondents, testing fieldwork arrangements, estimating response rate and interview time, and testing analysis procedures.

For experiments, validity is about ruling out factors which raise doubt as to whether change in the dependent variable can be attributed entirely to the independent variable or treatment. Internal validity (experimental design-related) can be compromised in various ways including a change to the subject during the study period (maturation); external change during study, e.g., weather conditions (history); the observation process itself may influence subjects (instrumentation); control groups significantly different (selection bias); and attrition of subject from a research (motility). External validity (generalised beyond the research subjects and setting) has two main threats: reactive effects of testing (i.e., observation may sensitise subjects) and effects of selection (i.e. subjects may not be representative of the wider population).

9

So far we have discussed primary quantitative collection following an experiment or a survey strategy. However, secondary quantitative data can be also used in a research project. The use of primary data gives the researcher the ability to control the formation of the sample aand the nature of the data that are collected. Consequently the researcher can be more confident that the data will fit the aim and objectives of the study. However, the collection of primary data can be a time-consuming process that requires great effort from the researcher. This can prove to be problematic for projects with tight time limits. This obstacle can be overcome by the use of secondary data which can be collected in a more time efficient way and in many cases will lead to larger sample sizes (compared with the primary data). Nevertheless, the researcher will face the problem that the data might not be a perfect fit for the research aim and objectives. Additionally, some issues might occur with the quality of the data as the researcher will not be actively involved either in the sample selection or the data collection process (Easterby-Smith, Richard Thorpe, & Jackson, 2012).

Summary

In this chapter, we have introduced the tools that are needed for collecting quantitative data. The key issues that should be related to your research question are a) defining what are your dependent and independent variables; b) how to sample your participants; and c) how to design appropriate questions to elicit the data that you need to answer your research question. The next chapter discusses the quantitative methods that are at your disposal to analyse the data that you have so painstakingly collected.

Further reading

Adams, H., Edelman, B., Valentin, D. and Dowling, W. J. (2009) *Experimental Design and Analysis for Psychology*, Oxford University Press Oxford.

Anderson, D. R., Sweeney, D. J., Williams, T. A., and Martin, K. (2010) *An Introduction to Management Science: Quantitative Approaches to Decision Making*, South-Western Cengage Learning.

Canavos, G. C. and Koutrouvelis, I. A. (2008) *An Introduction to the Design and Analysis of Experiments*, Prentice Hall Higher Education.

De Vaus, D. (2007). *Surveys in Social Research* (5th ed.). Australia: Routledge.

Neuman, W. L. (2014). *Social Research Methods: Qualitative and Quantitative Approaches* (7th ed.). England: Pearson

Walter, M. (2013). *Social Research Methods* (3rd ed.). Australia: Oxford.

References

Alexander, M., MacLaren, A., O'Gorman, K., & White, C. (2012). Priority queues: Where social justice and equity collide. *Tourism Management*, **33**(4), 875-884. doi: http://dx.doi.org/10.1016/j.tourman.2011.09.009

De Vaus, D. (2007). *Surveys in Social Research* (5th ed.). Australia: Routledge.

Easterby-Smith, M., Richard Thorpe, & Jackson., P. (2012). *Management Research* (4th ed.). London: Sage.

Hair, J. F. J., Black, W. C., Babin, B. J., & Anderson, R. E. (2010). *Multivariate Data Analysis: A Global Perspective* (7th ed.). USA: Pearson.

Oppenheim, A. N. (2000). *Questionnaire Design, Interviewing and Attitude Measurement*. London: Pinter.

Sarantakos, S. (1988). *Social Research* (2nd ed.). Melbourne Macmillan

Walter, M. (2013). *Social Research Methods* (3rd ed.). Australia: Oxford.

Zikmund, W. G., Babin, B. J., Carr, J. C., & Griffin, M. (2010). *Business Research Methods* (8th ed.): South-Western Cengage Learning.

9

10 Quantitative Data Analysis Approaches

Babak Taheri, Catherine Porter, Christian König and Nikolaos Valantasis-Kanellos

In order to understand data and present findings in an accurate way, researchers and managers need to develop an awareness of statistical analysis techniques. The previous chapter concentrated on quantitative data collection, this chapter delves into the statistical tools used to analyse the data once collected. It focuses on two sets of the most widely used statistical tools – exploring relationships and comparing groups – as shown in the 'Deductive' section in the Data Analysis area of the Methods Map (see Chapter 4). Finally, we briefly explain the nature of Big Data.

Data preparation

Real-life data generally cannot be used directly for data analysis – they are unorganised and filled with different types of problems and errors. We discuss three pre-processing steps that prepare data for further analysis: data entry, data cleaning and data formatting.

■ Data entry

A conventional way to organise data is to use tables, with *records* as rows and *attributes* as columns. A record is an identifiable piece of information which contains a set of values of attributes to the record. For example, one may organise the information collected from questionnaires in the following way: each record corresponds to all the answers from a respondent, with each attribute associated with the answer to one question.

No matter how careful one is, it is difficult to avoid making mistakes when entering data. To maintain a certain level of precision, one could use *double entry*. Its idea is very simple – let two individuals enter the same content and compare their inputs. When discrepancies are found, one shall verify and maintain the correct copy. By doubling efforts, double entry is very efficient in preventing entry mistakes. Another method is to use encoding to avoid entering text data directly. For example, when entering gender information such as 'male' or 'female' in text forms, some may introduce typos such as 'mael' and 'femeal', and some may capitalize the first letters as 'Female' and 'Male', which could be interpreted as different words. Alternatively, one can encode 'male' as '0' and 'female' as '1', so that one could enter 0s and 1s instead. The encoding function is explicitly provided in many data analysis software such as SPSS (Statistical package for the social sciences). SPSS can be used to analyse questionnaire-based and other data organised as cases with particular variables. Figure 10.1 illustrates a snapshot of variable view (information on variables is entered in the SPSS) and data value (data entered directly or can be imported from a spreadsheet file) on SPSS. Table 10.1 explains the information required for each variable in the questionnaire.

Table 10.1: Information required for each variable in the questionnaire in variable view in SPSS

Variable Label	Short Description
Name	Up to 8 characters (no spaces), starting with a letter Not allowed: ALL, AND, BY, EQ, GT, LE, LT, NE, NOT, WITH, OR, TO Can be: short version of item description e.g., var01, Q1a
Width	Max. no. of characters
Decimal places	Decimal places for numbers
Label	Longer version of name
Values	Values for coded variables
Missing	Blanks, no answer, etc
Columns	No. of columns in data view screen
Alignment	Left, right, centre
Types of measure	Nominal, ordinal, scales

10

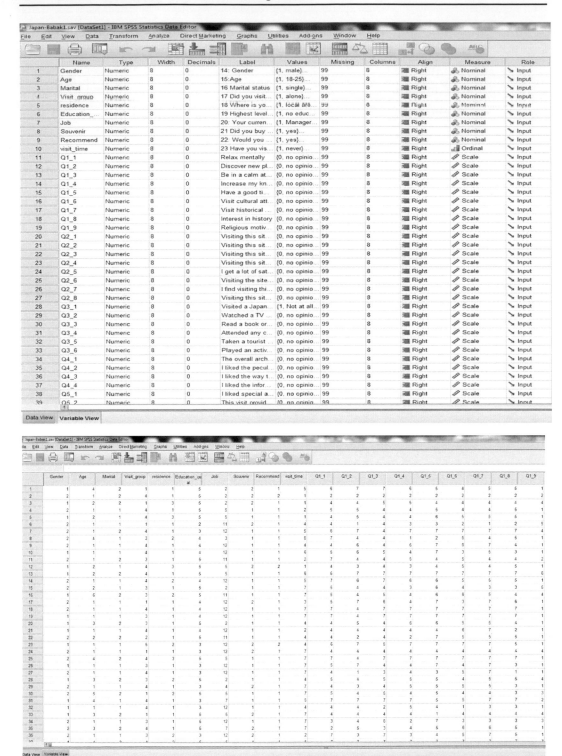

Figure 10.1: Example of (top) variable view and (bottom) data view in SPSS software

■   **Data cleaning**

Even if there are no errors introduced during entry phase, real-life data need to be cleaned because they are often *incomplete, noisy* and *inconsistent* (Han, Kamber, & Pei, 2011). Incompleteness arises when for some records the values for some attributes are missing. There are mainly two ways to deal with this issue. First, delete the whole record that misses data; this could be viable when the number of records with missing data is relatively small compared to the whole dataset. Second, fill the missing values; one can use the expected value on the corresponding attribute or regression on other attributes to predict the missing value. Noises refer to random factors that can only be quantified in a probabilistic way. Noises confound observations and cause *outliers* that are far away from normal observations. A primary task of data cleaning is to identify and 'smooth' out these outliers. Inconsistencies often arise when one combines information from different sources. For example, combining datasets with both American and British date information may cause confusion (i.e. the 3rd of April 1990 could be displayed as both 4/3/90 and 3/4/90).

Preliminary analysis

■   **Describing data**

To present a sample in an illustrative way one can either use descriptive statistics (numbers) or graphs, or both; it is a matter of personal preference – some prefer descriptive statistics because they are quantifiable while others prefer graphs because they are more intuitive. Therefore, when deciding which form to present data, it is important to know who your target audience is.

If the sample is of a nonmetric type (for example an ordinal scale as described in Chapter 9), *frequency* and *ratio* are two commonly used descriptive statistics. Frequency counts the number of occurrences of a specific category, and ratio calculates the corresponding percentage of frequency in the entire sample. Nonmetric data can be visualised through pie charts or bar charts. We give an example on the cut quality of diamonds based on a dataset with 53940 records (Source: http://vincentarelbundock.github. io/Rdatasets/datasets.html). The cut quality of diamonds is a nonmetric measurement and has five categories: fair, good, very good, premium and

10

ideal. Table 10.2 summarises the frequencies and ratios of all five categories. Figure 10.2 plots both with a bar chart and a pie chart.

Table 10.2: Cut quality of diamonds: frequencies and ratios

Cut quality	Frequencies	Ratios
Fair	1610	2.98%
Good	4906	9.10%
Very good	12082	22.40%
Premium	13791	25.57%
Ideal	21551	39.95%

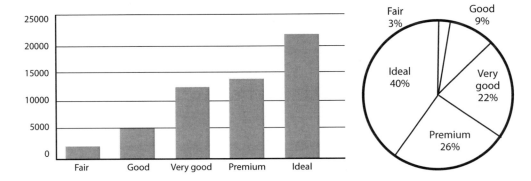

Figure 10.2: Cut quality of diamonds: bar graph and pie chart

If the sample is of a metric type, it makes sense to calculate all sorts of statistics measuring the basic characteristics of the sample such as *centre* and *dispersion*.

■ The centre denotes a typical value that represents the entire sample and can be measured by the *mean* (arithmetical average) and *median* (the value of the middle case in a series) of a particular sample.

■ Dispersion accesses the variation across the sample and can be measured by *variance* (the average of the squared differences from the mean), *standard deviation* (a measure of how spread-out numbers are), *coefficient of variation* (a measure of the dispersion of data points in a data series around the mean), *range* (the difference between the lowest and highest values), etc.

Further information and a more detailed explanation of quantitative measures and statistics can be found in Wisniewski's (2010) textbook on *Quantitative Methods for Decision Makers*.

To visualise metric measurements, a histogram and boxplot is appropriate. It is worthwhile to note that histograms and bar charts are quite similar in that they are all used to describe the distribution of a sample; with one minor difference that in a histogram the scale of the horizontal axis must be *equally* spaced. Using the same dataset on diamonds, we plot the distribution of another attribute 'carat' using a histogram and boxplot in Figure 10.3.

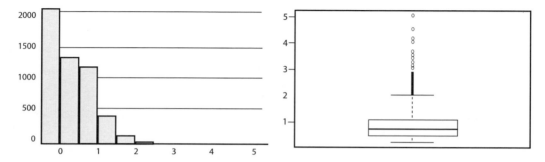

Figure 10.3: Carat of diamonds: histogram and boxplot

■ Statistical significance, null and alternative hypothesis

There are also three terms which you will see a lot in quantitative analysis:

- *Statistically significant*: means it is unlikely to have happened by chance (highly improbable). It can be strong or weak. The level of significance is influenced by sample size (not by population size). Statistical significance is usually measured with a P-value of the appropriate test. Researchers commonly accept the results are probably true if the statistical test has a P-value less than 0.05. For example, a finding from a study showed that individuals who had dementia with agitation had a somewhat lower rate of blood pressure problems when they took drug X compared to when they took drug Y. The difference in outcomes between X and Y drugs was not considered to be statistically significant because p=0.2. The probability that the finding were due to chance was high enough to assume that the two drugs did not vary in causing blood pressure problems.

- *Null hypothesis*: there is *no* significant difference or relationship (H_0).

- *Alternative hypothesis*: it means there is a significant difference or relationship (H_1). There might be more than one alternative hypothesis in a study based on the research question and aim. For example:

  H_0: Football and rugby participation levels are the same.

  H_1: Football and rugby participation levels are significantly different.

10

■ ## Parametric versus non-parametric analysis

There are two commonly known statistical techniques in social science research: *parametric* and *non-parametric*. Parametric tests follow four main assumptions: normally distributed data (data are from one or more normally distributed population), homogeneity of variance (each of several groups of participants comes from a population with the same variance), interval data and independence (the behaviour of one participant does not influence the behaviour of another) (see also Field, 2009 for more information). For example, Partial Correlation, Multiple Regression, Factor Analysis, Paired Simplest *t*-test, ANOVA, MANOVA are well-known parametric techniques. On the other hand, nonparametric techniques do not have such stringent requirements, for example, Chi-square, Spearman's Rank Order Correlation, Wilcoxon Signed Rank Test, Kruskal-Wallis Test, Friedman Test. Table 10.3 shows the non-parametric alternative techniques. This chapter mainly focuses on parametric data analysis.

Table 10.3: Non-parametric techniques, parametric alternative and variables

Non-parametric	Parametric alternative	Independent/dependent variable
Chi-square	None	One categorical dependent variable/ One categorical independent variable
Spearman's Rank Order Correlation	Correlation Coefficient	Two continuous variables
Wilcoxon Signed-Rank	None	One categorical independent variable (two levels)
Kruskal-Walls	One-way Between Groups ANOVA	One categorical independent variable (three or more levels)
Friedman Test	One-way Between Measures ANOVA	One categorical independent variable (three or more levels)

Statistical techniques part I: Exploring relationships

The techniques introduced in this section are based on the analysis of independent and dependent variables and address multiple purposes, such as testing theories and models, predicting future outcomes and trends, and assessing the reliability and validity of primary and secondary data scales.

■ *Correlation analysis* explores the association and relationship between two variables in terms of strength and direction.

- *Partial correlation analysis* explains the relationship between a pair of variables, which are or might be influenced by a third variable.

- *Multiple regression analysis* is used to predict the value or score of a single dependent variable from multiple independent variables.

- *Factor analysis* explores the structure of relationships within a large group of related variables. It reduces them to a limited number of dimensions and determinants.

■ Correlation analysis

Correlation analysis is used to quantify the strength of a linear relationship between two variables (which is also referred to as Pearson correlation). Correlation can be measured by the correlation coefficient r that ranges from -1 (i.e., a strong negative relationship) to +1 (i.e., a strong positive relationship). If $r = 0$, there is no correlation between the two variables. In addition, r^2 represents the proportion of variation in one variable that can be explained by the other variable and is more accurate in determining any correlation. Figure 10.4 illustrates a sample of different relationships between two independent variables representing different values of the correlation coefficient; see Cohen, Cohen, West, and Aiken (2013) for more information.

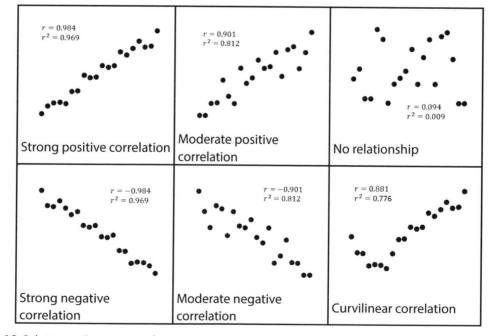

Figure 10.4: Interpreting scatterplots

10

Example: Correlation analysis helps to determine whether any event affects another event. Let us illustrate a simple situation, where a student wants to know if studying longer hours will result in better exam results. After collecting data from a sample, the data must be displayed in a scatter plot with the hours of study on the y-axis (horizontal) and the exam grade on the x-axis (vertical). The resulting diagram will look similar to one of the above diagrams. A strong positive correlation in this example means that according to your data set, the longer you study, the better your exam grade will be. A strong negative correlation means that the longer you study, the worse your exam grades will be. No relationship in this case means that the number of hours the student studies has no effect on his or her grade. A moderate correlation means that the hours a student studies have an effect (positive or negative) but only a very weak one. In all cases other factors might be relevant, and may need to be included in a more complex model.

■ Partial correlation

As an extension to the Pearson correlation, the partial correlation analysis allows us to explore the relationship between two variables, which are or might be influenced by a third. The analysis focuses on removing the impact of any additional variables on the two of the researcher's interest. Sometimes, a third variable impacts any relationship to some extent and therefore increases or decreases the value of the correlation coefficient. In other words, if variables A and B look strongly related to each other, their relationship might be influenced by a third variable C. The statistical control of variable C would show that the original correlation between A and B is much weaker, which results in a smaller value of the correlation coefficient.

The partial analysis of correlation requires at least three continuous variables and addresses the issue, if there is still a significant relationship between two variables, after controlling the impact of an additional factor. The objective of this technique is to point out and identify any hidden correlations that are explained by the effect of external variables not related to the unit of analysis.

Example: Referring to the above example of determining the effect that studying more hours has on the results of an exam, partial correlation considers the effect that other factors have on the outcome of an exam. These factors might for example be the student's previous education, ability to learn in general, or the working and learning environment, to name a few.

■ Multiple regression analysis

Multiple regression analysis is a technique for exploring the relationship between one continuous dependent variable and various independent variables. Similar to Pearson and partial correlation analysis, multiple regression measures the correlation between variables. However, the analysis is not limited to two variables but allows the researcher to explore the interrelationships between a larger number of variables. In particular, when using multiple regression, we can interpret the relationship between two variables (e.g. sales and advertising expenditure) whilst controlling for all other factors that may also influence the dependent variable (e.g. location, time of year, advertising expenditure of competitors). A more detailed description and explanation of assumptions can be found in Tabachnick and Fidell (2012).

Research that aims to predict a particular outcome of a phenomenon usually uses these kinds of techniques. Complex constructs, based on theoretical or conceptual models, can be measured and therefore, multiple regression analysis is capable of dealing with more complex real-life problems; analysing a theoretical model gives a more detailed insight into a phenomenon and the individual contribution of variables and constructs by considering the whole. Multiple regression analysis measures how much of the variance in the dependent variable can be explained by the independent variables. Each variable needs to be evaluated individually in order to find out its contribution to the whole, based on the value of the correlation coefficient.

Example: We assume the same situation where a student wants to determine what factors affect his or her exam results the most. Using a multiple regression analysis helps to identify and evaluate the level of correlation between the independent variables on the dependent variable. The dependent variable in this case would be the exam grade. The independent variables could be the hours of study, the previous education, gender or age of the student, or any other factor that distinctly characterises the sample population, or that the researcher hypothesises would affect exam grade.

■ Factor analysis

Unlike the previous techniques, factor analysis does not measure correlations for testing hypotheses but the method evaluates a large set of variables in order to synthesise it into a smaller, more summarised and manageable set of factors or components. Factor analysis is based on the comparison of interrelationships among variables in order to identify groups that belong together and is applied to problems that cannot be directly measured. However, the valuable information still remains in the smaller data set. Hence, the resulting number of variables or factors is more manageable and can be used for other methods such as regression or correlation analysis. The main concerns of factor analysis are three-fold.

1 It helps to understand the structure of certain variables,

2 It helps to build constructs and questionnaires to test variables, and

3 It reduces the number of variables from a large set to a more manageable number of components.

For example, Alexander et al. (2012) found underlying constructs of bullying and job satisfaction after running factor analysis in their study. The four factors were for buying scale labelled 'psychological bullying', 'verbal bullying', 'gender/sex bullying' and 'devaluing'. The eight factors were named as 'rewards', 'satisfaction with supervisor', 'promotion prospects', 'organisational feelings', 'working culture', 'co-workers', 'stress and pressure' and 'bureaucracy'.

The *R-matrix* is the commonly used arrangement including correlation coefficients (such as used in the correlation analysis) between each pair of variables or factors. The analysis focuses on exploring the maximum amount of common variance in a correlation matrix utilising the smallest number of explanatory scales.

Summary of statistical techniques to explore relationships

Table 10.4 summarises the main characteristics of the required variables and an example research question for each statistical technique that is used to compare groups. The general assumptions for statistical analysis are introduced in the previous section.

Table 10.4: Summary of statistical techniques to explore relationships

Variables	Example question
Correlation	
Two continuous independent variables	Is there a relationship between age and motivation scores?
Partial correlation	
Three continuous independent variables	Is there a relationship between tourist motivation scores and involvement after controlling for the effect of expectations?
Multiple regression	
Two or more independent variables; one continuous dependent variable	What is the relationship between involvement scores, tourist motivation and perception?
Factor analysis	
Set of related continuous independent variables	What is the underlying structure of the items that make up the tourist motivation scale and how many factors are involved?

Statistical techniques part II: Comparing groups

The aim of this section is to describe and explain the main statistical techniques in social science research that are used to explore differences between groups or conditions. The purpose of testing and comparing a set of two or more groups is to identify statistically significant differences in the means of the analysed groups. Using these kinds of techniques helps to make statistical inference about any population from a randomly chosen sample.

- *t-test analysis* compares the value of the mean scores (variables) for only two groups.
- *Analysis of variance (ANOVA)* compares the values of one or two independent variables for more than two groups with different or independent participants.
- *Multivariate ANOVA (MANOVA)* is used to compare the mean scores for two or more groups with more than one dependent variable.
- *Analysis of covariance (ANCOVA)* explains the difference between independent variables and one dependent variable influenced by an additional variable that has to be controlled.

10

■ *t*-test analysis

The *t*-test analysis technique is used to explore if there is a significant difference in the means of two groups, based on the analysis of one categorical independent and one continuous dependent variable. Hypotheses are tested from means, not individual scores, therefore the distributions demonstrating hypothetical conditions of reality are distributions of means not of individual scores. As a measurement unit, the *t statistic* is the ratio of the difference between two sample means ($\mu_1 - \mu_2$), divided by an estimate of the standard error (SE). The standard error is a measure of the dispersion of both samples, and is calculated by a formula that includes the variance of each, and the total sample size. The size of the *t*-statistic relative to a benchmark concludes whether the difference between two means is statistically significant. For example, Alexander et al. (2012) found the effects of different types of bullying scales by length of time in current job. In doing so, they conducted a series of independent *t*-tests using a median split of length of time in post as a grouping variable. The results highlighted a significant difference between individuals who had been employed for less than or equal to five years and those who had been employed for longer. Also, significant differences were strongest for psychological and verbal bullying factors.

The different levels of significance are described by Hair et al. (2010). The calculation of the statistics can be described as follows:

$$t \text{ statistic} = \frac{(\mu 1 - \mu 2)}{SE_{\mu_1 \mu_2}}$$

where

$\mu 1$ = mean of group 1

$\mu 2$ = mean of group 2

$SE_{\mu_1 \mu_2}$ = standard error of difference in group means, which is based on the square root of the average variance of the groups, and divided by the square root of the sample size.

The *independent-sample t-test* compares the difference in the means for two dissimilar population groups, such as males and females, or children and adults, meaning that independent sample groups are compared on different conditions. The *paired-sample t-test* is used when the data collection process of one sample group takes place on two different occasions or situations, meaning that two different conditions are applied to the same participants. For further details on the different techniques see Field (2009).

■   ## Analysis of variance (ANOVA)

Comparing the means of two different groups or conditions is not always sufficient and needs to be extended in order to compare the means of three or more sample groups. The use of analysis of variance (ANOVA) is suitable for this, as it compares the variance between different groups with the variability within each of the groups. As a measurement unit, the *F statistic* is the ratio that expresses the differences in the variances of different groups. For a more detailed explanation of the logic behind the *F statistic*, see the discussion by Field (2009) about experimental designs with different groups, or the interpretation by Hair et al. (2010) on how to determine when the ratio is large enough to reject the null hypothesis. Concluding, ANOVA analysis tests the null hypothesis that the means of different groups are not equal. If the *F statistic* is significant, the null hypothesis can be rejected and the population means are equal.

One-way between-groups analysis of variance compares different groups or conditions and tests the impact of one independent variable (or factor) on one continuous dependent variable. *Two-way between-groups analysis of variance* compares different groups or conditions and tests the impact of two independent variables on one continuous dependent variable.

■   ## Multivariate analysis of variance (MANOVA)

Sometimes, testing one single dependent variable from different groups does not properly answer the research questions or address real-life problems. Multivariate analysis of variance (MANOVA) extends the previous approach and is adequate in situations where there are several dependant variables. However, it is important not to just test all possible variables and put them together in a MANOVA, unless the model is based on good theoretical or conceptual constructs. Analysing multiple variables at the same time reduces the risk of errors. Rather than just running separate ANOVA models for individual variables, MANOVA represents a more complex and a single method of testing a wider range of questions (Hair, Black, Babin, & Anderson, 2010). It can be used in a one-way and two-way design. In real life, finding a significant result is more likely if you run a series of individual analyses at the same time. Therefore, the application of MANOVA gives more realistic results that are not inflated by these errors.

10

■ Analysis of covariance (ANCOVA)

In situations where an additional variable, also referred to as *covariate*, may influence the outcome scores of the dependent variable (similar to the partial correlation analysis), the analysis of covariance (ANCOVA) as an extension to ANOVA is an adequate technique to use. Assuming that the covariate is measured without error is not realistic in social science research. ANCOVA is a combination of regression analysis and the analysis of variance, and removes the influence of any additional variable in order to control the score of the dependent variable. The analysis can be designed as one-way and two-way between-groups ANOVA. Furthermore, the appropriate use of two or three covariates is suggested by Stevens (2012) in order to reduce errors and increase the significance between the groups. The right choice of the covariate is crucial in order to eliminate errors that bias the results. Therefore, an effective covariate is highly correlated with the dependent variable(s), however it is not correlated with the independent variables. As a result, the influence of differences between individual groups will be reduced and controlled, which leads to an increased power of the *F statistic* (Tabachnick and Fidell, 2012).

Summary of statistical techniques to compare groups

Table 10.6 summarises the main characteristics for the required variables and gives an example research question for each statistical technique that is used to compare groups. The general assumptions for statistical analysis are introduced in the previous sections.

Table 10.5: Summary of statistical techniques to compare groups

Technique	Variables	Example question
t-test analysis	One categorical independent variable; One continuous dependent variable	Is there a change in tourists' satisfaction scores from time 1 to time 2?
ANOVA (one-way)	One categorical independent variable; One continuous dependent variable	Is there a difference in satisfaction scores for different age groups of tourists?
ANOVA (two-way)	Two categorical independent variable; One continuous dependent variable	Is there a difference in satisfaction scores for different age groups and genders of tourists?

MANOVA	One or more categorical independent variables; Two or more related continuous dependent variables	Is there a difference between genders, across different age groups, in terms of their scores on satisfaction and motivation measures?
ANCOVA	One or more categorical independent and one covariate variable; One continuous dependent variable	Is there a significant difference between three age groups on tourist motivation, while controlling for the scores on repeated visits at time 1?

Structural Equation Modelling (SEM)

There are two different generations of data analysis techniques available for finding relationships between scales (Hair, Hult, Ringle, & Sarstedt, 2014). *First generation* techniques can only analyse one layer of linkages between independent and dependent variables at a time, e.g., linear regression, analysis of variance, analysis of covariance and principal components. *Second generation* techniques answer a set of research questions in one single, systematic and comprehensive analysis by modelling the relationships among multiple independent and dependent scales at the same time, e.g., partial least squares, covariance based structural equation modelling and redundancy analysis.

Second generation data analysis with latent variables has been used in social science, e.g., consumer behaviour, marketing, management and tourism studies in the last decade (Alexander et al., 2012; Hair et al., 2014; Henseler, Ringle, & Sinkovics, 2009; Taheri, Jafari, & O'Gorman, 2014). It defines the structure of the relationships among variables. It is a technique for examining a unique combination of both interdependence and dependence in multivariate data analysis and its foundation lies in two well-known multivariate techniques, namely, multiple regression analysis and factor analysis.

Hair et al. (2010, p. 634) define structural equation modelling as "a family of statistical models that seek to explain their relationships among multiple variables. In doing so, it examines the structure of interrelationships expressed in a series of equations, similar to a series of multiple regression equations. These equations depict all of their relationships among constructs (the dependent and independent variables) involved in the analysis. Constructs are unobservable or latent factors represented by multiple

10

variables (much like variables representing a factor in factor analysis)…".
Figure 10.6 illustrates these relationships.

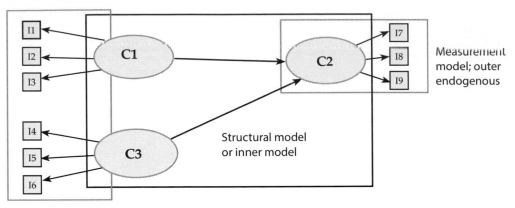

Measurement model; outer exogenous

Figure 10.5: Visual demonstration of SEM

Information about the Figure

Exogenous variables: are independent variables not presumed to be caused by other variables in the model.

Endogenous variables: are variables assumed to be caused by other variables in the mode. Unlike the first generation of regression tools, SEM not only assesses the structural model, but in the same analysis also evaluates the measurement model, loadings observed items (measurements) on their expected latent variables constructs.

C1, C2 and C3 are the constructs or latent variables: they represent an abstract concept, presumed to underlie selected observed behavior; cannot be measured directly.

I1…I9 are the items or observed variables: represent observed behaviour in the very broadest sense and measured directly.

SEM is also sometimes executed using specialised software packages such as AMOS and SmartPLS. There are two methods to estimate the relationships in a structural equation model: Component-based SEM (PLS-SEM) vs. Covariance-based SEM (AMOS-SEM). Each of these methods may be appropriate for different research contexts, and researchers need to understand the dissimilarity before using them. Unlike co-variance based structural equation modelling (e.g., AMOS), which uses the structure of variables, PLS is a component-based approach suitable for both predictive applications and theory building (Hair et al., 2014). PLS can be modelled in formative (i.e., based on classical test theory where the measured indicators are assumed to be caused by the construct) and reflective (i.e., indicators cause changes in the construct) modes (Taheri et al., 2014). For example, Taheri et al., (2014) establish relationships between drivers of visitors' engagement (prior knowledge, cultural capital, recreational motivation and reflective motivation) and level of engagement with heritage sites using PLS, whereby both formative and reflective scales are included. Whilst prior knowledge, recreational motivation and cultural capital positively affect visitors' level of engagement, there was no significant relationship between reflective motivation and level of engagement. Table 10.6 illustrates the main differences between Component-based and Covariance-based SEM.

Table 10.6: Differences between Component-based SEM vs. Covariance-based SEM

Basis of comparison	PLS-SEM (e.g. SmartPLS)	CB-SEM (e.g. AMOS)
Objective	Prediction oriented	Theory oriented
Approach	Variance based	Covariance based
Assumption	Predictor specification (nonparametric)	Multivariate normal distribution and independent observations (parametric)
Relationship between a latent variable and its measures	Can be modelled in either formative or reflective	Usually only reflective indicators
Implications	Optimal for prediction accuracy	Optimal for parameter accuracy
Model complexity	Large complexity (e.g., 100 constructs, 1000 indicators)	Small to moderate complexity (e.g., < 100 indicators)
Sample size	Power analysis based on the portion of the model with largest number of predictors. Recommendations for minimum number of observations can range from 30 to 100 cases	Ideally based on power analysis of specific model. Recommendations for minimum number of observations can range from 200 to 800.

10

Large scale – big data

■ Nature of big data

We consider big data as a type of secondary data that can be utilised by students in research projects. Big data can be seen as deductive or inductive analytics approach based on the nature of a potential study. Big data are generated by various methods and means around us every second of every day in forms beyond imagination. According to Gartner's report, "big data is high volume, high velocity, and/or high variety information assets that require new forms of processing to enable enhanced decision making, insight discovery and process optimization" (Laney, 2012).

◼ Forms of big data

Big data can be sourced by various means and ways. A main distinction lies between the data type (structured or unstructured) and source (machine or human generated):

- *Structured data* are those data with precise length and format.
- *Unstructured data* are those that do not follow any specified format.
- *Machine generated data* are created by machines without human interaction
- *Human generated data* are created by the interaction of humans with machines.

It must be mentioned that machine and human generated data can be created both in structured and unstructured ways. Thus, for example sensor data (RFID, GPS), web log data, point of sale (POS) and financial data are characterised as structured machine generated data, while input data (age, sex, income etc.), click stream data and gaming related data can be characterised as human generated structured data. On the other hand, satellite images, scientific data, photographs and videos, radar or sonar data are perceived as unstructured machine generated data, while a company's internal documents, social media data and website content are perceived as unstructured human generated data.

A framework that shows the most relevant sample of technological companies is provided by Nair and Narayanan (2012), which adds the internal/external dimension in the data sources classification. Figure 9.1 depicts this framework. According to this framework, the nature of the company and its main strategic focus will determine what kind of data should be considered in their decision making. However, a complete analysis of these choices does not fall into the scope of this book. For more information consult Nair and Narayanan (2012).

	Structured		Unstructured	
External	Mobile phone/GPS	Public surveys	Google + Twitter	Facebook
	Purchase History	Credit history	Pinterest	Instagram
			Personal life events	Blogs
	Travel History	Life event records		
	Real Estate Records			Foursquare
		Census data	External sensor data	
Internal	Customer relationship management (CRM)	Web profiles	Online company forums	Web feeds
		Sales records		
			SharePoint	
	HR records	Expense records		
	Financials	Customer profiles	Text documents	Sensor data

Figure 10.6: Four dimensions of big data. (Source: Nain and Narayanan, 2012)

■ Big data application and analysis tools

In a business management context big data enable managers to measure and directly enhance their understanding about their business, thus they are able to convert this quickly gained knowledge into valuable information that helps to make decisions, and potentially creates a competitive advantage (Bughin, Chui, & Manyika, 2010).

The collection of huge amount of data led companies to the need to develop ways to handle these data and make sense of them. Companies such as Yahoo, Google and Facebook developed several tools to analyse big data. These tools enable them to process enormous amounts of data in efficient, cost effective and time-sensitive ways. Companies commonly use tools such as MapReduce, BigTable and Hadoop. However, the use of these programmes requires advanced knowledge and computing skills. A thorough description of these tools falls outside of the scope of this book. For a comprehensive discussion about advanced analytic tools please see Zikopoulos et al. (2012). Instead, a more basic analysis tool such as Google Analytics can be used.

The concerns regarding big data can be divided in three categories; these are privacy related issues, technological issues and managerial reluctance.

10

In particular big data has been characterised as the 'Big Brother' disguised in corporate clothing (Lohr, 2012). This characterisation implies questions regarding the level of trust that consumers show to organisations when organisations are not yet sure of how they can use and combine the data they collect in vast amounts on a daily basis. The very famous WikiLeaks scandal is just an example of how high security measures can be compromised.

Summary

In this chapter, we have discussed your data preparation approach, preliminary (descriptive) analysis as well as introduced some of the main statistical techniques used in quantitative research in business management. The key issues that should be related back to your study question are a) how to prepare your data; b) how to use preliminary data analysis; c) what analyses are appropriate for comparing groups; d) what techniques are most appropriate for exploring relationships.

Further reading

Hair, J. F. J., Black, W. C., Babin, B. J., & Anderson, R. E. (2010). *Multivariate Data Analysis: A Global Perspective* (7th ed.). USA: Pearson.

Field, A. (2009). *Discovering Statistics using SPSS* (Vol. 3). London: SAGE Publications Ltd.

Nair, R. and Narayanan, a. (2012) *Getting Results From Big Data: A Capabilities-Driven Approach to the Strategic Use of Unstructured Information.*

Pallant, J. (2007). *SPSS: Survival Manual - A Step by Step Guide to Data Analysis using SPSS for Windows* (3rd ed.). UK: Open University Press.

References

Alexander, M., MacLaren, A., O'Gorman, K., & Taheri, B. (2012). "He just didn't seem to understand the banter": Bullying or simply establishing social cohesion? *Tourism Management, 33*(5), 1245-1255.

Bughin, J., Chui, M., & Manyika, J. (2010). *Clouds, Big Data, and Smart Assets: Ten tech-enabled business tends to watch*: McKinsey.

Cohen, J., Cohen, P., West, S. G., & Aiken, L. S. (2013). *Applied Multiple Regression/Correlation Analysis for the Behavioral Sciences*: Taylor & Francis.

Field, A. (2009). *Discovering Statistics using SPSS* (Vol. 3). London: SAGE Publications Ltd.

Hair, J. F. J., Black, W. C., Babin, B. J., & Anderson, R. E. (2010). *Multivariate Data Analysis: A Global Perspective* (7th ed.). USA: Pearson.

Hair, J. F. J., Hult, G. T. M., Ringle, C. M., & Sarstedt, M. (2014). *A Primer on Partial Least Squares Structural Equation Modeling (PLS-SEM)*. UK: Sage.

Han, J., Kamber, M., & Pei, J. (2011). *Data Mining: Concepts and Techniques*. USA: Morgan kaufmann.

Henseler, J., Ringle, C. M., & Sinkovics, R. R. (2009). The use of partial least squares path modeling in international marketing. *Advances in International Marketing, 20*, 277-319.

Laney, D. (2012). *The Importance of 'Big Data': A Definition*. Gartner.

Lohr, S. (2012). The Age of Big Data. *The New York Times*. http://www.nytimes.com/2012/02/12/sunday-review/big-datas-impact-in-the-world.html

Nair, R., & Narayanan, A. (2012). Getting results from big data: a capabilities-driven approach to the strategic use of unstructured information. http://www.strategyand.pwc.com/

Stevens, J. P. (2012). *Applied Multivariate Statistics for the Social Sciences, Fifth Edition*: Taylor & Francis.

Tabachnick, B. G., & Fidell, L. S. (2012). *Using Multivariate Statistics*. Boston: Pearson Education.

Taheri, B., Jafari, A., & O'Gorman, K. (2014). Keeping your audience: Presenting a visitor engagement scale. *Tourism Management, 42*, 321-329.

Zikopoulos, P., deRoos, D., Parasuraman, K., Deutsch, T., Giles, J., & Corrigan, D. (2012). *Harness the Power of Big Data The IBM Big Data Platform*: Mcgraw-hill.

Wisniewski, M. (2010). *Quantitative Methods for Decision Makers*, Essex: Pearson Education, Limited.

10

Managing Ethics in Research Projects

James Richards, Lakshman Wimalasena and Gavin MacLean

In recent years, universities and a variety of other organizations have begun to introduce procedures that seek to ensure that their research meets key ethical requirements. So far the focus of this book has been on generating research ideas and considering a range of possible research methods and methodologies in order to explore those very research ideas. Aside from the actual management of the dissertation (see Chapter 12 and Appendix 1), the ethical dimension of your planned research is the one other major topic you should address before progressing much further. In practice, what this means is that your research, which is likely to involve you distributing questionnaires, conducting interviews or conducting focus groups, brings with it various dilemmas in terms of your moral conduct towards the people you are expecting to fill in questionnaires, be interviewed or take part in focus groups. Such dilemmas will be dependent on the design of your particular study, but, typical ethical dilemmas in relation to business management research include: the manner in which you intend to recruit people to your study, the extent to you will inform participants of what your research is about, and dealing with research participants who may be concerned about how they are portrayed in your final dissertation.

There are some simple steps which can help ensure that your research embodies the kinds of ethical principles that many institutions require, and we will use a range of real life ethical dilemmas to help you as you formulate your own research. The chapter concludes with checklist of questions to consider.

The importance and relevance of ethics in business management research

Being clear about the ethical dimensions of your research is important for three main reasons: navigating sensitive topics, improving research outcomes, and ensuring professional conduct.

■ Navigating sensitive research topics

The first reason for considering ethics is that you may be researching something which is seen as sensitive. Many of you, perhaps even the majority, will be conducting research on topics that are not seen as particularly sensitive in relation to business organisations. What is meant by sensitive is wide-ranging and may also be defined or viewed differently by different parties. These differences in perspective are important in making ethical choices. For example, imagine wishing to conduct research that looks at the potential for unlawful discrimination in the promotions process. In such situations you many have a senior management team who believe their promotions procedures negate the possibility for discrimination on gender, religious or other grounds. The management team may have conducted research or collected data that underpins their confident claims that discrimination does not occur. In this situation senior managers may be willing to talk openly about topics such as sexual discrimination. However, lower level management or non-management employees within the organization may feel differently. They may believe they have been unlawfully discriminated against, but they may not be willing to voice their concerns for fear of recriminations should they speak out about a failed promotion application. Whilst discrimination seems an overtly sensitive issue, there are many other issues which may evoke sensitivities on behalf of those involved in the research. There are ethical dilemmas where the interests of different groups diverge, e.g. those commissioning the research and those being asked to participate in the research. A commitment to research ethics allows researchers to foresee the potential impact their research may have on their participants and make plans to off-set such concerns.

■ Improved research outcomes

A second reason to consider ethics in your research is that it will improve the quality of the outcomes that you achieve. Imagine yourself as a business

11

manager facing an organisational problem where you, your colleagues or professional peers have little or no expertise. In such situations, a possible solution is to ask whether academic research has been conducted that might offer some guidance or insight to the problem. However you would still need to attempt some kind of evaluation of the merits and relevance of such research. As such, it is assumed here that you will be looking for primary research that is based on studies involving willing participants, studies involving a high number of participants, studies involving participants sharing many characteristics, as well as studies written in a fashion that does not compromise the reputations of participating organisations.

None of the above would be possible without research ethics. In other words, the best business management research is based on recruiting participants who fully understand what the research is about and can fully relate it to their own experiences. Such participants may also be eager to refer researchers to colleagues or peers with similar or unique insights and experiences, and feel safe in the knowledge that involvement in such research projects will not compromise personal or wider reputations. As such, research ethics is also an important aspect of achieving a good grade for your dissertation.

Professional affiliation and conduct

A third reason to note the importance and relevance of research ethics goes beyond the individual and the present moment. As prospective business managers you will be aware that you will sometime soon be expected to join and be governed by a professional body. Students of business management can expect to be members of, for example, the Chartered Management Institute, the Chartered Institute of Personnel and Development, or the Chartered Institute of Marketing. Such institutes tend to have codes of conduct that relate in most part to day-to-day professional conduct, but also refer in some way to conduct in relation to research. As prospective business management researchers you are, as such, expected to abide by the standards set out by organisations that directly or indirectly govern business management research and practice. As further evidence that ethics matter, professional research associations such as the British Academy of Management (2013) also have codes of practice. The British Academy of Management sets out seven key principles (see Box 11.1) that should be followed in the conduct of research and wider professional practice.

Compliance with the requirements of a professional body or association may be regarded as a sensible precaution and such guidance has typically served business management practitioners and researchers over many years. Adopting good practice will help with the credibility of your research and will help you make the transition from student of business management to business management practitioner.

Box 11.1: British Academy of Management Code of Ethics and Best Practice

- Responsibility and accountability

- Integrity and honesty

- Respect and fairness

- Privacy and confidentiality

- Avoidance of personal gain

- Conflict of interest

- Collegiality

Source: British Academy of Management (2013)

Exercise 11.1

Referring to the British Academy of Management's Code of Ethics and Best Practice in Box 11.1, what principles of the code are most relevant to the project you have planned?

Ethical principles in business management research

A range of ethical principles can be closely associated with business management research. Central to most of the ethical principles is the well-being of research participants. In the preface of this book, we discussed Barry Marshall's unusual research protocol where he aimed to give himself a gastric ulcer so that he could treat himself. His research went on to win a Nobel Prize and one could argue that he only put himself at risk. How this research would fare in relation to the principles of ethical research

11

aimed at minimising harm to participants is an interesting case. More dramatically, the Stanford Prison experiment conducted in 1971 would almost certainly fall foul of modern ethical approval processes. The experiment took a group of students and randomly assigned some the role of guards and others the role of prisoners in a simulated prison. The planned two week experiment was abandoned after six days as 'guards' began to engage in sadistic and abusive behaviours toward their 'prisoners.' Whilst much may have been learned about the tendency of roles to influence behavioural norms, the experiment clearly caused harm (in the form of severe stress reactions) amongst the participants. Ethical approval today typically covers harm prevention as well as informed consent, the avoidance of deception, participants' rights to privacy, fraud and academic misconduct, such as plagiarism. Issues of academic integrity are a source of major concern for both students and universities. Your institution will offer detailed guidance on what is viewed as inappropriate practice and many institutions will routinely pass dissertation submissions through software such as Turnitin to check whether unattributed content is being reproduced.

In the remainder of this chapter the principles of ethical research will be discussed in turn. It should be noted as well how such principles link in with the next section that looks at ethics in real life business management research.

■ Harm to participants

Put simply, to conduct research that causes harm to participants is unethical. Harm in business management research could be physical, but far more likely to take on a less obvious form. The most common potential for harm in business management research is of a psychological nature, such as threats to self-esteem, stress or feeling guilty (Bryman, 2008). Preventing harm, however, can involve common strategies, such as assurances of anonymity at all stage of the research process. This could include the ongoing use of pseudonyms in field notes, transcripts and the final presentation of findings in the dissertation. In some cases it may not always be possible to know in advance whether harm is likely to happen. Strategies here could involve piloting interview or focus group questions and looking for signs of harm by debriefing research participants. The following sub-section further contemplates how harm can be avoided in business management research.

■   Informed consent

A second key principle that can ensure the well-being of research participants is *"informed consent"*. Gaining informed consent for your study can go a long way to preventing harm coming to your research participants. This principle concerns providing prospective research participants with sufficient information for them to decide whether to take part or not in your study. Sometimes it may not be possible or even desirable to provide prospective participants with full or partial information before a study commences, but we shall return to such points later in the current section, and cover them further in the following section.

Box 11.2: Sample information sheet

Thank you for showing interest in taking part in my dissertation. The information below provides details of what my study is about and your potential role in my study.

The aim of my project/dissertation is to [provide concise and jargon free details of your study].

Participation in my study involves [include details of what this involves plus an estimation of the time required of the participant].

The benefits of taking part in my study include [provide a range of benefits that relate to both you and the participant]. The study, however, comes with minor risks [if applicable, state what these may be for the participant].

Information provided by you will only be used for my university project/dissertation. The information you provide will be kept secure [provide details] and the information will not be used in a manner that will reveal your identity [where there is a possibility of partial identification you should detail what this may involve]. Only my project/dissertation supervisor and I will have access to such information in its original format. All such information will be destroyed one year after the completion of my dissertation.

Participation in this dissertation is completely voluntary and you have the right to withdraw at any time without any prejudice or negative consequences.

This study has been approved by [insert details of research ethics committee at your institution].

If you have any questions or queries about my study please contact me through the details below.

[Name, telephone/email address]

11

In most instances the advance provision of information about the study, including things such as what your study is about, what involvement looks like, what the risks of taking part involve, and the details of a right to withdraw from the study at any time, is sufficient (see Box 11.2) to gain informed consent from prospective research participants. However, there will be instances, particularly involving research that covers known sensitive topics or vulnerable individuals, where it would be good practice to clearly demonstrate that the prospective research participant fully understands what they are committing themselves to by taking part in your research project. In such situations a consent form could be used (see Box 11.3).

Box 11.3: Sample consent form

Title of project/dissertation: [insert the title of project/dissertation here]

I have been informed of and understand the purposes of the study.

I have been given an opportunity to ask questions about the study.

I understand that I can withdraw from the study at any time without prejudice or negative consequences.

Any information which might potentially identify me will not be used in the final report/dissertation.

I agree to participate in the study outlined to me.

Name of participant:

Signature of participant:

Date:

■ Deception

Deception in relation to business management research can take a range of forms and may be an option for a variety of reasons. First, deception can be an option for the business management researcher in situations where full or even partial awareness of the true nature of the study could distort the occurrence of natural reactions. For example, it would be reasonable to argue that a lot could be learned from observing the behaviour of consumers who are not aware they are participating in a research project. A degree of deception could be an option for the business management researcher wishing to provoke or observe responses that may be hampered by the full and prior disclosure of details of the study. A further example of where a lack of information may be permissible concerns when it may be impractical to inform all research participants taking part in a study. This could be a reality when undertaking an ethnographic study of an organisation, which may involve observing and having informal, unplanned conversations with many employees. However, even if such practices can be defended, there remains the possibility that such practices could lead to business managers acquiring a reputation as 'snoopers.' Further, it is evident that drawing a line between what is acceptable and what is not acceptable remains problematic (Bryman, 2008). However, it should be noted that deception in relation to research must be fully thought through, should not be seen as a first or easy option, and will need to be fully justified when ethical approval is sought for your research (see section on research ethics approval process).

Participants' right to privacy

A fourth ethical principle largely surrounds the notion of privacy. This ethical principle concerns how far the researcher can ensure participants' right to the privacy, as well as similar concerns, such as, confidentiality, safety and anonymity of participants. This principle is strongly linked to the ethical principles previously discussed, including harm and informed consent. Indeed, it could also be said that deceptive research methods are clear examples of where the privacy of research participants could be violated (Bryman, 2008), although such a problem could be overcome to a point if all possible steps are taken to protect the true identity of the participants (Haggerty, 2004). That said, even practices associated with attaining informed consent do not act as an absolute guarantee of participant privacy. For instance, informed consent does not mean that in a research situation, such as an interview, that the research participant will always feel comfortable avoiding or refusing to provide answers to sensitive questions. This may also occur in focus groups, where researchers may not be able to control situations involving peer pressure, leading to the potential for participants to reveal private or compromising details that may not have been shared during interviews or questionnaires.

11

Exercise 11.2

Using the examples in boxes 11.2 and 11.3, design an information sheet and consent form for your prospective study. Evaluate your work by sharing your ideas with fellow students.

Ethics in real life business management research

The importance of research ethics, as well as key research ethics principles, have already been discussed in this chapter, yet it is likely that many business management students, having limited or no experience of conducting a major piece of primary research, will find it difficult to imagine applying research ethics principles to actual research ideas and practice. In this section, the key aim is to take you through real life examples of business management research, where important ethical principles are central to research design and eventual fieldwork. It may help to source the original journal articles under discussion as an accompaniment to this section.

■   Ethics in business management practice research

The first case is a study of what looks to be at first a rather innocuous business management practice: introducing open plan offices. A summary of the study is detailed in Box 11.4.

Box 11.4: Researching business management practices

The focus of the research conducted by Baldry and Barnes (2012) is a common trend and feature of business management practice, that of an increased introduction of open plan offices to the workplace. In many situations this may attract little if any consternation from relevant parties, yet would this be the case in situations where the employees expected to work in open plan offices traditionally had very different office arrangements? How would such employees look upon those changes, especially if they were given little if no say on changing work space arrangements that affected them? The researchers, as such, expected to find the practice of introducing open plan offices in the context of the planned study, that of academics working in higher education, to be a sensitive topic for all concerned.

Baldry, C. and Barnes, A. (2012) The open-plan academy: space, control and the undermining of professional identity, *Work, Employment & Society*, **26**(2), 228-245.

In this situation the researchers in question faced a major dilemma – whether or not to seek access to research participants through their employers. A key feature of the dilemma concerned the high probability that the organisations implementing new office space arrangements were unlikely to provide unrestricted and unconditional access to their academic employees. Furthermore, even if the organisations did grant full access to their academic employees, then there was the possibility of causing harm to research participants who voice deeply critical views concerning new working space arrangements. In other words, the researchers believed academic employees could be victimised or even face disciplinary action for taking part in a study that would allow them to be openly outspoken about new office space arrangements. The researchers decided that the best approach was not to involve representatives of the organisations implementing such practices in the process of recruiting research participants to the study.

What actually happened was the researchers covertly recruited research participants (academics affected by changing work spaces) through informal networks and interviewed 18 university employees on personal aspects of the introduction of open plan offices. The researchers were aware that covert research or a lack of informed consent is broadly frowned upon in academic circles, yet also aware that covert research could be justified in exceptional circumstances. The researchers, however, also needed to consider ways of protecting their prospective research participants from potential harm. In order to prevent possible harm to research participants the researchers adopted pseudonyms for individuals and organisations throughout their research paper.

The journal paper that emerged from the research in question was evidently limited by the covert approach. Even after the publication of the paper in a top ranking journal, it is also reasonable to suggest that there is unlikely to be a consensus on whether the researchers were right to adopt the covert approach in the first place. However, it could be said that the study sheds new and important light on a growing business management practice and at the same time no apparent harm came to the research participants.

■ Ethics in employment and Internet research

In the second case we see an example of what was then a very new and emergent trend in business and human resource management. Summarised details of the research in question can be found in Box 11.5.

11

Box 11.5: Researching employee use of the Internet

The focus of the research conducted by Richards (2008) concerned what was then a new Internet phenomenon – employees blogging about the jobs that they do. The first reports of employee blogging, typically provided by the popular media and trade journals, tended to portray such activities in a negative light – activities of this kind could, for example, damage the reputation of the employer. Many other accounts of the time reported employees being disciplined for revealing details of their employment on new social media platforms. The researcher believed existing accounts over-emphasised employer views at the expense of employee/blogger views of this new Internet phenomenon.

Richards, J. (2008) 'Because I need somewhere to vent': the expression of conflict through work blogs, *New Technology, Work and Employment*, **23**(1-2), 95-109.

It was evident that the researcher expected employee views to contrast to a larger or greater extent from the views expressed by the popular media and trade journals on this new Internet phenomenon. As such, the researcher believed an efficient manner in which to canvass those views was to recruit a good sample and spread of employees/bloggers and request participating employees/bloggers to complete a self-reporting e-questionnaire designed to draw out the variety of reasons to blog about jobs and employers. The researcher also believed any such findings would be strengthened by the gathering of blog posts to further demonstrate the variety of reasons to blog about employment.

While it was crucial to consider an efficient manner to gather information on the blogging habits of employees, it quickly came apparent that a range of ethical dilemmas would need to be addressed before commencing such a study. For instance, how could the researcher enlist the trust of would be participants when there was no easy or straightforward way in which to establish the credentials and impartiality of the researcher? What if prospective research participants were suspicious of attempts to contact them, interpreting outsider attempts to contact them as the entrapment tactics of employers or the popular media? A second ethical dilemma concerned protecting the privacy of blogging communities, in that while these activities were potentially accessible to hundreds of millions of Internet users, very few users knew of their existence. In other words, it was possible that attempts to contact many hundreds of bloggers would be overly intrusive and potentially cause irreparable harm to a thriving, yet hidden range of interlinked Internet communities. A third ethical dilemma identified by the researcher considered the ethics of both using and interpreting blog extracts.

To overcome these ethical dilemmas the researcher did the following. First, the researcher set up a blog/database linking to many hundreds of employee blogs, including information to confirm the researcher's credentials on the blog, as well as regularly updating the blog with articles and views on such blogs. Collectively, this allowed the researcher to build up an insider and trusted status among prospective research participants. Prospective participants were recruited individually – typically via a short message on the participant's blog —with the immediate option to visit the researcher's blog to verify that this was a bona fide academic study. Finally, in order to ensure an accurate interpretation of blog postings, bloggers were contacted concerning permission to use blog extracts and at the same time requested to provide examples based on key themes emerging from preliminary analysis of the survey data.

The journal paper that emerged from the research in question effectively demonstrated that employee blogs were indeed a multi-faceted phenomenon. The paper, however, made a further contribution to knowledge and research practice as it demonstrated how it was possible to conduct effective and ethical research in emergent and hard to access settings.

Exercise 11.3

Download the paper detailed below from your university library website and complete the following tasks. Summarise what the article is about. What are the key research dilemmas of this study? How was the research dilemmas addressed in the study? Do you feel that the research dilemmas are adequately resolved in this research?

Langer, R. and Beckman, S. (2005) Sensitive research topics: netnography revisited, *Qualitative Market Research: An International Journal*, **8**(2), 189 - 203.

11

The research ethics approval process

The previous section looked at the realities of ethics in business management research. We now consider how to go about gaining ethical approval for your dissertation. This section is designed to inform you of what to expect in terms of acquiring ethical approval for your research and why it is important to give this aspect of your dissertation careful consideration.

Universities are likely to insist on students delaying fieldwork until ethical approval has been granted. Some universities may even insist on ethical approval being granted as a part of a dissertation proposal, which may be several months before the dissertation actually officially begins. Students are typically informed of such arrangements, but it is up to you to make sure you understand and comply with these arrangements. Failure to comply with ethical procedures is typically treated as an academic offence – similar to cheating in an examination or plagiarising coursework, so do not take the ethical approval process lightly, especially as there is more to be gained from the approval process than complying with university rules and regulations.

A key issue with regard to the approval process is anticipating how your application for ethical approval will be viewed by the reviewing individual or committee. By reading this chapter, as well as guiding information provided by your university, you should be aware of the ethical dilemmas associated with your planned research and therefore set aside sufficient time to make a strong ethical approval application.

The approval process, however, may vary somewhat from university to university, so what is provided here is an attempt to at least broadly prepare you for the ethical approval process for your study. In most cases you will be expected to fill in a standard form (see Box 11.6), with the information you are expected to provide varying in terms of detail, nature and amount of information. You may be expected to download a template of the approval form and submit a copy manually, yet some universities have an entirely electronic submission process.

The form is likely to be made up of several sections. The first section will typically involve basic details, such as your name, project/dissertation title and name of your project supervisor. It is unlikely that you will need to provide a final version of the title to your project, but you should aim to provide a title that adequately summarises what you plan to do. In the second section of a typical research ethics approval process, it is probable that you will need to provide important details of your study, such as aims and objectives, your planned methodology, as well as details of prospective research participants. It is important to provide a good level of detail as without sufficient detail your application may well be rejected or returned to you at this point. A third and final section of research ethics approval forms tends to focus on typical research ethics dilemmas and often there is an opportunity to explain why, for example, all participants in your research may not be or only partially informed of what your study is about. If you plan to involve participants who are widely considered to be vulnerable, such as children, then this is the place to set out the particular steps you will take to make sure no one is harmed in the process of your research.

Box 11.6: Example research ethics approval form

Section A: Dissertation details, researcher and supervisor

Dissertation title:

Name of student:

Student registration number:

Dissertation supervisor:

Section B: Project/dissertation summary

Dissertation aims and objectives:

Methodological details:

Details of research participants:

Section C: Ethical considerations (provide further details where necessary)

Will the study involve vulnerable groups, e.g. children, disabled people, ethnic minorities, the elderly?

Will participants be informed of the aims of your study?

Will participants be informed of their rights?

Will participants be informed of their expected contribution?

Will participants be debriefed (if applicable)?

Will participants be exposed to any stressful or unpleasant situations?

Will participants be paid to take part in your study?

Will the collection of information from research participants potentially compromise the interests of the research participant?

Are there any potential negative outcomes to the study, e.g. harm to you or the research participant, criminal proceedings or civil liability?

Are there any other ethical issues that have potential implications for your study?

11

There could be a range of outcomes to the research ethics approval process. Probable outcomes include the following: pass and proceed, re-work and re-submit, rejection on the grounds of having serious and insurmountable ethical implications, and rejection on the grounds of a poorly presented and detailed application.

Exercise 11.4

Find out about the relevant research ethical approval at your university. Prepare a draft application based on this information.

Checklist questions for an ethical study

In the preparation for a dissertation involving research participants you should consider answering the following questions.

1   Have you consulted the research ethics guidance provided by any professional organisation you belong to or are seeking to join in the near future?

2   Do you understand what is expected of you in terms of gaining ethical approval where you are studying?

3   Have you identified both obvious and potential ethical dilemmas associated with your planned research?

4   Have you developed a plan to navigate both obvious and potential ethical dilemmas associated with your planned research?

5   How do you intend to get informed consent from your research participants?

6   If full informed consent is not possible or problematic, how do you intend to negotiate such a dilemma?

7   Do you need to gain clear evidence of consent from participants in your study?

8   Are you confident you can fully protect the privacy of your participants?

9   How do you plan to protect and keep your data safe?

10 What do you plan to do in terms of anonymising your data?

11 What measures do you plan to put in place if your study involves vulnerable research participants?

12 What plans will you put in place if participants wish to seek more information about your study or make a complaint?

References

British Academy of Management (2013) *The British Academy of Management's Code of Ethics and Best Practice.* www.bam.ac.uk

Bryman, A. (2008), *Social Research Methods*, 3rd edition, Oxford: Oxford University Press.

Haggerty, K. (2004), Ethics creep: governing social science research in the name of ethics, *Qualitative Sociology*, **27**(4) 391-414.

Further reading

The following literature provides both a wide and deep understanding of research ethics.

Farrimond, H. (2013) *Doing Ethical Research*, Basingstoke: Palgrave Macmillan.

Israel, M., & Hay, I. (2006) *Research Ethics for Social Scientists*. London: Sage.

Oliver, P. (2010) *The Student's Guide to Research Ethics*, Maidenhead: OUP.

These are more specialised and provide example of literature specifically related to business management research and dissertations, as well as key research ethics themes, such as, harm, consent, deception, vulnerability, and Internet phenomena.

Altinay, l. and Wang, C. (2009) Facilitating and maintaining research access into ethnic minority firms, *Qualitative Market Research: An International Journal*, **12**(4), 367 - 390.

Bell, E. and Bryman, A. (2007) The ethics of management research: an exploratory content analysis, *British Journal of Management*, **18**, 63–77.

Berry, D. (2004) Internet research: privacy, ethics and alienation: an open source approach, *Internet Research*, **14**(4), 323 - 332.

Downey, H., Hamilton, K. and Catterall, M. (2007) Researching vulnerability: what about the researcher?, *European Journal of Marketing*, **4**(7/8) 734-739.

Hair, N. and Clark, M. (2007) The ethical dilemmas and challenges of ethnographic research in electronic communities, *International Journal of Market Research*, **49**(6), 781-800.

Polonsky, M. (1998) Incorporating ethics into business students' research projects: a process approach, *Journal of Business Ethics*, **17**, 1227–1241,

Taras, D. & Steel, P. (2007) We provoked business students to unionize: using deception to prove an IR point, *British Journal of Industrial Relations*, **45**, 179–198.

11

12 Writing Up Your Research Project

Robert MacIntosh, Thomas Farrington and John Sanders

For many people, their dissertation represents the largest piece of written work they will have had to produce to date. Writing tens of thousands of words is a qualitatively different problem than writing shorter essay or assignment style pieces. With scale comes the challenge of making sure that the document as a whole flows, is clearly structured and reads like a single integrated piece. In reality, you will find yourself writing different sections at different times, sometimes months apart. It is not uncommon for these different sections to vary slightly in focus, structure or tone and this can mean that the final project reads as somewhat disjointed. The problem is that both projects and writing styles differ, so there is no single recipe for success. The research topic, methods, supervisors and your own way of working are all key aspects of developing a high quality document that will be assessed against the kinds of criteria set out in Appendix 2.

The purpose of this chapter is to highlight a few key points about the process of writing up your research project, as distinct from the process of doing the research itself, and offer some advice on writing effectively. Though obviously interrelated, it is worth teasing these two tasks apart since it can make the whole process more productive. The chapter begins with a look at mapping out your writing, before offering suggestions on how to find your focus and maintain it. The chapter then looks at overcoming writer's block, rewriting and editing, and the use of technology. This is followed by a series of writing tips, before the chapter concludes with some practical advice on the relationship between you and your supervisor.

Getting started

At some point, you'll find yourself facing a blank page. More accurately, it will likely be a blank screen since almost everyone writes via a keyboard, screen and word processor today. Finding a way to get started is often the first challenge. You may have had to put a research proposal together before starting the dissertation proper. If so, then you'll have an outline structure from which to work. A sensible first step is to create a contents page, which sets out those aspects of a research project that are commonly recognised such as an abstract, introduction, literature review, etc. Appendix 3 sets out some examples of typical project structures and includes details of indicative word count for each section. Whilst not cast in stone, these are a helpful guide and can offer you a way of gauging progress. Many students begin with the anxiety that they cannot imagine finding enough to write about. In practice, the reverse is often true, and finding a way to compress your project is more of a problem than the lack of words available.

Take each of the chapter headings from your contents page and break them down into subsections. For example, the methods chapter might open with an overview of the nature of knowledge claims, before moving on to the range of possible choices that you considered for your own research project. A justification for the methods that you have chosen might follow, then a detailed account of how you will operationalize these methods in the research. Chapter 4 would offer a clear structure for such a chapter and you would be able to make a rough estimate of how many words each theme or subsection might require. The order and titles of these sections and subsections are likely to change as your project progresses, yet producing this map of your dissertation will allow you to see where you are headed, and what you need to do to get there. Writing the content is a slightly more involved undertaking, and the following observations and exercises are designed to simplify that process, and encourage you to write regularly.

Writing as thinking

12

> *With the door shut, downloading what's in my head directly to the page, I write as fast as I can . . . If I write rapidly [then] I find that I can keep up with my original enthusiasm and outrun the self-doubt that's always waiting to settle in.*
>
> *Stephen King (2002, p. 210)*

The language we use when we talk about our interests and goals is typically much less formal than that which we use when writing the same things down, yet informal writing can actually be a very helpful way of thinking through ideas. When there's nobody else there to listen or read, use the blank page to communicate with yourself. Using the first person, write down what it is you want to look at, what you want to find out, and what you want to say. Try to write for a few minutes without thinking about the rules of language, or deleting or editing anything. Ignore your internal critic, and allow yourself to write freely. You can use as many or as few words as you like, and if you get stuck then you can just start a new line. The aim of this exercise is to relax, make a record of your ideas, and work your way up to writing formally for an audience. Rowena Murray (2006, p. 89) notes that this 'freewriting' technique can help writers "work out their relationship to knowledge [and] help us test how much we have actually understood." Over time, you may find this practice of 'writing as thinking' offers a quick way of bringing your aims into focus and kick-starting your writing sessions.

Murray (2006, p. 104) offers the following seven prompts, which can help refine your thoughts into more formal language. By completing these sentences, you will develop a set of statements to keep you focussed as you write your dissertation. You will likely revise and clarify these statements several times throughout the duration of your project, so don't feel you have to get this right first time.

- My research question is . . . (50 words)
- Researchers who have looked at this subject are . . . (50 words)
- They argue that . . . (25 words) Smith argues that . . . (25 words) Brown argues that . . . (25 words)
- Debate centres on the issue of . . . (25 words)
- There is still work to be done on . . . (25 words)
- My research is closest to that of X in that . . . (50 words)
- My contribution will be . . . (50 words)

Although you will probably find it helpful to return to these exercises as you progress through your dissertation, it is important to remember that these are designed to stimulate your writing sessions, and should not be seen as a substitute for regular, formal written work. The key to completing a dissertation on time and to the best of your ability is getting into the habit of writing every day.

Making writing a habit

You might not write well every day, but you can always edit a bad page. You can't edit a blank page.

Jodi Picoult (Charney, 2012).

By the time you come to write a dissertation, you will have been writing since childhood and will have accumulated years of experience of what works best for you. We each typically have habits and contexts which enable us to write. It may be that the library, your home or a coffee shop is your venue of choice. Most people who write professionally, e.g. novelists, journalists, playwrights, have an established writing routine.

Children's author Roald Dahl went to his 'writing hut' at the bottom of his garden and wrote for two hours in the morning, broke for lunch and wrote for another two hours in the afternoon. The ritual and routine of space and time can be an important enabler for writing. Some manage to write quickly. Others write painfully slowly. J. K. Rowling writes whenever and wherever the inspiration takes her, the names of the Harry Potter characters first drafted on an air sickness bag. Graham Greene would write meticulously neatly without crossing out anything, and in neat, square handwriting. His editor described this process as producing handwriting so tiny and cramped that it looked like an attempt to write on the head of a pin. Greene would write five hundred words exactly in a day and would stop for the day when he reached this target, even if he were in mid-sentence. Ernest Hemingway and Vladimir Nabokov wrote standing up, while Truman Capote wrote lying down. There is no way to tell what works for you. Try to find the best time of day for you and stick to it where possible. It is important to schedule time for writing. You should also try to calculate how quickly you write and use this as a guide when working out how long it will take to complete individual chapters and the project as a whole.

Of course, today's technology allows us to write in a number of different ways. You can dictate, type or hand-write. You can write almost anywhere and at any time. One common experience when tackling an extended piece of writing like a dissertation for the first time is that ideas will strike you at the most unexpected of times. You may be in the midst of something completely unrelated when you realise that you need to connect some point from the literature review to some detailed point in your analysis. It is important to capture these moments and you may find yourself making

12

notes, recording voice memos or using some other technique to capture your thoughts on the move.

Although it may seem peculiar at first, scheduling clear and manageable tasks every day will soon become as normal as checking your email. Speaking of checking your email, one tactic employed by many writers is to make writing their first task of the day, and to see any online social interactions as rewards for successfully completing their writing task. Unless there is a good reason for making contact with the outside world, you are eating into what may be the most productive hour of your day. Nathan Englander (Charney, 2013a) gives the following advice:

> *Turn off your cell phone. Honestly, if you want to get work done, you've got to learn to unplug. No texting, no email, no Facebook, no Instagram. Whatever it is you're doing, it needs to stop while you write.*

At first, the time you spend away from social networks may only be 15-30 minutes each day, and this will probably feel like much longer. Although this will quickly become easier, and the length of time will naturally increase, you should maintain 15-30 minutes of writing time as a daily minimum. Once you are in the habit of writing, a common mistake is to try to block out whole days of writing time. In practice this rarely works as planned, and it may be more realistic to set yourself a more modest task, e.g. write 300-500 words on the justification of your research techniques in a two hour window. By adopting this approach you are effectively taking one very large document and breaking it down into a series of smaller writing tasks. Not only does this make it less intimidating to write, it also makes it easier to schedule, since you can allocate shorter periods of time during which you will write shorter pieces of text.

Give yourself small rewards for sticking to your daily writing schedule (e.g. food, exercise, entertainment), take regular breaks, and don't write to the point of exhaustion. Hemingway (Plimpton, 1958) suggests that you "write until you come to a place where you still have your juice and know what will happen next". As such, a successful writing session is not necessarily one in which the tasks were completed to the highest standards, or even entirely completed. James Joyce saw the composition of three sentences as a good day's work. While Joyce's satisfaction is perhaps characteristically unusual, Karen Russell (Charney, 2013b) nonetheless notes that:

> *You need to give yourself permission to write badly, just to get something down . . . if you can make peace with the fact that you will likely have to throw*

out ninety percent of your first draft, then you can relax and even almost enjoy 'writing badly.'

Hopefully you will manage to retain more than ten percent of your writing from each session, but the general acceptance of one's writerly imperfections is a crucial stage of your academic development, and points to perhaps the most important principle of writing: **write first and edit second**. When you allow that internal critic to stop you from writing, you are interrupting the flow of thoughts both onto the page and within your head. It may well be that what you write is too simplistic or unclear, but getting these thoughts out as a first draft could lead you to conceive new ideas or forge unforeseen links between parts of your research. Rowling notes that in this respect writing is "like learning an instrument, you've got to be prepared for hitting wrong notes occasionally . . . or quite a lot."

Of course, it will not be long before you are sending your work to your supervisor for feedback. Although it may be tempting to ruthlessly cut any and all sentences that you do not consider to be suitably developed or relevant, there remains the possibility of your supervisor noticing something useful within these less certain notions. As such, you and your supervisor might like to agree upon a system that indicates your more tentative sentences and thoughts. For example, you could highlight in yellow those parts that you are unsure about, and highlight in red those parts that you really don't like. This extra level of communication about your writing will prevent you from losing potentially valuable ideas, whilst allowing you to show your supervisor that you are able to be self-critical.

For Russell (Charney, 2013b), the true measure of a good writing session is therefore a positive answer to the following question:

> *Was I able to stay put and commit to putting words down on the page, without deciding mid-sentence that it's more important to check my email, or 'research' some question online, or clean out the science fair projects in the back of my freezer?*

Writing is as much about discipline and practice as running a marathon or learning to bake a soufflé, both of which make fine extracurricular rewards. Just as one wouldn't succeed in either of these without first conducting considerable research, one cannot expect to perfect academic writing without first taking the time to read the writing of others.

Of course, when writing, you expose your underlying thought process and assumptions to critical review. We often make assertions, generalisa-

12

tions and (perhaps dubious) connections in speaking, but writing is an altogether more disciplined genre. As such, it is important to think carefully about the extent to which your research sets up something of a self-fulfilling prophecy. In the context of research, a self-fulfilling prophecy is when the researcher begins with a particular idea of what they want their research to prove, and steers or interprets various aspects of the process towards achieving those results. This is most visible in advertising campaigns for health and beauty products, where the aim of research is to produce a figure that reflects favourably upon the product. You might see the claim that 72% of consumers saw a reduction in wrinkles by using a particular face cream. Yet the researchers can fairly easily lead the majority of a group towards the opinion that a product (which is presumably free to the testers, who are likely to be paid for their time) is working for them. They might ask leading questions (see Chapter 7) or simply run several test groups at the same time and choose the most favourable results.

The temptation of money provides an easy example of how research may be biased, but there are less tangible influences that may have similarly distorting effects. For example, you may feel very passionately about the topic at hand and this may lead you to inadvertently create a sense of researcher bias. In can be very difficult to remain emotionally removed from topics that touch on issues such as consumer rights or inequality, but research that is biased can only stall future progress in your chosen area. Think carefully about the extent to which you have created leading questions or assumptions in either your data gathering process or your analytical process. Have you adequately considered alternate explanations of the same phenomena? Have you reflexively acknowledged your own biases and opinions in the construction of your argument? It is not uncommon for these kinds of critical comments to become clear either when you ask a peer or your supervisor to review early drafts, or simply because you take a little time away from the research project and return with a more dispassionate perspective.

Reading as writing

> *The real importance of reading is that it creates an ease and intimacy with the process of writing . . . It also offers you a constantly growing knowledge of what has been done and what hasn't, what is trite and what is fresh, what works and what just lies there dying (or dead) on the page.*
>
> *Stephen King (2002, p. 145)*

At times, completing a review of the relevant literature may seem like a fairly mechanical task, particularly if you are diligent in the good practice of writing short summaries of robust articles and chapters as you find them. Yet the act of reading these pieces is also one of educating yourself about how to write to the highest academic standards. As you engage critically with the argument or approach of a publication, you should try to also engage with the language used to convey the points, and move between them. While you must never duplicate another person's work and present it as your own, the best way to get a working idea of academic writing conventions in your field is by reading highly regarded scholarship. You will notice certain words and phrases are frequently used by various authors in order to guide the reader through the structure of the piece. Take a note of the most commonly used examples and try using them at similar points in your own work.

At the same time as reading good writing motivates you to write well, discovering the scholarly positions and findings of other writers in your field will allow you to more clearly define your own critical voice. As such, you should note down your thoughts and any questions you think of as you read. As you may note above, several of Murray's (2006) seven writing prompts stem from your responses to the work of others. Reading and understanding the relevant literature will prevent you from spending time writing about that which has already been said, so making your writing sessions more efficient. Scheduled reading time is therefore crucial to the improvement of your writing. Stepping away from your dissertation to read is also one every effective way of tackling the dreaded writer's block, to which we now turn.

Writer's block

There is some disagreement about what exactly causes writer's block, but it's an experience that most writers experience or at least appreciate. This is something worth bearing in mind: everybody has to write several drafts before they get to the finished article. Murray (2006, p. 169) gives a number of reasons for experiencing writer's block:

- They think they must work out what they think – and what they want to say – before they can write . . . and get stuck at that point . . .

    . . . instead of using writing to sort out what they want to say.

12

- They struggle to work a point out logically, or scientifically or objectively . . . and get stuck at that point . . .

   . . . instead of working it out in words.

- They want to be sure before they write . . .

   . . . instead of writing when they are not sure.

- There is no end to the project in sight.

Thankfully, writer's block is a temporary and solvable problem, and by this point in the chapter you are already equipped with many of the tools to help you move past it. If you have tried all of the above and are still feeling unable to write about your dissertation topic, then simply try writing about anything that comes to mind. You might find it useful to write about why you feel unable to write, but even writing about what you had for breakfast and why will at least get some words on the page. Spend five minutes on this, and then try some freewriting around your research questions, before returning to the scheduled tasks. Remember to keep your aims clear, realistic, and flexible: you don't have to finish an entire section before moving on to another part of your dissertation. Keep a list of less immersive writing tasks to carry out when you are feeling at your least creative, such as checking and adding missing references, writing transitional or linking sentences, or ensuring the contribution of each section to your overall argument is clear throughout. If you are able to reschedule your writing for a little later, then you may find that ten minutes of exercise helps to clear the mind. Haruki Murakami (2008) famously runs or swims every day, finding the routine of writing and exercise a crucial regulator of his productivity levels. Of course, you may have no inclination to run or swim, but even a short trip to the shops may deliver the change needed to get you writing; just make sure you do get writing!

General tips for better writing

- **Tell the reader what you are going to do and do it**. Write a paragraph that briefly guides the reader through what they are about to read. The body of the essay then follows this structural map. You will probably revise this paragraph, and the structure, several times.

- **Make your argument obvious**. As well as providing a paragraph explaining what you are going to do, explain to the reader the way in which the information presented and how each point made contributes to your overall argument.

- **Be clear with language**, define new terms when you introduce them then stick to these terms. Avoid minor variations that will confuse both you and the reader.

- **Stay on topic**. It's easy to drift off on a tangent when the ideas are flowing, and could be useful during the writing process, but be ruthless when it comes to editing. Save your cuttings though, as you might be able to use the less relevant ideas elsewhere.

- **Transitional or linking sentences are crucial.** They often serve a dual function in both linking one section to the next, and signposting why this transition contributes to your argument.

- **Write literally and be concise**. Avoid metaphors, appeals to common sense, sayings and stock phrases.

- **Read your work aloud.** This will help to show you where punctuation has been over or underused.

- **Take regular breaks.** Some suggest a break from writing every forty-five minutes, and the whole point of setting the daily writing tasks and targets above is to avoid the seriously harmful effects of a forty-eight hour break-free writing session towards the deadline.

- **Always be critical, but never be insulting.** In finding your own critical voice, you are likely to disagree with the work of other scholars. Be professional about this, and avoid value-laden terms that denigrate the work of others. Remember, if it wasn't for their work then you'd have nothing to disagree with.

- **Your conclusion must provide your answer to the research question**, by summarising your approach, findings, and discussion. Don't bring in any new material at this stage. If you find you wish to bring in some new theory here, then you must find a place to introduce this much earlier in the piece.

- **When proof-reading** a draft, do something to **distance yourself from your work**. This might be to print it out in a different font, or in booklet form. This will give you a fresh perspective on your work, closer to that of an outside reader.

12

- **Most importantly: write first and edit second!** If you can write three to five hundred words every day then you will feel like you have mastered the art of writing. Don't let your editorial voice steal the spotlight!

(re)Writing skills and sub-editing

Easy reading is damn hard writing. But if it's right, it's easy. It's the other way round, too. If it's slovenly written, then it's hard to read. It doesn't give the reader what the careful writer can give the reader.

Maya Angelou (Charney, 2013c)

It is worth noting that academic writing is quite different to other kinds of writing. The relationship between writing and academic writing is akin to the relationship between writing a novel and writing a legal document. The former is aimed at a general audience whilst the latter is aimed at a specific and targeted audience familiar with jargon, linguistic conventions, etc. One of the key differences is the need to cite the work of others when reviewing concepts, theory and literature. This tendency to "write with brackets" is one of the most obvious signs that you are reading an academic document. From earlier assignments you'll have learned to use citations to demonstrate that you are familiar with the work of relevant scholars. You'll need to master the Harvard style or some similar citation protocol and it is worth checking the style specified for your dissertation. But that is just the basic grammar. Beyond this, you need to learn to summarise and critique other people's work and to write with an appropriate **citation density**. If you're not sure, then pick up any peer-reviewed article from a management or organizational journal, squint your eyes such that the text is almost out of focus (or if you're of a certain age, just taking your glasses off achieves the same effect) then look at the pattern of the text. The ratio of words to (citations, 1993) is critically important. Most good scholars have mastered the art of summarising the literature by using citations. They don't under cite with only one or two citations appearing sporadically. Equally, they don't over cite where every statement or claim is supported by dozens of citations. Instead, writing with the appropriate citation density is one of the things that marks out a well-researched dissertation. You should also avoid citing the same text book repeatedly, since this indicates a lack of background reading and a relatively poor grasp of the literature.

Bear in mind who will read your eventual dissertation. It would be safe to assume that the academics reading your dissertation are familiar with the process of reading research papers. It is unlikely that they are reading about the concepts or theories that you are using for the first time. Rather, assume that they are familiar with most of the literature that you've reviewed. To take one simple example, when you say that Mintzberg's (1973) views on strategy downplay the extent to which key strategic actors can exert control or predict the consequences of their actions, you are assuming that the reader will have read and remembered the contents of *The Nature of Managerial Work* by Henry Mintzberg. If you want to make a more specific point, use a direct quotation.

Typically, textbooks assume that you are starting from scratch in an area of theory. Academic articles or literature reviews assume that you've read the original citation and that the author of the article is trying to help lead the reader through a particular take on the literature, or to synthesis it, or to develop a critique. As a result, most of the words available to the author are used to develop an argument, not to re-tell what someone else said. Therefore, good academic articles tend to appear impenetrable to novice readers because they aren't designed with that audience in mind. Gradually, as you spend time getting to know your own field of study, you'll become familiar with this shorthand style of citation writing. You should then find yourself better able to emulate it, but bear in mind that the marking process also has realistic expectations. Scholars publishing in top-tier journals have typically spent many years studying, reading, writing and publishing research in their chosen field. The vast majority of people preparing a dissertation have not yet spent the same amount of time and you are not expected to attain such standards in your first piece of extended, research-based writing.

Returning to the theme of writing practice, it is also worth considering the relationship between the processes of writing, reading, rewriting and editing. The award winning novelist and screen-writer John Irving claims that he is a modestly talented writer but a dedicated editor of his own work. In his own words he says "I began to make progress as a writer once I began to take my own lack of talent seriously". Our strong advice would be to factor the process of (re)writing into your project plan. Many people find it helpful to write through a series of progressively more refined stages from rough notes and bullet points, to a rough draft supplemented by useful quotes from the literature, to a finished draft, to a final draft. Often the final drafting stage is helped enormously by stepping away from the original text

12

for a short period. Zadie Smith suggests that whenever possible you "leave a decent space of time between writing something and editing it." When the text has just been completed we are often blind to everything from small typos to major sequencing or content errors. Yet a few days later we are able to read our own text afresh and spot these flaws. In many of the weakest dissertations, the first person to read the assembled dissertation is the person who will mark it. Your project plan should allow time for revising your own text either on the basis of comments from your supervisor, or simply on the basis of your own proof-reading.

Finally, academic writing relies on a strong narrative thread just as any other form of writing does. Where a novelist may look for a story arc, a hook or an interesting situation, an academic writer looks for a strong research question to orient the reader. Ideally, research questions make it obvious why the research is being conducted and in what way the project will generate useful insights. Often a dissertation will run to thousands of words but the underpinning logic of the dissertation is embedded in a few sentences in and around the research question(s). It is therefore worth spending a disproportionate amount of time on producing a clear, concise and compelling research question. Relating each significant point back to this question will keep the reader engaged with and aware of the overall narrative.

Software issues

In the last ten years or so, it has become more commonplace to use software to structure the large amounts of information from articles, interviews, etc. Some people find 'mind-mapping' tools useful, others cannot stand them. Again, these can be based on specific software such as Inspiration, or utilising MS Word. For managing the literature that you'll be reading you may wish to use software such as Endnote, Reference Manager or Mendeley. Independent of what type of literature, e.g. books, industry reports or journal articles, we would advise you to consider using referencing software. Spending a little extra time on this during your project could save you days of work at the end. Finally, there are software packages that help with the analysis of data. Some packages (such as SPSS) are helpful for quantitative datasets others (such as NVivo) are especially designed to help with qualitative data. As with our earlier recommendations, you may find that other packages suit your needs.

Of course, you'll also need to type your project up and, these days, it would be almost impossible to find someone who did not routinely use a word processing package to do this. You may wish to create a document template at the outset that manages all of the details of page layout, formatting, font type and size, page margins for binding, etc. Again, check the departmental guidelines on these conventions, and if possible then look at some well-regarded examples. While the careless use of irregular fonts and the online thesaurus can ruin otherwise good writing, the sensible use of technology to manage your project can save a considerable degree of stress and frustration. If in doubt about any aspect of your dissertation then ask your supervisor, with whom you should regularly communicate. The next section offers advice on keeping this unique relationship productive.

Managing feedback from your supervisor

Managing feedback from your supervisor is critical to successfully completing a research project. If students expect to create a successful research project, obtaining feedback should not not be left to chance. There are a number of proactive strategies that students should employ to manage the feedback they obtain from their supervisors.

First, students should organize regular meetings to discuss their research projects with their supervisors. Some degree programmes stipulate that supervision sessions are logged with agreed actions and a summary of key discussion points. This is a sensible approach which is often overlooked. Typically supervisors expect to meet with their research students every four to six weeks. Of course this may vary depending on the research project's stage of development. For example, in the initial stages of the dissertation, weekly or fortnightly meetings to determine its scope and purpose may be required; on the other hand, during its write-up few if any meetings are needed. Frequent meetings provide opportunities for students to address problems and then modify their work for further consideration by the supervisor. Without frequent feedback, understanding of key topic ideas and issues can be forgotten.

Second, in order to get the best out of your supervisor it is important that you allow sufficient time between setting-up a meeting and its actual date. Sometimes students forget that their supervisors need time prior to a meeting to think about their student's research, and to read anything that

12

he or she has sent to them in advance. It is important to show that you are aware of these things and appreciate the hidden time and effort that your supervisor gives to you. Therefore, if you want to enhance the opportunity of receiving high-quality feedback, you should allow your supervisor sufficient time to think about your research work. It is a good strategy to agree dates for the next meeting during the course of the current one.

Third, it is a good idea to actually turn up at the agreed time and date. If you turn up late to a scheduled meeting it will probably be cut short and mean the opportunity to gain insights from your supervisor's feedback is lost. In addition, even if a student still manages to obtain a meeting after being late, it will be likely that the supervisor will be worrying about other work that he or she should be attending to, but which is being neglected because of the time given to you. Therefore, being late increases the likelihood of lowering the quality of feedback received from your supervisor. Meetings not only provide valuable feedback, but also help to establish what kind of student-supervisor relationship you are going to have. If you cancel a meeting at short notice, the time and thought that your supervisor has already invested in it is wasted. Lateness and missed meetings have a negative impact on the future relationship between supervisor and student. Certainly it will harm the degree of seriousness and commitment with which the supervisor approaches future meetings.

By respecting your supervisor's time and other commitments you are encouraging them to take you seriously. In a positive way you are demonstrating to your supervisor that you expect meetings to be well prepared and treated with respect. Some students even phone or e-mail a day or two before the planned meeting to confirm with their supervisor that everything is okay and whether there is anything else they should be thinking about or preparing that may not have been mentioned previously.

Fourth, students should always present work to a high standard of presentation, i.e. it should be logically structured and not contain proof-reading errors. A high standard of presentation is important as it enables the supervisor to focus his or her energy on evaluating the quality of the ideas presented rather than struggling to decipher it due to awkward structuring and/or proofreading errors. High standards of presentation allow the supervisor to maximize his or her time with you during meetings by discussing substantive issues and making suggestions, rather than wasting time highlighting grammatical issues. Therefore, taking the time to present ideas in a readable format pays dividends, as it ensures more of your supervisor's time is paid to the quality of the ideas presented. Moreover, a positive aspect of proofreading is that it strengthens your overall writing skills. Proofreading your work will also make it look more professional and accomplished. Many writers spend more time editing and proofreading than they do on the actual creative process. The overall feel of the finished product lies within how well your work has been proofread and edited. As stated above, your supervisor will appreciate the effort. Therefore, having the discipline to ensure that all written work given to your supervisor is of a high standard is a necessary activity and good practice for the future.

It may seem an obvious observation but supervisors expect students to follow the advice given. It is surprising how often advice is disregarded. If you disagree with the feedback provided then it is important that you confront the issue with your supervisor rather than ignore him or her and continue to write what you think is right. Disagreement is nothing to worry about, as long as you can defend your position through reason and argument. Your supervisor will accept that your views differ from his or her own. But you should listen to what your supervisor says to you. Remember, he or she will have considerable experience and broad knowledge of your discipline. In some cases, disagreements can prevent successful cooperation, which can again harm the feedback received.

Moreover, it is essential that students be enthusiastic and excited about their work. Enthusiasm and excitement works to the advantage of the student, as it will encourage your supervisor to produce high quality feedback. When students are really excited about what they are doing, it stimulates those around them. If you succeed in maintaining your enthusiasm it will make your research project enjoyable for your supervisor. Certainly students will be investigating subject areas in the normal course of events that enable them to gain more depth and detailed knowledge on a topic than their supervisor. Therefore, it is no exaggeration to state that your supervisor will expect to be intermittently surprised by new information, evidence and ideas that you are able to supply. Accordingly supervisors gain benefits from having a research student as a means of keeping them up-to-date with new developments and at the forefront of knowledge in their field. Gaining new information and evidence will enhance your supervisor's enjoyment and encourage them to spend additional time reading and thinking about your topic area. In other words, enthusiasm and surprises will inspire your supervisor to commit more time and energy into the feedback he or she provides.

12

One way to improve the quality of feedback you receive from your supervisor(s) is to take some responsibility for the content of your supervisory sessions. It is advisable that students enter a meeting with a proposed list of topics or questions for discussion. Preparing a list of topics or questions serves a number of purposes: it provides a basic agenda for the meeting; it forces the student to clarify issues that may remain vague; and it prevents the accumulation of a number of small issues becoming a single insurmountable obstacle.

It is hoped that the suggestions and exercises above will promote good writing practices for those undertaking their first major writing project. While there is no guidance that can guarantee dissertation success, and no approach that cannot be compromised by careless writing and research methods, daily writing and regular communication with your supervisor will give you the best chance of producing your strongest work.

References

Charney, N. (2012). Jodi Picoult on Writing, Publishing, and What She's Reading. Retrieved 1 June, 2015, from http://www.thedailybeast.com/articles/2012/04/03/jodi-picoult-on-writing-publishing-and-what-she-s-reading.html

Charney, N. (2013a). How I Write: Nathan Englander. Retrieved 1 June, 2015, from http://www.thedailybeast.com/articles/2013/03/27/how-i-write-nathan-englander.html

Charney, N. (2013b). Karen Russell: How I Write. Retrieved 1 June, 2015, from http://www.thedailybeast.com/articles/2013/02/06/karen-russell-how-i-write.html

Charney, N. (2013c). Maya Angelou: How I Write. Retrieved 1 June, 2015, from http://www.thedailybeast.com/articles/2013/04/10/maya-angelou-how-i-write.html

King, S. (2002). *On Writing*: Pocket Books.

Mintzberg, H. (1973). *The Nature of Managerial Work*. Harper & Row

Murakami, H. (2008). *What I Talk about When I Talk about Running*: Vintage.

Murray, R. (2006). *How to Write a Thesis*: McGraw-Hill Education.

Plimpton, G. (1958). The Art of Fiction XXI: Ernest Hemingway. *Paris Review*, **5**(18), 68.

A1 Managing Your Research Project

John Sanders, Vera Tens and Robert MacIntosh

> Managing a research project is similar to managing any other type of project: following some basic rules minimises the chances of things going wrong as well as making the whole process more enjoyable and productive.

Project planning: Phases, tasks and milestones

One of your first activities should be to map out the key phases, tasks and milestones that will make up your research project. Combined, these three items form the basis of the project plan.

Phases tend to be interpreted by many researchers as groups of activities. Listed below is one view of the key phases in your research project.

1 Establishing your topic

2 Building an understanding of the literature

3 Choosing your method(s)

4 Gathering data

5 Doing the analysis

6 Writing and re-writing

7 Formatting and submission

There may be small variations based on the type of qualification that your dissertation sits within. For example, research-based degrees such as a PhD or MPhil typically incorporate an oral defence of the thesis whereas this only occurs in very rare circumstances in a taught programme. Similarly, in some degree programmes, topics are assigned rather than chosen. Nevertheless, this list of key phases, or a close variant of it, offers the first building block with which you can prepare a project plan. A simple first step is to check the submission date and work backwards from there, allowing time as you see fit for each of the phases that are as relevant to your project.

Tasks are those activities that go to make up an individual phase. Tasks are therefore shorter, more precise, and should be described in a level of detail that would make it clear to anyone reviewing your project plan what is going on and when. Task descriptions should not be long sentences or even paragraphs, but key points that identify necessary activities. For example, phase 2 listed above suggests that you will need to develop a solid grasp of the key literatures pertaining to your chosen topic. This phase will be made up of a number of specific tasks, often stated in the form of a list, using some form of numbering or similar as identifier. For example:

Phase 2: Building an understanding of the literature (see Chapter 3)

Tasks

2.1 Identify key concepts

2.2 Identify seminal authors and contributions

2.3 Identify key journals

2.4 Agree search terms and the boundaries of a structured review of the literature

2.5 Summarise key debates and points of agreement/disagreement

2.6 Establish a research question

Depending upon your own preferences, tasks may contain subtasks and can be broken down into a sensible number of sub-levels. Whilst this level of detail is partly dependent upon your choices it also relates to the nature of the research project. The example given above is typical in that tasks are ordered in sequence that they will likely occur over time, e.g. the first task that is to be executed appears at the top of the list, and the last one at the bottom. Bear in mind that tasks or subtasks may overlap and that some iteration will probably occur between tasks.

Finally, milestones are events that usually attached to a particular deadline such as a submission date, or the point by which ethical approval must be secured. In many cases, milestones are linked with finishing a phase. To some degree, they can be regarded as objectives, and one of their key purposes is to allow you to monitor whether the project as a whole is on time or not. Milestones often indicate that a new task or phase can or should be started. Identifying milestones is just as subjective as the process of identifying tasks and subtasks. Our strong advice would be to discuss phases, tasks and milestones with your supervisor(s) to strike an agreement over the way in which your project will be delivered.

Even the simple process of identifying phases, tasks and milestones in list format is a big step in the right direction. It creates a rudimentary project plan and it is worth noting that experience suggests that students following a rudimentary project plan tend to be better organised and achieve better outcomes than those who approach their project informally. From here, we will refer to this basic project plan as 'Plan A'. A student following Plan A has a clear view of what they should be doing, by when, in order to complete their research project in time and to a high standard. This can be regarded as approaching your project in an organised manner. That said, no project plan is static, and most projects of this scale and duration experience setbacks and unexpected delays. Tasks which at first appeared sequential in nature may in fact need to be done in parallel and vice versa. A common experience for students is that the start of one task is put on hold until other tasks in the project plan progress or even finish. But sometimes data collection takes longer than expected, analysis is more challenging or ethical approval slows things down.

We have given an example of a dissertation project plan below. We would stress that this example is not definitive; rather it is one of many possible project plans. It does however demonstrate the general point that research projects can be divided into phases, tasks and sub-tasks.

Plan A: Tasks

1. Project organisation/planning
    1.1. Identify your research area
    1.2. Identify your research question
    1.3. Identify tasks and milestones
    1.4. Identify resources, e.g. time, financial, etc.
2. Literature
    2.1. Search the literature
    2.2. Review the literature

2.3.   Search and review more literature

3. Data

   3.1.   Research approach

   3.1.1. Review research philosophies

   3.1.2. Identify philosophical stance

   3.1.3. Identify research method and methodology to be used

   3.1.4. Get ethical approval for planned data collection

   3.2.   Data collection

   3.2.1. Identify potential samples, i.e. people or organisations

   3.2.2. Identify ways of accessing samples, e.g. interviews face-to-face, interviews via Skype, field work etc.

   3.2.3. Data collection according to research method(ology)

   3.3.   Data evaluation

   3.3.1. Validity and reliability

   3.3.2. Triangulation

   3.3.3. Comprehensiveness

   3.4.   Data analysis

   3.4.1. Document data collection process

   3.4.2. Document data collected, e.g. transcribe interviews, etc.

   3.4.3. Analyse data collected, e.g. use statistics software, content analysis or similar

4. Writing

   4.1.   Writing requirements

   4.1.1. Word count

   4.1.2. Page layout

   4.1.3. Font type and size

   4.1.4. Referencing style

   4.1.5. Other

   4.2.   Write literature review

   4.3.   Write research methodology

   4.4.   Write discussion and conclusion

   4.5.   Write other necessary chapters

   4.6.   Write the introduction

    5. Review and revise

        5.1.   Revisit earlier tasks as often and when necessary

        5.2.   Edit written chapters and sections

        5.3.   Check references, citations and quotes

        5.4.   Check formatting, spelling, grammar

        5.5.   Re-read and re-write sections and chapters

    6. Submission of report/thesis

The milestones that you set for your research project will obviously vary with the topic, but will also be based on the views of both you and your supervisor(s). For illustrative purposes, we have translated the example above into milestones.

Example milestones and timeline

1 Identify research area and topic and prepare project plan (3rd year, 2nd semester)

2 Provide an extended research proposal to supervisor (4th year, by week 4 of 1st semester)

3 Discuss literature review findings with supervisor (ongoing until submission, starting as early as possible)

4 Provide first draft of literature review chapter to supervisor (no later than week 4 of 1st semester in year 4)

5 Prepare first draft of research methodology chapter (4th year, by week 8 of 1st semester)

6 Submit on-line Research Ethics Approval form (4th year, by week 8 of 1st semester)

7 Prepare first draft of data collection and analysis chapter (4th year, no later than week 1 of 2nd semester)

8 Prepare first draft of discussion and conclusion chapter (4th year, no later than week 4 of 2nd semester)

9 Prepare first draft of dissertation (4th year, no later than week 8 of 2nd semester)

10 Submit final version of dissertation (4th year, by week 12 of 2nd semester)

    No matter what your own plan and milestones look like, it would be wise to remember that they are not set in stone.

A

Managing resources

Developing the initial project plan, Plan A, is the first step into managing the research project. However, every project also requires the identification, allocation and management of resources.

Resources can be related to time, people, finance, knowledge and skills or others. They may be required or provided by the researcher and/or another party such as supervisors or other third parties. It is always useful to identify resources for each task and to keep information relating to these resources in a single overview document rather than having them stored in different forms or locations.

Perhaps the single biggest resource at your disposal is time. Your project will require you to identify and allocate your time wisely, e.g. who is executing which tasks and how long are they likely to take. The identification and allocation of time to each task in the project plan is critical if you are to avoid the experience of cramming too much activity into too little time close to the submission deadline. In project management terms, time allocation can be done 'forward', where there is no existing deadline, or 'backwards' where a specific and known time constraint is in place.

Forward planning means that time is allocated to each task at the lowest level; the sum of each task on that level will define time for the higher level task, and so forth. This forward planning process allows the creation of a finish date for the project. It may be useful to allow for overrun on some tasks and therefore push the finish date out a little.

The backward planning approach is used when a deadline, i.e. a time constraint such as a submission deadline, already exists. Some projects have a number of externally driven time constraints, e.g. a date by which a draft literature review must be completed, a final submission date for the project as a whole, etc. In such circumstances you will have to work backwards by dividing up the available time between the tasks required to ensure that you meet the final deadline and any interim deadlines that you face. Using this approach, it is necessary to start at the highest task level or even phase and then work downwards to the lowest level of task.

Examples for each using some of above Plan-A tasks and milestones are shown below.

Task #	Task	Est. duration	Start date	Est. finish	Comments
1	Project organisation/ planning				Requires info from all subtasks first
1.1	Identify your research area	2 days	Day 0	Day 2	
1.2	Identify your research question	5 days	Day 2	Day 7	Assumes tasks are done in sequence
1.3	Identify tasks and milestones	10 days	Day 7	Day 17	Assumes tasks are done in sequence
1.4	Identify resources, e.g. time, financial, etc.	15 days	Day 17	Day 32	Assumes tasks are done in sequence
1	Project organisation/ planning	32 days	Day 0	Day 32	Once all subtasks are identified, the sum will define the task duration and estimated end date

N. B. It is good project management practice to allow for overrun, e.g. in above example for instance to allow for an additional 3 days for Task 1.

Figure A1.1: Forward planning

Milestone 7 "Submit on-line Research Ethics Approval form" has to be done in 4th year, by week 8 of 1st semester. In order to fill in and submit the on-line form, it is necessary to be clear about the research methodology to be employed though.

Milestone 5 "Prepare first draft of research methodology chapter" would have to be finished before this milestone is reached. Furthermore, additional time maybe required as your supervisor might want to read and comment on the methodology. Assuming that this will require 4 weeks, it thus means that Milestone 5 has to be done by week 4 of 1st semester in year 4.

Figure A1.2: Backward planning

▪ Other approaches to planning

A project plan need not be restricted to the two approaches described above. It is possible for some tasks to be time constrained, whereas others may not. Milestones in general tend to be linked with a deadline, and thus are most likely to require the backward planning approach. In addition, time constraints by, for example, third parties will add to the complexity of the

A

planning and managing process and needs to be reflected in the project plan.

As with any other project, research projects may also require financial resources. These can be related to the purchase of data, costs of travel, accommodation, transcription or having to pay for access to specific books or literature. It is therefore good project management practice to plan for financial expenditure by developing a project budget, which also identifies where the finances are likely to come from.

Another crucial type of resource of any research project is literature (see Chapter 3). Access to project relevant literature is a basic requirement and therefore needs to be considered at the start of each project.

Overall, no matter how detailed or crude a project plan is, it should always be revisited as the project itself unfolds. Furthermore, it is good management practice to get the buy-in from everyone who will be involved in the project. Giving early notice of any requests for people's time is always a good idea, e.g. interviews that you wish to schedule, requests for feedback on written drafts from your supervisor(s), etc.

Useful resources

People manage projects of all kinds across almost every industry, geography and size of organization. As a result, there are a plethora of helpful tools available to anyone looking to manage a project. Academic research projects are, in principle at least, no different and you may well choose to use software or other specialist project management resources to help you manage your work.

You may already know one particular type of project planning software, in which case use what you already know and spend the time you would have invested in learning the software on completing your project. If you have never used project management software you might find that the time invested up front more than repays itself when you come to execute the project plan. One commonly used example is Microsoft's Office Project. This has the advantage of being relatively easy to use, but, whilst those managing complex industrial projects may need specialist features, the less experienced project manager will find that the basic functionality of something like MS Excel is sufficient. To a certain degree, it comes down to personal preference. The timing of a project is often visualised by using a Gantt-chart, which is built into MS Project already. A simple example – using MS Excel –

may look similar to the below table using data from above example of Plan A tasks.

#	Milestone	Week 1	Week 2	Week 3	Week 4	Week 5
1	Project organisation/planning	■	■	■		
1.1	Identify your research area	▓				
1.2	Identify your research question		▓			
1.3	Identify tasks and milestones			▓		
1.4	Identify resources, e.g. time, financial, etc.			▓		
2	Literature				■	■
2.1	Search the literature				▓	▓
2.2	Review the literature					▓

Figure A1.3: Project planning using a Gantt chart

Contingency planning: when Plan A goes astray

It would be a mistake to assume that Plan A will come together exactly as formulated. Indeed, experience indicates that each phase, task or milestone usually takes longer than planned. This can have a profound effect on student motivation, as what once seemed an achievable and highly manageable plan of action can start to seem hopelessly optimistic given the time remaining. Below are a number of common challenges encountered with suggested contingencies.

Challenge #1: Employment

Before accepting, or extending, any work commitments, you should consider the total demand which it will make on your time. Essentially the most important determinant of the amount of part-time employment or outside activity in which you can safely engage is your ability to organise your own time effectively. There are students who manage a substantial part-time commitment to research whilst at the same time being employed. In contrast, many students find it difficult to organize their time effectively even on a single task such as a research project. Therefore, you must make a realistic personal assessment of what you can and can't do. If you feel that you have overcommitted yourself, then take immediate action to remedy the situation. The worse thing to do is to hesitate and let the stress of over-commitment force you to miss deadlines. This is where a project plan is

A

useful. A project plan at least alerts you to where you are in relation to both self-imposed and externally imposed deadlines.

Challenge #2: Unforeseen illness

Perhaps because research projects can be time-pressured, you can find that exhaustion makes you prone to illness. Whether the illness is relatively minor or something more significant, it can affect your ability to complete the project. Equally, the illness of a close relative can detract from your ability to focus on your research work. Generally universities are very sympathetic towards students who suffer from medically certified illnesses. If an illness is starting to affect progress this should be notified to the university as soon as possible. The worst thing to do is nothing, as the longer the notification is left the more difficult it becomes for the university to reconstruct timings and dates for later evaluation. The decision becomes even more difficult if shorter periods of illness are involved when there may be a preference to absorb the time lost and at the same time maintain any grant payment. If illness is going to cause long-term problems it is much better to make a decision about suspending studies earlier rather than later.

Challenge #3: Motivation

What may have seemed a fascinating or exciting project can quickly become dull or difficult as you face the reality of writing an extended piece of work. While it is difficult to make a contingency plan for a loss in motivation, it is important to realize that it will happen. Conducting a research project can be an extremely arduous process and no student can maintain the same level of enthusiasm for it throughout his or her studies. Perhaps you can set current tasks to one side and switch attention to another element of the research study. Possibly you can focus on the initial reasons for choosing the topic and remind yourself why it seemed interesting, or maybe you need to accept that it isn't as exciting as you first thought and focus instead on the role this project plays in reaching graduation.

Challenge #4: Feasibility

Whether it is a lack of access, or the quality of the data that you eventually capture, there can be the gradual realization that the planned conclusions cannot be drawn from the available data. You may discover that the envisioned relationships between variables are unclear or do not exist; an outcome which would be judged unacceptable. Alternatively, the promises of interviews or focus groups may fall through and you are left with either no or limited data. In these circumstances, early advice from your supervisor can help you to reframe your research to design research aims and objectives that remain achievable.

Challenge #5: Computing difficulties

Most of us rely, most of the time, on computers to create documents, capture and analyse data, communicate, etc. Computer problems can also cause considerable delays and problems to researchers. Alarmingly computer software related problems occur at the most inconvenient of times. It goes without saying that maintaining up-to-date backups of all data and word processing files is a sensible precaution especially given the scale of the writing task.

A

A2 Assessing Your Research Project

Nigel Caldwell and Robert MacIntosh

Whilst each individual college or university will have its own particular marking process and criteria, there are large areas of common ground when it comes to the assessment of research projects. We have studied an extensive set of marking guides and combined features of these to produce three fictitious examples (which we refer to here as universities A, B and C). Our purpose in doing this is to illustrate some key points about assessment. These marking guides are reproduced in Table A2.1 below.

Table A2.1: Anonymised research project marking guides

Guide A	Guide B	Guide C
Identification of the research area, aim, objectives and/or research questions [20%]	How well chosen and well justified are the research methods employed in the project ? [25%]	Is the purpose of the research clear, justified and achievable? [30%]
Does the literature review inform the research? [40%]	Literature or body of knowledge has been thoroughly investigated, understood and incorporated [45%]	Technical content including use of literature and methods [30%]
Is the chosen methodology appropriate? Are valid and reliable analysis methods used? [30%]	Initiative, originality, imagination and skill in construction and execution [10%]	Evidence of the effort involved and of originality [30%]
Writing style and presentation: (English grammar, reporting style, presentation of tables, figures, equations, etc.) [10%]	Presentation of relevant and well-founded conclusions and recommendations [20%]	Implications for practice, for theory and limitations to the work [10%]

It is worth noting that we are examining general principles, not specifics, since these would vary with the nature of your programme of study. A very sensible next step would be to find and read the specific equivalent from the course handbook of the programme that you are studying.

Of course, what interests you as a student is the mark that you will eventually obtain for your research project, and how that mark is constructed. The primary concern of those marking your research project is ensuring fairness and consistency in the allocation of marks. Consider for a moment a cohort of 100 students, each working on a research project in their final year of study. Naturally, the 100 projects will vary in terms of topics, methods, types of data, etc. From the university's perspective, marking 100 research projects is qualitatively different from marking 100 exam scripts, because of the inherent variations from one project to the next. To deal with this, most universities involve multiple markers to ensure consistency. First, your research project will likely be marked by your supervisor. Then, typically, a second copy of your project is given to an independent second marker who forms their own view of the grade in relation both to the kinds of criteria set out in Table A2.1 and to more generic grade descriptors that set out the characteristics of an A, B or C grade piece of work (see Table A2.2). Where the marking guide sets out weightings for individual aspects of the project, each aspect would be graded individually then weightings applied to arrive at an overall grade. Once both markers have arrived at an independent assessment of the project, their written comments are compared. The second marker role is a safeguard against bias (positive or negative) from the first marker. Where there is agreement the mark is confirmed. Where the first and second markers disagree, a third marker is usually asked to offer an opinion, often with sight of the written reports from the first and second markers. This process is time consuming but helps ensure that there is a consistent standard such that all distinction or first class projects are of a comparable standard, and all fails are confirmed as deficient in relation to the grading scheme, etc. All of this occurs within the university and is then endorsed by an external and independent examiner from another university. Typically, a representative sample of all research projects are considered by the external examiners, alongside a statistical analysis of the spread of marks, standard deviation, comparison with previous years, etc. External examiners are appointed for a fixed period of 2 or 3 years and cannot fulfil the role of examiner indefinitely, to ensure that there is always a fresh perspective on the marking process.

Table A2.2: Indicative grade descriptors

A Grades [typically 70%-100%]	Exceptionally good work that is distinctive and goes beyond run of the mill. Rich in conceptual sophistication, independent insight, pertinent information or understanding of relevant issues. Demonstrates an easy familiarity with concepts and sources.
B Grades [typically 60%-69%]	Very good standard of work demonstrating an obvious and consistent understanding of the topic or problem at hand. A convincing grasp of relevant literature combined with effective use of evidence and argumentation. Some indication of critical scrutiny and independent thinking, and a high standard of presentation.
C Grades [typically 50%-59%]	A good performance, offering an accessible and well structured discussion of relevant issues or arguments, suitably illustrated with original or appropriate secondary source material. Presentation will be coherent, well structured and literate, with accurate and effective referencing of the material used.
D Grades [typically 40%-49%]	Competent work offering a routine treatment based on limited reading or a heavy reliance on lecture notes. Though a basic understanding will be apparent, the work may lack depth, breadth, clarity or focus. Communication may be hampered by a poorly structured presentation.
E Grades and below [typically 39% and below]	Submissions showing some awareness of the topic under investigation, yet with limited conceptualisation, discussion and/or articulation. May not distinguish between relevant and irrelevant material and tends to be superficial in the treatment of both concepts and data. Poorer work may be plagiarised, inaccurate or misleading.

From your point of view, it pays to realise that whilst your supervisor will usually have some expertise or interest in the specific topic of your research project, very often the second marker will not. Also, whilst your supervisor will have helped in the evolution and shaping your research project by offering comment and advice, the second marker will come to the project cold. The document must stand on its own merits with no prior assumptions or knowledge on the part of the reader. Rather than being a disadvantage, this aids the objectivity of the marking process. The processes described above occur at what are variously called assessment, award or exam boards that take place after the degree programme or course has completed. Securing the agreement of the external examiners is a necessary pre-condition to confirming the award of individual marks, degree classifications, etc. All universities have an appeal process in place but typically such appeals centre on the process rather than the academic integrity of the grades awarded.

Why should you care about the assessment process, beyond a vague sense of reassurance that consistency and fairness is built into the process? Well reading about this 'backstage' process should help you with understanding the challenge you face in writing a research project. Try to keep in mind that there is a wider audience for your study, that it will be read and the mark validated by someone who will have little or no contact with you, your work or your topic, and that this internally validated mark then has to be validated by an external authority. Understanding this process should make you put a premium on clarity – being able to clearly explain what you are proposing to study and why, what the relevant literature tells you and what it doesn't, the way you approached the research in terms of any methods used, clear presentation of any data collected and analysis and conclusions that are patently linked to the original research questions or issues. Whilst you cannot fully predict the outcome of the marking process, there are things that you can do to get feedback. Your supervisor should be your primary source of feedback (as discussed in Chapter 12) but you can also test out the sense of the project by asking someone else to read either a complete draft or a sample section/chapter. If they struggle to see the purpose of the project, find it too dense or obtuse, then it is likely that your markers will too. Typos don't materially influence the overall grade but they do create an impression that little care was taken in the production of the project. The best projects are those which are easiest to read and follow, offering the reader clear signposting about the journey ahead, the route the research will take them on, and where the research – and reader – will end up.

Example marking guides

The point that clarity is central brings us to the first issue in assessment – that the research problem being addressed is at an appropriate level of challenge. Whilst many students start their research project with lofty ambitions, there is no requirement to change the world. Marking guidance often asks whether the student has designed a study with enough challenge to be interesting but also do-able within the time frame and available resources. Guides A and C explicitly mark against this theme, though the weightings applied vary. Framing your project is important and choosing a topic which is too diffuse has negative knock-on effects throughout the development and writing of your project. Chapter 2 offers clear guidance on shaping a suitable project.

A

The quality of the literature review is assessed explicitly in all three guides. Note that the emphasis on the *use* made of the literature; it has to *guide and inform* the dissertation. There is therefore an obvious link between the extent to which a clear brief has been specified (see previous paragraph) and the extent to which a precise and detailed literature review has been conducted. The literature review represents the largest portion of the overall grade in guides A and B. Guide C combines what is described as the 'technical content' including literature and methods, whilst guides A and B take the choice of methods as a separate theme for assessment. The originality of the work attracts 30% of the grade in guide C, only 10% in guide B and doesn't feature as an explicit criterion in guide A.

Presentation is mentioned in guides A and B but it is worth observing that many students write research projects in a second, or even third language and any critique of your grammar would be placed in that context. Guides B and C draw specific attention to conclusions reached, with guide C focusing particularly on implications for both theory (linking back to the literature review) and practice.

Our point in dissecting both marking guides and grade descriptors is twofold. First, it establishes that whilst each individual marking guide or set of grade descriptors is different, there are certain common themes which tend to recur in most universities or colleges. This is understandable given that the process of arriving at judgements of quality occurs in all universities and colleges. Within the wider curriculum, research projects are commonly used to provide a detailed analysis of your individual ability to think and write coherently, to draw together insights from the literature and to work with data to develop findings. How you develop a research design, link this to the literature, gather and analyse data and present findings are the underlying features of all research projects. Our second purpose in examining three different marking guides is to encourage you to find the specific guide that your research project will be assessed against. Whilst it is tempting to focus on the need to press ahead and meet the deadline, looking at assessment criteria should be one of the first things that you do. Indeed, it can be done before you reach the research project since marking guides are available in advance. At the very least, you should be paying attention to any explicit signals about the relative weighting associated with individual aspects of your research project by those doing the assessment.

A3 Project Structure and Word Counts

The following table offers a suggested structure and approximate word counts for dissertations, relative to the degree being pursued. This is designed to be altered according to the needs of the researcher, and the stipulations of their supervisor and institution. It is important to understand that the table is offered here only as a set of non-specific suggestions for your (hopefully!) very specific project. All dissertations are different, and your supervisor is the best person to talk to about your specific institutional, school, or college requirements, which may vary quite significantly. Creating your own outline through discussion with your supervisor gives you both a sense of where you are in the process and what needs to be done, whilst also functioning as a reference point when completing smaller intermediary targets. The examples below illustrate a general principle of successful research espoused by this book: a larger project becomes much more manageable when broken down into smaller, clearly defined sections. This approach is likely to prove helpful even beyond PhD level, when writing papers for publication in academic journals, for instance, or even when completing the second edition of a textbook!

Section	Word count			
	Hons Dissertation	MSc Dissertation	MPhil	PhD
Introduction	**1500**	**1500**	**5000**	**8000**
Pre-theoretic overview	500	500	1000	1500
Why this is interesting?	100	100	500	500
Research purpose	600	600	1500	2000
Aim and objectives	300	300	500	500
Something	0	0	1500	1500
Something else	0	0	0	2000
Literature review	**3000**	**3500**	**12,000**	**23,000**
Historical overview (of theory)	500	500	1000	8000
Contemporary review of theory	1500	2000	7000	10000
Context for study	1000	1000	5000	5000
Methodology	**2000**	**2000**	**6000**	**17,000**
Philosophy	500	500	1000	3000
Methodological options	0	0	0	4000
Data collection technique	600	600	2000	4000
Sourcing and selecting data	200	200	500	750
Research ethics	200	200	500	750
Data analysis tool(s)	500	500	2000	5000
Empirical material	**2000**	**2500**	**6000**	**12,000**
Presentation of data	500	750	1500	3000
Analysis	1000	1000	3000	6000
Findings	500	750	1500	3000
Discussion	**2000**	**2500**	**6000**	**12,000**
Discussion	1800	2000	5000	8000
Theory development	200	500	1000	4000
Conclusion	**1500**	**2000**	**5000**	**8000**
Reviewing the aim and objectives	300	500	1500	2000
Contribution - theory				2000
Contribution - context	300	500	1500	1000
Contribution - method				
Contribution - management practice				
Methodological review	300	300	500	1000
Limitations and further research	300	300	1000	1000
Overall conclusion	300	400	500	1000
Total	**13,000**	**15,000**	**40,000**	**80,000**

Index